Platform Supply Chains in the AI Era

Digitalization, big data analytics, automation, and cloud computing have transformed traditional supply chains into **Platform Supply Chains (PSCs),** which redefine coordination, enhance efficiency, and accelerate innovation across the entire value network. In the AI era, platform supply chains are digitally orchestrated. AI-empowered ecosystems integrate diverse stakeholders (producers, consumers, service providers, logistics, etc.) through a "centralized" digital platform, facilitating interactions, coordination, and value co-creation. Some well-known platform supply chains include Amazon and Wayfair (e-commerce marketplaces aggregating brands and managing fulfillment), Alibaba and Pinduoduo (platforms digitizing the entire supply chain from production to sales), Uber and Meituan (on-demand service platforms coordinating drivers, service providers, and customers), and Huawei and Haier (manufacturers integrating industrial machinery, devices, and sensors with the Internet and data analytics)

Artificial intelligence supports platform supply chains by automating decisions and managing conflicting objectives among stakeholders. Using tools like machine learning (ML), natural language processing (NLP), computer vision, reinforcement learning (RL), Internet of Things (IoT), blockchain, and Generative AI, these supply chains can automate tasks, forecast demand, personalize services, and adapt quickly to change.

This book series explores the evolving landscape of platform supply chains (PSCs), with a focus on how AI empowers platforms to optimize operations, enhance collaboration, and drive innovation across industries. It aims to deepen our understanding of how AI and digital platforms are redefining the future of supply chain management. The series adopts an interdisciplinary scope, encompassing theoretical modeling, empirical research, experimental studies, and real-world applications.

Topics

The book series covers, but is not limited to, the following topics:

Foundations of Platform Supply Chains

- Conceptual models of platform-based supply chains
- Ecosystem perspectives in supply chain orchestration
- AI-enabled value creation and capture in digital platforms

AI Technologies in Platform Supply Chains

- Machine learning for demand forecasting and inventory optimization
- Natural language processing for automation and communication
- Computer vision for quality control and warehouse automation
- Reinforcement learning for dynamic logistics and decision-making
- Generative AI for documentation, training, and decision support
- Edge AI and IoT integration in supply networks

Platform Design, Operations, and Governance

- Matching algorithms for supplier-buyer coordination
- Pricing mechanisms, commissions, and incentive design arising from platform supply chains
- Trust, reputation, and rating systems in multi-sided markets arising from platform supply chains
- Supply chain visibility and traceability enabled by digital platforms
- Platform supply chains governance and control mechanisms
- Blockchain and smart contracts in platform supply chain logistics

Behavioral and Organizational Perspectives

- Human-AI collaboration in platform supply chain operations
- Behavioral biases in platform-based decision-making
- User preferences and customization in service design arising from platform supply chains
- Motivation, trust, and coordination among platform supply chain participants
- Labor dynamics and gig work in logistics and fulfillment arising from platform supply chains
- Crowdsourced logistics and human-in-the-loop systems

Policy, Ethics, and Strategic Implications

- Data privacy and AI ethics in platform supply chains
- Regulation and competition in platform supply chains
- Strategic management of platform supply chains

Industry Applications and Case Studies

- E-commerce and retail platforms (e.g., Amazon, Alibaba, JD.com)
- Logistics tech platforms

Yugang Yu · Shengming Zheng · Ting Wang ·
Ye Shi

Platform Supply Chains 1

Predict-then-optimize Paradigm

Springer

Yugang Yu
School of Management
University of Science and Technology of China
Hefei, China

Shengming Zheng
School of Management
University of Science and Technology of China
Hefei, China

Ting Wang
School of Management
University of Science and Technology of China
Hefei, China

Ye Shi
School of Management
University of Science and Technology of China
Hefei, China

ISSN 3091-4795 ISSN 3091-4809 (electronic)
Platform Supply Chains in the AI Era
ISBN 978-981-95-9964-6 ISBN 978-981-95-9965-3 (eBook)
https://doi.org/10.1007/978-981-95-9965-3

This Springer imprint is published by the registered company Springer Nature Singapore Pte Ltd.
The registered company address is: 152 Beach Road, #21-01/04 Gateway East, Singapore 189721, Singapore

Editorial Board for Platform Supply Chains 1–5

Preface

We stand at an inflection point in the history of commerce and operations. The digital platform—that seemingly simple architectural concept of connecting disparate groups through technology—has become the dominant organizing principle of our economic age. From the way we hail rides and book accommodations to how we purchase goods, access services, and consume content, platforms have reshaped not just individual industries but the fundamental structure of market interaction itself.

This transformation has been swift, profound, and often disorienting. Traditional supply chain managers, trained in the art of optimizing linear pipelines, find themselves confronting a new reality: they must now orchestrate ecosystems they do not own, coordinate agents they do not employ, and govern interactions they do not directly control. Meanwhile, platform architects and data scientists, masters of network effects and machine learning, discover that their elegant digital designs must ultimately contend with the messy, physical realities of moving goods through space and time, of delivering services in real-world contexts, and of managing the human dynamics of trust, quality, and fairness.

This book emerges from the convergence of these two worlds. It is born from the recognition that the platform revolution demands nothing less than a reinvention of supply chain management—and that this reinvention requires a new methodological paradigm. The Predict-then-Optimize (PTO) framework represents exactly that: a fundamental shift in how we think about decision-making in complex, data-rich, uncertain environments. It is not merely another tool in the operations research toolkit, but a new way of integrating what we know (through prediction) with what we should do (through optimization) in a world where data is abundant but perfect information is impossible.

This book grew from our own journey through the evolving landscape of platform operations. As researchers and consultants, we have spent the past decade observing, studying, and sometimes participating in the rapid transformation of supply chains across sectors. We witnessed early e-commerce platforms struggling with inventory placement, ride-hailing companies grappling with driver incentives, marketplace platforms wrestling with fraud detection, and service platforms attempting to balance supply and demand in real time.

What struck us was a recurring pattern: traditional optimization methods, designed for more stable, controlled environments, were consistently failing to capture the dynamic complexity of platform ecosystems. Meanwhile, sophisticated machine learning models were producing ever-more-accurate predictions, but these predictions were often disconnected from the actual decisions they were meant to inform. The "predict-then-optimize" approach—where prediction and optimization were treated as separate, sequential steps—was producing suboptimal outcomes and leaving significant value on the table.

Our motivation in writing this book is threefold:

- To provide a unified theoretical framework that bridges the often-separate worlds of machine learning, operations research, and platform economics. We believe the PTO paradigm offers exactly this unification.
- To offer practical guidance for platform operators, data scientists, and supply chain managers who are building and managing these systems in the real world. Too often, academic research remains siloed from practical implementation; we strive to bridge this gap.
- To establish a research agenda for the next generation of scholars who will shape the future of platform operations. The questions raised by platform supply chains are both fundamentally important and intellectually rich, spanning computer science, economics, operations, and ethics.

This book is designed to serve multiple audiences:

- Academic researchers and graduate students in operations management, computer science, industrial engineering, and business analytics will find a comprehensive treatment of the PTO paradigm and its applications, complete with formal models, methodological approaches, and references to the growing literature.
- Practitioners and platform leaders—including chief technology officers, heads of supply chain, data science leads, and product managers—will find actionable insights, real-world examples, and strategic frameworks for implementing PTO in their organizations.
- Entrepreneurs and innovators building new platform businesses will gain a deeper understanding of the operational challenges they will face and the methodological tools available to address them.
- Policymakers and regulators seeking to understand the inner workings of platform economies will find valuable insights into how algorithmic decision-making shapes market outcomes, competition, and social welfare.

We have structured the book to be accessible to readers with diverse backgrounds. While some sections delve into mathematical formalisms, we always provide intuitive explanations and real-world context. Key concepts are introduced gradually, with each chapter building upon the foundations laid in previous ones.

The platform economy is still young. The PTO paradigm is still emerging. What we present in this book is not the final word, but rather a snapshot of a rapidly evolving field at a particularly exciting moment of convergence. We have tried to capture both the established foundations and the cutting-edge innovations that are shaping the future.

We invite you to join us on this exploration of one of the most important developments in modern commerce. Whether you are a student seeking to understand this new world, a practitioner building it, or a scholar seeking to advance it, we hope this book provides both useful tools and inspiring questions.

The platform revolution has transformed how we connect; the Predict-then-Optimize paradigm may well transform how we decide. Together, they are reshaping the very nature of supply chains—and through them, the global economy itself.

Hefei, China

Yugang Yu
Shengming Zheng
Ting Wang
Ye Shi

Acknowledgements The authors gratefully acknowledge the financial support from the National Natural Science Foundation of China (Grant Numbers 72091215/72091210, 72201261, 72571255).

Competing Interests The authors have no competing interests to declare that are relevant to the content of this manuscript.

Contents

Chapter 1
Introduction

Abstract Driven by the widespread adoption of next-generation technologies—including the Internet of Things, blockchain, artificial intelligence, and cloud computing—platform supply chain systems are undergoing a profound shift toward greater digitalization, intelligence, and operational efficiency. These advancements support real-time data capture, sophisticated analytics, and intelligent decision-making across the entire supply chain. Beyond basic digital upgrades, platform supply chains are evolving from traditional linear structures into dynamic, interconnected networks. This transformation enables broader data sharing and deeper integration across stakeholders. As a result, modern platform supply chain management is characterized by end-to-end digital intelligence, systemic complexity, and network-wide collaboration. By establishing or participating in such platforms, companies can significantly enhance their capabilities in intelligent decision-making, rapid response, resource orchestration, and risk control. Within this context, the predict-then-optimize (PTO) paradigm has gained considerable traction in platform supply chain operations. This book offers a comprehensive and systematic examination of platform supply chain management through the lens of the PTO approach, integrating theoretical foundations with practical implementation. To frame the scope and flow of the book, Chap. 1 opens with an overview of the background and evolution of platform supply chains. Section 1.1.2 introduces the PTO paradigm, and Sect. 1.1.3 examines its specific applications in platform supply chain management. Finally, Sect. 1.1.4 outlines the structure of the book and summarizes the focus of subsequent chapters, providing readers with a clear guide to the content ahead.

1.1 The Evolution and Architecture of Platform Supply Chains

Digital platforms are accelerating the transformation of industries worldwide (Li et al., 2026). Exemplified by leaders such as Alibaba, Facebook, Apple, and YouTube, these entities—though distinct in their markets—leverage the platform model to redefine economic landscapes. Their influence is expanding from business into critical social domains like education, healthcare, and government. The dominance of

Y. Yu et al., *Platform Supply Chains 1*, Platform Supply Chains in the AI Era,
https://doi.org/10.1007/978-981-95-9965-3_1

platform businesses among the fastest-growing global brands underscores this shift (Parker & Van Alstyne, 2018; Van Alstyne et al., 2016). This trend signals a profound societal transformation, heralding the arrival of a new era: the age of platformization. Under the background of digital economy and platformization, the rapid rise of digital platforms has fundamentally reshaped the architecture of modern supply chains (Cui et al., 2023; Wang et al., 2023; Xia et al., 2024; Zhang et al., 2023, 2024).

1.1.1 The Historical Trajectory: From Traditional to Platform Supply Chains

The evolution of supply chain management is a chronicle of humanity's relentless pursuit of efficiency in the movement of goods, information, and capital. For the bulk of industrial history, this quest was confined within the paradigm of the **linear, firm-centric pipeline**. This model, theoretically grounded in transaction cost economics (Coase, 1937) and perfected in the 20th century by manufacturing titans like Ford and Toyota and retail giants like Walmart, conceived of the supply chain as a sequential, managed flow. Raw materials moved to manufacturers, finished goods to distributors, and products to retailers, finally reaching the consumer in a largely unidirectional "push" system. Information flow was often analog, lagged, and followed the physical product, leading to the infamous "bullwhip effect" where small demand fluctuations amplify upstream, causing inefficiencies (Lee et al., 1997). Optimization focused on minimizing cost and maximizing throughput within this controlled hierarchy—a system epitomized by concepts like Just-In-Time (JIT) inventory (Ohno, 2019) and Enterprise Resource Planning (ERP) systems that sought to bring monolithic order to complex operations. Relationships were predominantly **dyadic** (firm-to-firm) and long-term, governed by contracts and stable, often inaccurate, forecasts.

The dawn of the digital age introduced connectivity as a transformative variable. The first wave of digital transformation (1990s-early 2000s) fostered **digitally integrated supply chains**. Technologies like Electronic Data Interchange (EDI), RFID, and Advanced Planning and Scheduling (APS) software injected greater visibility, coordination, and speed into the traditional pipeline (Simchi-Levi et al., 1999). Firms could track shipments in real-time, share demand forecasts with key suppliers via CPFR (Collaborative Planning, Forecasting, and Replenishment), and respond more agilely to market changes. Yet, the fundamental architecture remained largely intact—a chain, albeit a faster, more visible, and better-coordinated one, still orchestrated by a single focal firm exercising vertical control. The internet initially served as a powerful communication and transaction layer atop these existing linear structures, as seen in B2B procurement exchanges and early B2C e-commerce models (e.g., Amazon as a retailer, Dell's configure-to-order).

The true architectural rupture, however, commenced with the emergence and explosive growth of **multi-sided digital platforms**. This was not merely a technological upgrade but a paradigmatic shift in economic organization, challenging the very notion of the firm's boundaries (Parker et al., 2016). The platform model, grounded in theories of multi-sided markets (Evans, 2003; Rochet & Tirole, 2003), network effects (Katz & Shapiro, 1985), and the reduction of transaction costs through digital mediation, did not seek to optimize a proprietary pipeline. Instead, its core function was to **facilitate, enable, and govern direct value-creating interactions** between independent, often fragmented, groups of users (Gawer, 2014). Where a traditional firm internalizes production and manages a proprietary inventory (the"pipeline"), a platform externalizes production to its ecosystem—to drivers (Uber), hosts (Airbnb), third-party sellers (Amazon Marketplace, Alibaba's Taobao), or content creators (YouTube, Instagram). The platform's core assets thus underwent a fundamental transmutation: from physical capital and inventory to **software, data, algorithms, and community governance**.

This shift precipitated the birth of the **platform supply chain**. Unlike a traditional supply chain, which is a managed *process*, a platform supply chain is a curated, adaptive *ecosystem*. It is a dynamic, self-organizing network where the platform firm does not own the primary means of production or inventory but owns the critical **interface, the interaction protocols, the data infrastructure, and the trust mechanisms** that enable millions of decentralized micro-transactions to occur with coherence, efficiency, and scalability (McIntyre & Srinivasan, 2017). The evolution, therefore, is not linear but convergent and transformative: the logic of platform-mediated exchange began to permeate and reconfigure the very domain of physical logistics and operations management, giving rise to a hybrid, powerful new structure that blends digital coordination with decentralized physical execution.

1.1.2 Defining the Architectural Core of Platform Supply Chains

A platform supply chain can be formally defined as *a multi-sided, digitally-intermediated network structure in which a platform entity orchestrates the matching, transaction, and fulfillment of goods, services, or information among multiple independent participants—such as manufacturers, suppliers, retailers, and consumers, while governing the ecosystem through data-centric coordination mechanisms and modular operational protocols*. This architecture is built upon several interdependent, foundational pillars that distinguish it decisively from its predecessors.

1. Multi-Sided Participation and Cross-Side Network Effects: The platform explicitly designs its system to serve two or more distinct but interdependent user groups (e.g., riders and drivers, buyers and sellers, streamers and viewers). The core economic engine is the **cross-side network effect**: the value to a user on one side (e.g., a buyer) increases with the number, quality, and diversity of users on the other side (e.g., sellers) (Eisenmann et al., 2006). This creates a powerful, non-linear feedback loop for growth—the classic "chicken-and-egg" problem—but also introduces a fundamental operational challenge: managing **dynamic liquidity**. The platform must constantly balance supply and demand not just in aggregate, but in hyper-localized contexts (a specific neighborhood at 5 PM on a rainy Friday) and for specific niches (a rare collectible, a specialized freelance service). This dynamic, two-sided (or multi-sided) marketplace, governed by the platform's "invisible hand" of algorithms, is the defining economic unit and operational arena of the platform supply chain (Cusumano et al., 2019).

2. Modularity, Decentralization, and Ecosystem Innovation: Interactions within the platform supply chain are intentionally designed to be modular and loosely coupled. A third-party seller on an e-commerce platform operates as an independent micro-enterprise, choosing their own inventory, pricing (within platform rules), and packaging. A driver on a ride-hailing platform owns their vehicle and decides their working hours and general location. The platform provides standardized **Application Programming Interfaces (APIs)** and modular service "blocks"—such as a payment gateway, a tracking software development kit (SDK), a standardized rating system, or a fraud detection service—that these decentralized agents plug into (Tiwana et al., 2010). This architectural modularity allows for immense scale, flexibility, and rapid innovation at the "edges" of the network, as complements can innovate without requiring permission from the platform core. However, it also means the platform exerts control not through direct hierarchical command, but through the **strategic design of the interaction protocols** (what data is shared, how transactions are settled) and **algorithmically administered incentive structures** (e.g., search ranking, promotional visibility, service tier benefits) (De Reuver et al., 2018).

3. Data as the Central Nervous System and Core Asset: If the traditional supply chain ran on schedules and purchase orders, the platform supply chain operates on **continuous, real-time data streams**. Every search query, click, hover, booking, review, GPS ping, payment attempt, and chat message generates structured and unstructured data. This data serves a triple, intertwined purpose, transforming it from a byproduct into the platform's most valuable strategic asset (Iansiti & Lakhani, 2020):

- **Matching and Discovery:** Sophisticated algorithms use contextual and historical data to connect a specific consumer request with the most suitable provider (product, driver, service professional) in milliseconds, optimizing for factors beyond simple proximity, such as predicted satisfaction, likelihood of transaction completion, and long-term value.
- **Coordination and Trust Building:** Real-time tracking data (e.g., live package location, driver ETA) coordinates physical movement and sets accurate expectations, while algorithmic reputation systems (reviews, ratings, trust scores) mitigate the profound trust deficit inherent in decentralized transactions between strangers (Bolton et al., 2013).
- **Intelligence, Prediction, and Ecosystem Design:** Aggregated and anonymized data is analyzed using machine learning to forecast demand surges, detect sophisticated fraud patterns, optimize dynamic pricing, design efficient service zones, and guide strategic ecosystem growth initiatives. Data is the fuel for the predictive models that drive the platform's operational intelligence.

4. Algorithmic Governance and Dynamic Control: Platforms govern their sprawling ecosystems not through middle managers but through encoded rules—algorithms. These algorithms make or critically inform a vast array of operational decisions: real-time dynamic pricing (surge pricing), matching priorities and batching, search ranking and visibility, fraud detection and account flagging, content moderation, and even the allocation of promotional subsidies (Kellogg et al., 2020). This represents a historic shift from **managerial fiat and human discretion** to **algorithmic policy and automated governance**. The platform's "control" is indirect but pervasive and instantaneous, exercised through the constant, automated adjustment of the digital environment in which all participants operate. The rules of the game are encoded in software and can be A/B tested and updated continuously, creating a system of dynamic, adaptive, and often opaque governance that raises significant questions of fairness, accountability, and power (Zuboff, 2019).

1.1.3 Typology and Manifestations: A Spectrum of Platform Supply Chains

Platform supply chains are not monolithic; they exist across a spectrum defined by the nature of what is exchanged (goods, services, information) and the depth of the platform's involvement in the physical fulfillment or service delivery. We can identify several key archetypes, each with distinct operational implications:

- **Transaction Platforms (Digital Marketplaces):** These focus primarily on facilitating the matching and financial transaction of goods or services. Their involvement in physical fulfillment can range from minimal to fully integrated.
  - *E-commerce Marketplaces (e.g., Amazon Marketplace, Alibaba's Taobao/Tmall, eBay):* Connect buyers with a vast array of sellers. The platform may provide optional, integrated logistics services (Fulfillment by Amazon, Alibaba's Cainiao Network) as a modular service, but the core value proposition is discovery, trust, and transaction efficiency (Zhu & Liu, 2018).
  - *Service-on-Demand Platforms (e.g., Uber, Lyft, DoorDash, TaskRabbit):* Match consumers with service providers for real-time, localized services. Here, the coordination of the service delivery itself (the "last mile" of the ride or delivery) is central to the value proposition, requiring sophisticated spatio-temporal matching and tracking algorithms (Cachon et al., 2017).
  - *Asset-Sharing Platforms (e.g., Airbnb, Getaround):* Facilitate temporary access to underutilized physical assets. The platform's operational role extends deeply into trust-building (through reviews, verifications, and insurance), quality standardization through photography and listing guidelines, and dispute resolution.
- **Innovation/Developer Platforms:** These provide a foundational technological infrastructure upon which other firms build complementary products and services, creating a nested, layered supply chain of innovation.

  - *Cloud Computing Platforms (e.g., AWS, Microsoft Azure, Google Cloud Platform):* Provide modular, on-demand computing, storage, and AI services that form the indispensable digital backbone of virtually all modern digital supply chain operations and analytics.
  - *Operating Systems and App Stores (e.g., iOS, Android):* Orchestrate a global supply chain of software (applications) from millions of developers to billions of end-users, managing discovery, distribution, updates, and financial settlement.

- **Integrated Social-Commerce and Livestreaming Platforms:** These blend social interaction, content creation, and real-time commerce, creating dynamic supply chains for influence, entertainment, and products simultaneously (e.g., Instagram Shopping, TikTok LIVE Shopping, Pinduoduo's social team-purchase model). Here, the "supply chain" includes the flow of attention and influence, which is then monetized through instant transactions (Luo et al., 2025).
- **Logistics Orchestration Platforms:** These are platforms specifically architected to coordinate the physical movement of goods across multiple, fragmented carriers, warehouses, and customs agencies (e.g., Flexport, FourKites, project44). They add a critical layer of data-driven visibility, coordination, and optimization atop traditional, often siloed, logistics assets, effectively creating a "control tower" for global trade.

1.1.4 The Operational Imperatives and Inherent Tensions

The unique architecture of platform supply chains generates a new set of operational imperatives and inherent tensions that traditional Operations Management (OM) theory, designed for pipeline control, is often ill-equipped to handle:

1. **Managing Scale, Liquidity, and the Congestion Problem:** How does one ensure a reliable, high-quality "supply" (of drivers, products, hosts) is available to meet fragmented, spiky, and unpredictable"demand" across millions of micro-markets and microseconds? This is a continuous, two-sided yield management problem of unprecedented granularity. Congestion—where too many requesters face too few providers, or vice versa—can cause system failure (Guda & Subramanian, 2019).
2. **Quality Control and Standardization in a Decentralized System:** Without direct employment contracts, how can a platform ensure consistent service or product quality? This leads to the central, yet imperfect, role of **reputation systems, standardized service protocols, certification programs, and algorithmic de-platforming** as the primary tools for quality control. However, these systems can be gamed, can exhibit biases, and may not capture all quality dimensions (Cullen and Farronato, 2021).
3. **Optimizing for Ecosystem Health versus Short-Term Platform Profit:** Short-term profit maximization (e.g., extreme surge pricing, high commission rates) can

damage the long-term health and sustainability of the ecosystem by driving away users on either side. The platform must optimize for complex, long-term metrics like user lifetime value, overall platform engagement, and Gross Merchandise Value (GMV) health, often requiring subsidies and carefully balanced trade-offs (Edelman, 2015).

4. **Data Richness versus Strategic Information Asymmetry:** While the platform has a near-omniscient "god's-eye view" of aggregate data flows, individual participants (sellers, drivers) often operate with limited, asymmetric information. This can lead to strategic gaming, inefficient behaviors (e.g., driver clustering in known hotspots), and a perceived lack of fairness. Designing transparent yet strategy-proof mechanisms is a profound algorithmic and economic challenge (Benjaafar et al., 2019).
5. **The Physical-Digital Integration Gap ("The Last Inch Problem"):** The platform excels at digital matching, payment processing, and data analytics. However, the final moment—the physical handover of a package, the ride in a car, the stay in a home, the quality of a meal—remains analog, variable, and prone to friction and unpredictability. Bridging this"last-inch" gap between digital promise and physical reality is the critical, ongoing operational frontier for platform supply chains.

In conclusion, the evolution from the linear, integrated pipeline to the decentralized, platform-orchestrated ecosystem represents a fundamental change in the ontology of supply chains. The object of management is no longer a flow but a complex adaptive network; the primary lever of control is no longer a directive but an algorithm and an incentive; the core strategic asset is no longer inventory but data and community. This new architectural reality demands a correspondingly new paradigm for decision-making—one that can thrive on radical uncertainty, learn continuously from high-dimensional data streams, and optimize for the dynamic, multi-objective equilibria of a living ecosystem. This imperative sets the stage for the methodological revolution at the heart of this book: **the Predict-then-Optimize paradigm**.

1.2 The Predict-Then-Optimize Paradigm

This book adopts and develops the Predict-then-Optimize (PTO) paradigm as a unifying analytical framework for platform supply chains. In this section, we briefly introduce the PTO paradigm.

1.2.1 The Limits of Traditional Optimization in a Stochastic, Data-Rich World

Classical Operations Research (OR) and prescriptive analytics have long provided the methodological backbone for supply chain decision-making. The goal is theoretically pristine: given a well-defined set of constraints (capacity, budget, time) and an objective function (minimize cost, maximize revenue, etc.), find the provably *optimal* decision. Foundational models like linear programming (Dantzig, 1951), integer programming, and dynamic programming (Bellman, 1966) are powerful tools for this purpose within their domain of applicability. However, they typically rest on a critical, often heroic, simplifying assumption: that the key parameters of the problem (demand, travel time, conversion rates, costs) are **known with certainty** or can be reasonably represented by static, historical averages.

In the reality of modern, let alone platform, supply chains, this assumption is almost universally violated. Supply chains are intrinsically stochastic systems, awash in **deep, multi-layered uncertainty**. Demand is volatile and influenced by a myriad of factors. Travel and service times are highly variable. The likelihood of a user accepting a price offer or a driver accepting a dispatch is unknown and context-dependent. The future behavior of a new marketplace seller is unpredictable. Traditional OM has developed a suite of advanced methods to handle uncertainty, but each has significant limitations when applied to the platform context:

- **Stochastic Programming:** Incorporates probabilistic scenarios to model uncertainty explicitly (Birge & Louveaux, 1997). While powerful, it becomes computationally intractable ("curses of dimensionality") when the number of uncertain parameters is large or when decisions are high-frequency and real-time—precisely the case in platform operations.
- **Robust Optimization:** Seeks decisions that perform well under a worst-case scenario within an uncertainty set (Ben-Tal et al., 2009). This can lead to overly conservative, inefficient outcomes that waste the platform's potential for agile response, as it ignores distributional information beyond the worst-case bound.
- **The Ubiquitous *Ad Hoc* Approach: Using Point Forecasts:** The most common practice in industry is a disjointed, two-step process: (1) a data science team produces a point forecast (e.g., predicted demand = 100 units) using a statistical or machine learning model, and (2) this single number is plugged as a deterministic input into a downstream optimization model. This **decoupled approach** is fundamentally flawed because it ignores **decision-dependent uncertainty** (Elmachtoub & Grigas, 2022). The cost of a prediction error is not simply its squared deviation from the truth; its impact is entirely contingent on the downstream decision it informs. A prediction error for a high-margin, highly perishable item has catastrophic consequences different from the same magnitude error for a low-margin, stable good. By separating prediction from optimization, we train predictors to be statistically accurate (e.g., minimize Mean Squared Error) but not necessarily *decisionally effective*.

In the volatile, high-dimensional, and data-saturated environment of a digital platform, these traditional approaches fracture under pressure. Decisions must be made in milliseconds (matching a driver), are deeply personalized and contextual (dynamic pricing for a specific user), and are based on rich, high-dimensional feature sets (user history, location, device, time, weather, local events). The "uncertain parameters" are not just random variables with simple distributions; they are complex, non-linear functions of observable covariates that must be *learned* from massive datasets. This reality necessitates a tight, formal, and computationally feasible integration of the statistical learning of uncertainty with the prescriptive calculus of optimization. This integration is the essence of the Predict-then-Optimize paradigm.

1.2.2 Formalizing the Paradigm: Prediction and Optimization as Integrated Stages

The **Predict-then-Optimize (PTO)** paradigm, also emerging in the literature under names like *Smart Predict then Optimize (SPO)*, *Decision-Focused Learning*, or *End-to-End Learning for Optimization*, offers a principled framework for this necessary integration (Donti et al., 2017; Elmachtoub & Grigas, 2022; Wilder et al., 2019). It formally recognizes that in a business or operational context, the ultimate goal is **not the most accurate prediction in an abstract statistical sense, but the most useful prediction for making a high-quality decision.** The criterion for success is the value of the decision outcome, not the fidelity of the intermediate prediction.

The paradigm can be decomposed into two conceptually sequential but, in advanced implementations, algorithmically intertwined stages:

Stage 1: The Contextual Prediction (Learning) Problem

In this stage, we leverage historical data $D = \{(x_i, y_i)\}_{i=1}^N$ to learn a mapping from **observable context or features (x)** to an **uncertain target parameter (y)** that is a crucial input to the subsequent decision problem. The feature vector x is rich and may include: contextual details (timestamp, GPS coordinates, weather), user profile attributes, product/service characteristics, and market indicators. The target y is the unknown we need to estimate for optimization, such as *demand quantity*, *service completion time*, *customer conversion probability*, *driver supply elasticity*, or *customer lifetime value*.

We train a predictive model $f_\theta(x)$, parameterized by weights θ, that outputs a prediction $\hat{y}$. This model can range from interpretable linear or logistic regression to powerful, non-parametric methods like gradient boosting machines (e.g., XGBoost) or deep neural networks, chosen based on the complexity and structure of the data.

Stage 2: The Prescriptive Optimization (Decision) Problem

This is the prescriptive core where value is created. We have an optimization problem with decision variable z, an objective function $c(z, y)$ that depends on both our decision and the true (unknown) parameter y, and constraints $g(z, y) \leq 0$.

The naive, decoupled approach simply substitutes the true y with its point prediction $\hat{y}$ and solves $z^*_{naive} = \arg\min_z c(z, \hat{y})$.

The foundational insight of PTO is that we must explicitly account for the **loss function of the downstream decision problem** when training our predictor. The "cost" of a prediction error is not its squared deviation, but the *suboptimality it induces in the final decision*. Formally, let $z^*(y) = \arg\min_z c(z, y)$ be the true optimal decision if we knew y. The decision made using prediction $\hat{y}$ is $z^*(\hat{y})$. The **regret** or **decision loss** is the difference in actual cost incurred:

$$\mathcal{L}_{decision}(y, \hat{y}) = c(z^*(\hat{y}), y) - c(z^*(y), y) \geq 0.$$

The goal of the PTO paradigm is to train the predictive model parameters θ to minimize the *expected decision loss* over the distribution of future data, i.e., $\min_\theta \mathbb{E}_{(x,y)}[\mathcal{L}_{decision}(y, f_\theta(x))]$, rather than the expected prediction error like MSE $\mathbb{E}[(y - f_\theta(x))^2]$.

1.2.3 Methodological Approaches Within the PTO Paradigm

Translating this paradigm into practice requires novel techniques that bridge the traditionally separate fields of machine learning and mathematical optimization. Three principal methodological strands have emerged:

1. **Two-Stage Stochastic Programming with Data-Driven Scenario Generation:** This approach maintains the two-stage structure but connects them via scenario generation. The predictive model $f_\theta(x)$ (or an associated generative model) is used to produce a representative set of scenarios $\{y_s\}$ for the uncertain parameter y, often capturing its conditional distribution $P(y|x)$. These scenarios are then fed into a two-stage stochastic program: the first-stage ("here-and-now") decision z is optimized against the expected cost over these data-driven scenarios, accounting for recourse actions in the second stage (Shapiro et al., 2021). This method is powerful and interpretable but can be computationally demanding for real-time applications with many scenarios.
2. **Decision-Focused Learning (Differentiable Optimization):** This is a more deeply integrated and rapidly advancing approach. It aims to train the predictive model end-to-end by directly minimizing the decision loss. The key innovation is to treat the optimization problem as a **differentiable layer** within a neural network architecture (Agrawal et al., 2019; Amos & Kolter, 2017).

   - **Forward Pass:** Context $x \rightarrow$ Predictive model $f_\theta(x) \rightarrow$ Prediction $\hat{y} \rightarrow$ Optimization solver $\rightarrow$ Optimal decision $z^*(\hat{y})$.
   - **Loss Computation:** The actual cost $c(z^*(\hat{y}), y)$ is computed using the true y.
   - **Backward Pass (Key Step):** The gradient of this decision loss with respect to the predictive model parameters θ, $\nabla_\theta c(z^*(\hat{y}), y)$, is computed. This requires propagating gradients *back through the optimization solver*, which is non-trivial as solvers are typically not differentiable. Techniques like implicit differentiation (using the KKT conditions of the optimization problem) and the development of differentiable convex optimization layers (e.g., CVXPYlayers) have made this feasible for a broad class of problems (Amos, 2022). The model learns to make predictions that "bend" towards steering the optimizer to decisions with better actual outcomes, even if the predictions themselves become slightly biased when judged by statistical metrics.

3. **Contextual Stochastic Optimization and Reinforcement Learning:** This framework often circumvents the explicit prediction of y altogether. It directly seeks a policy $\pi_\phi(x)$, parameterized by ϕ, that maps from the observed context x directly to a decision z. This is a "predict-then-optimize" process collapsed into a single policy. Methods like **contextual bandits** and **Reinforcement Learning (RL)** are used, where the policy is trained to maximize cumulative reward (negative cost) through exploration and interaction with the environment (Sutton & Barto, 1998). This is particularly powerful for sequential decision-making problems under uncertainty, such as dynamic pricing or multi-period matching, where the impact of a decision affects future states.

1.2.4 The Symbiotic Fit: Why PTO Is the Indispensable Paradigm for Platform Supply Chains

The PTO paradigm is not merely a useful technical upgrade for platform operations; it is a necessary adaptation, as the features of platform supply chains multiply its advantages:

- **Native Handling of High-Dimensional Context:** Platform decisions are profoundly contextual. PTO seamlessly integrates these rich features x into the decision-making pipeline via the predictive model, moving far beyond time-series forecasts to contextual, personalized estimates of uncertain parameters.
- **Direct Alignment with Complex, Multi-Objective Business Goals:** Platform success metrics are rarely simple. They involve trade-offs between liquidity, profit, user growth, equity, and long-term ecosystem health. PTO allows the optimization stage's objective function $c(z, y)$ to be precisely this complex business KPI. The predictive model is then trained to support *this specific objective*, not a generic statistical goal.
- **Scalability to High-Dimensional State and Decision Spaces:** The state space of a platform (all possible configurations of users, locations, inventory) is astronomically large. PTO methods, particularly those leveraging deep learning for the prediction stage, are uniquely capable of learning effective representations and patterns within this high-dimensional space to inform tractable optimization.
- **Enabling Real-Time, Adaptive Learning Systems:** The integrated, often differentiable nature of modern PTO systems allows for rapid online learning and adaptation. As new data streams in from the ecosystem, the predictive models can be updated continuously via mini-batch learning or reinforcement, ensuring the decision engine remains aligned with a non-stationary reality—a critical capability for platforms in fast-moving markets.

In essence, the PTO paradigm provides the mathematical and computational foundation for building the "central nervous system" of an intelligent platform. It is the methodology that enables a system to continuously *learn from* the ecosystem's rich data exhaust in order to *prescribe optimal governance actions* for that same ecosystem. It closes the feedback loop between observation, prediction, and action in a principled, automated, and value-driven way. Having established this powerful conceptual and methodological framework, we now turn to its concrete, transformative applications in managing the unique operational challenges of platform supply chains.

1.3 Applying the PTO Paradigm to Platform Supply Chain Management

The theoretical power and necessity of the PTO paradigm find their ultimate validation and refinement in practical application. Platform supply chains, with their well-defined operational pain points and data-rich environments, provide an ideal proving ground. This section outlines the primary domains of application, illustrating how PTO is reshaping core platform functions from reactive management to proactive, intelligent orchestration. The literature in each area is rapidly growing, reflecting the paradigm's ascendance.

1.3.1 Dynamic Pricing and Revenue Management

Pricing in a platform is a high-stakes, high-dimensional, real-time optimization problem under deep uncertainty. The platform must set prices for millions of SKUs (e-commerce) or for a service in hyper-localized zones and times (ride-hailing), balancing the dual objectives of clearing the market and extracting revenue while managing cross-side network effects.

- **Traditional and Early Platform Approach:** Use historical averages to estimate a demand curve, then apply rule-based heuristics or classical revenue management algorithms (e.g., from airline industry) (Talluri & Van Ryzin, 2004).
- **PTO Approach:** Model the **contextual demand function**. Let feature vector x include: product/service attributes, competitor prices (scraped), user profile and purchase history, time of day, day of week, local events, weather, and real-time inventory/supply levels. The predictive model $f_\theta(x, price)$ forecasts the **price-dependent conversion probability** or demand elasticity—the uncertain parameter y. The optimization stage then solves for the price p^* that maximizes expected revenue $p \cdot f_\theta(x, p)$ (or a more complex objective including growth and fairness). This enables truly personalized, real-time pricing. Literature shows significant lifts: (Ban & Keskin, 2021) use a contextual bandits framework for dynamic pricing with demand learning, while (Ferreira et al., 2016) demonstrate the value of integrating forecasting and optimization for online retail. In ride-hailing, the pioneering work of Hu et al. (2022) models the equilibrium effects of surge pricing, a

problem naturally suited to a PTO framework that predicts driver supply and rider demand responses.

1.3.2 Matching and Dispatch Optimization

The core real-time operation of an on-demand platform is matching a request (a ride, a delivery order) to a provider (driver, courier). The objective is multi-faceted: minimize wait time, maximize provider utilization/earnings, minimize detour, and ensure service quality, all while considering the future state of the network.

- **Traditional Approach:** Greedy matching based on nearest Euclidean distance or first-available agent. Some platforms use simple batching to improve efficiency.
- **PTO Approach:** Frame matching as a **sequential stochastic optimization problem**. The predictive model forecasts key uncertainties conditional on context x: the **estimated time to completion** of a current job (highly dependent on dynamic traffic), the **acceptance probability** of a dispatch (based on driver's state, direction, and historical behavior), and the **short-term future demand** in nearby zones. The optimization stage (often formulated as a multi-period matching problem or solved via reinforcement learning) makes matches not myopically, but to position the supply network optimally for anticipated future requests. Liu et al. (2022) survey RL approaches for ride-hailing. Work by Özkan and Ward (2020) demonstrates a PTO-style approach where a predictive model of trip duration informs a stochastic matching optimization, significantly reducing passenger wait times and driver idle miles compared to greedy algorithms.

1.3.3 Inventory and Fulfillment Network Design

For e-commerce platforms, especially those offering fast (same-day/next-day) shipping promises, inventory placement is a billion-dollar optimization problem. The platform must decide which products to stock, in which fulfillment centers (FCs) or dark stores, and in what quantities, under highly uncertain, spatially-correlated demand.

- **Traditional Approach:** Forecast demand at a regional or FC level using ARIMA or similar time-series models, then solve a deterministic or two-stage stochastic multi-echelon inventory optimization (MIP) model (Graves & Willems, 2008).
- **PTO Approach:** Generate **granular, contextual demand predictions**. Features x include product trends, online search volume, seller promotions, social media sentiment, and socioeconomic data of the FC catchment area. The predictive model (e.g., a spatio-temporal graph neural network) outputs a probabilistic forecast for

demand $y_{i,t}$ for product i in location l at time t. The optimization stage then solves a large-scale stochastic inventory-location problem, minimizing the expected total cost (holding, transportation, stockouts, and repositioning) based on the *joint distribution* of demand provided by the predictive model. This can dramatically reduce safety stock needs while improving service levels. The work of Kaynov et al. (2024) on "deep learning for multi-location inventory management" and Yin and Dai (2022) on large-scale demand forecasting integrated with planning at Amazon are canonical examples of the PTO philosophy in action.

1.3.4 Service Region Design and Incentive Allocation

Platforms must proactively manage their supply side to ensure adequate coverage and service quality. This involves designing dynamic service zones (geofencing) and allocating monetary incentives (guaranteed earnings, streak bonuses, hotspot bonuses) to influence where and when independent agents work.

- **Traditional Approach:** Use historical "gap maps" (areas of unmet demand) to manually redraw static zones and allocate blanket, one-size-fits-all incentives.
- **PTO Approach:** Predict **supply elasticity and spatial activity patterns**. Build a predictive model where context x includes driver characteristics, historical incentive responsiveness, real-time and forecasted local demand, weather, and daypart. The target y is the predicted probability of a driver logging on, moving to a specific zone, or completing a number of trips in response to a proposed incentive structure. The optimization stage then solves for the optimal incentive scheme (amount, timing, conditionality) across the city's spatial grid to minimize a cost function that includes incentive payouts and the expected cost of unmet demand (modeled as lost revenue or customer attrition). This is a classic contextual stochastic optimization problem. Literature includes the work of Bimpikis et al. (2019) on spatial pricing and incentives in ride-sharing networks, and Zhao et al. (2023) on data-driven optimization of subsidy allocation in food delivery platforms.

1.3.5 Reputation, Fraud, and Risk Management

Trust is the currency of platforms. They must identify and mitigate fraudulent transactions (fake reviews, payment fraud, account takeovers, promo code abuse) and manage the risk posed by unreliable or malicious agents, all in real-time.

- **Traditional Approach:** Rule-based systems (e.g., flag transactions over $X) and simple logistic regression or decision tree models on a limited set of handcrafted features.

- **PTO Approach:** Treat fraud detection as a **contextual classification problem with asymmetric and decision-dependent costs**. The predictive model $f_\theta(x)$ (e.g., a graph neural network operating on a transaction-user graph) estimates the probability of fraud y, using a rich feature set x: transaction details, user behavior sequences, device fingerprints, IP addresses, and network graphs of connected accounts (Cheng et al., 2025). Crucially, the cost of a false positive (blocking a legitimate user, damaging their trust) is very different from the cost of a false negative (allowing fraud, losing money). The PTO optimization stage uses these probabilistic predictions to make the *decision* of whether to block, flag for review, or allow a transaction, minimizing the total expected cost (financial loss + reputational damage) to the platform. This moves beyond AUC as a metric to directly optimizing business value. The field of "cost-sensitive learning" and "learning with structured output" is highly relevant here (Elkan, 2001; Nam et al., 2014).

1.3.6 Content Moderation, Ranking, and Recommendation Systems

While not a "supply chain" in the physical sense, the flow of content and products is the core "inventory" of social and media platforms. Recommendation systems determine what content to "supply" to which user, directly driving engagement, ad revenue, and marketplace transactions.

- **Traditional Approach:** Collaborative filtering (Matrix Factorization) or shallow learning to predict user ratings (the prediction goal), then rank items by the predicted rating.
- **PTO Approach (Multi-Objective, Decision-Focused Recommendation):** The predictive model learns to estimate user engagement probabilities (clicks, watch time, likes, purchase) for items given context x. The optimization stage does not simply rank by predicted engagement. It solves for a slate of recommendations that optimizes a *blended, often non-linear objective* that might include: maximizing long-term user satisfaction and retention, ensuring diversity and serendipity, promoting new creators (for ecosystem health), satisfying fairness constraints, and maximizing downstream conversion value (e.g., for e-commerce recommendations) (Abdollahpouri et al., 2020; Schafer et al., 2001). The PTO paradigm, particularly through reinforcement learning (e.g., Deep Q-Networks for recommendation), trains the system end-to-end to directly maximize this complex, decision-focused objective, often outperforming systems that simply chain a prediction model to a greedy ranker (Zhao et al., 2018).

1.3.7 Synthesis: The Platform as a Self-Optimizing, Adaptive Organism

The application of the PTO paradigm across these diverse domains coalesces into a unified vision: the platform supply chain as a **self-optimizing, adaptive learning organism**. It is a cyber-physical system that embodies a continuous, automated loop of intelligence:

1. **Senses:** It observes its internal and external environment through perpetual, high-fidelity data streams (Stage 1: Contextual Prediction).
2. **Evaluates:** It simulates and evaluates potential actions against a complex, multi-stakeholder objective function that encodes the long-term health and performance of the entire ecosystem (Stage 2: Prescriptive Optimization).
3. **Acts:** It executes the chosen actions by adjusting its algorithmic levers—prices, matches, incentives, rankings, alerts—in real-time.
4. **Learns:** It measures the outcomes of those actions, using the new data to update its predictive models and refine its understanding of the world, thereby closing the loop.

This represents the pinnacle of data-driven operations management. The PTO paradigm provides the essential methodology to move beyond descriptive analytics ("what happened") and predictive analytics ("what will happen") to truly **prescriptive analytics ("what is the best thing to do, and why")** in the complex, dynamic, and multi-agent world of platforms. It transforms the platform from a passive marketplace infrastructure into an active, intelligent orchestrator of economic and social activity.

1.4 Organization and Contents of the Book

This book, *Platform Supply Chains: The Predict-then-Optimize Paradigm*, provides a systematic study of how the Predict-then-Optimize (PTO) framework transforms operations management in platform supply chains. The following outlines the book's organization and content, beginning with a motivational overview in Chap. 1 that introduces platform supply chains, the PTO paradigm, and its transformative impact on their operations. Next, it is structured into three core chapters, each addressing a crucial aspect of operations management in the platform supply chains. Below we briefly introduce the organization and contents. Chapter 1 first motivates the whole book by providing an overall introduction to the platform supply chains, PTO paradigm, and operations management in the platform supply chains with the PTO paradigm discussing how the PTO paradigm reshapes operations management in platform supply chains. Chapters 2–4 present data-driven analytics frameworks to address complex inventory and product management challenges in various industries. Each chapter follows the Predict-then-Optimize framework: using data-driven

Table 1.1 Main content of the book

Section	Industry focus	Prediction tool	Optimization tool	Primary goal
Chapter 2	Online retailer	Multinomial Logit (MNL)	Robust assortment model	Revenue growth and strategic design
Chapter 3	Food manufacturing	Time-series ensemble (DET/DIT/PCT)	Risk-averse multiperiod newsvendor	Profit maximization under volatility
Chapter 4	Cross-border fast fashion retailer	Random forest (machine learning)	Stochastic inventory model	Risk mitigation and cost reduction

analytics to forecast or estimate parameters, followed by prescriptive optimization models to make operational decisions. Table 1.1 summarize the main content of this book. Chapter 2 proposes an integrated framework for an online retailer that combines new product design with assortment optimization. By utilizing a Multinomial Logit (MNL) model to estimate consumer preferences and a robust assortment model to account for parameter uncertainty, this approach demonstrated a 31% improvement in expected revenue. Chapter 3 addresses a multiperiod risk-averse newsvendor problem for a food manufacturer by transforming nonstationary demand into predictable stationary series through detrending and differencing methods; by using an ensemble of these techniques, it achieves up to a 92.25% improvement in profit performance. Chapter 4 develops a two-stage predictive and prescriptive approach for a cross-border e-commerce fashion retailer, using machine learning (specifically random forests) to classify profitable items and optimize inventory in overseas warehouses, resulting in cost reductions of up to 20%. Together, these papers illustrate how integrating predictive and prescriptive analytics can significantly enhance operational decision-making and financial outcomes in real-world retail settings.

References

Abdollahpouri, H., Mansoury, M., Burke, R., & Mobasher, B. (2020). The connection between popularity bias, calibration, and fairness in recommendation. In *Proceedings of the 14th ACM Conference on Recommender Systems* (pp. 726–731).

Agrawal, A., Amos, B., Barratt, S., Boyd, S., Diamond, S., & Kolter, J. Z. (2019). Differentiable convex optimization layers. *Advances in Neural Information Processing Systems*, 32.

Amos, B. (2022). Tutorial on amortized optimization for learning to optimize over continuous domains. In *Proceedings of the 39th International Conference on Machine Learning*.

Amos, B., & Kolter, J. Z. (2017). Optnet: Differentiable optimization as a layer in neural networks. In *International Conference on Machine Learning* (pp. 136–145) (PMLR).

Ban, G. Y., & Keskin, N. B. (2021). Personalized dynamic pricing with machine learning: High-dimensional features and heterogeneous elasticity. *Management Science, 67*(9), 5549–5568.

Bellman, R. (1966). Dynamic programming. *Science, 153*(3731), 34–37.

Benjaafar, S., Kong, G., Li, X., & Courcoubetis, C. (2019). Peer-to-peer product sharing: Implications for ownership, usage, and social welfare in the sharing economy. *Management Science, 65*(2), 477–493.
Ben-Tal, A., El Ghaoui, L., & Nemirovski, A. (2009) *Robust optimization* (Vol. 28). Princeton University Press.
Bimpikis, K., Candogan, O., & Saban, D. (2019). Spatial pricing in ride-sharing networks. *Operations Research, 67*(3), 744–769.
Birge, J. R., & Louveaux, F. (1997). *Introduction to stochastic programming*. Springer.
Bolton, G., Greiner, B., & Ockenfels, A. (2013). Engineering trust: Reciprocity in the production of reputation information. *Management Science, 59*(2), 265–285.
Cachon, G. P., Daniels, K. M., & Lobel, R. (2017). The role of surge pricing on a service platform with self-scheduling capacity. *Manufacturing & Service Operations Management, 19*(3), 368–384.
Cheng, D., Zou, Y., Xiang, S., & Jiang, C. (2025). Graph neural networks for financial fraud detection: A review. *Frontiers of Computer Science, 19*(9), Article 199609.
Coase, R. H. (1937). The nature of the firm. *Economica, 4*(16), 386–405.
Cui, X., Li, Y., Li, X., & Fang, S. (2023). Livestream e-commerce in a platform supply chain: A product-fit uncertainty reduction perspective. *International Journal of Production Economics, 258*, Article 108796.
Cullen, Z., & Farronato, C. (2021). Outsourcing tasks online: Matching supply and demand on peer-to-peer internet platforms. *Management Science, 67*(7), 3985–4003.
Cusumano, M. A., Gawer, A., & Yoffie, D. B. (2019). *The business of platforms: Strategy in the age of digital competition, innovation, and power*. Harper Business.
Dantzig, G. B. (1951). Maximization of a linear function of variables subject to linear inequalities. *Activity Analysis of Production and Allocation, 13*, 339–347.
De Reuver, M., Sørensen, C., & Basole, R. C. (2018). The digital platform: A research agenda. *Journal of Information Technology, 33*(2), 124–135.
Donti, P., Kolter, J. Z., & Amos, B. (2017) Task-based end-to-end model learning in stochastic optimization. *Advances in Neural Information Processing Systems*, 30.
Edelman, B. (2015). How to launch your digital platform. *Harvard Business Review, 93*(4), 90–97.
Eisenmann, T., Parker, G., & Van Alstyne, M. (2006). Strategies for two-sided markets. *Harvard Business Review, 84*(10), 92.
Elkan, C. (2001) The foundations of cost-sensitive learning. In *International Joint Conference on Artificial Intelligence* (Vol. 17, pp. 973–978). Lawrence Erlbaum Associates Ltd.
Elmachtoub, A. N., & Grigas, P. (2022). Smart "predict, then optimize". *Management Science, 68*(1), 9–26.
Evans, D. S. (2003). The antitrust economics of multi-sided platform markets. *Yale Journal on Regulation, 20*(2), 325–382.
Ferreira, K. J., Lee, B. H. A., & Simchi-Levi, D. (2016). Analytics for an online retailer: Demand forecasting and price optimization. *Manufacturing & Service Operations Management, 18*(1), 69–88.
Gawer, A. (2014). Bridging differing perspectives on technological platforms: Toward an integrative framework. *Research Policy, 43*(7), 1239–1249.
Graves, S. C., & Willems, S. P. (2008). Strategic inventory placement in supply chains: Nonstationary demand. *Manufacturing & Service Operations Management, 10*(2), 278–287.
Guda, H., & Subramanian, U. (2019). Your uber is arriving: Managing on-demand workers through surge pricing, forecast communication, and worker incentives. *Management Science, 65*(5), 1995–2014.
Hu, B., Hu, M., & Zhu, H. (2022). Surge pricing and two-sided temporal responses in ride hailing. *Manufacturing & Service Operations Management, 24*(1), 91–109.
Iansiti, M., & Lakhani, K. R. (2020). *Competing in the age of AI: Strategy and leadership when algorithms and networks run the world*. Harvard Business Press.

Katz, M. L., & Shapiro, C. (1985). Network externalities, competition, and compatibility. *The American Economic Review, 75*(3), 424–440.

Kaynov, I., Van Knippenberg, M., Menkovski, V., Van Breemen, A., & Van Jaarsveld, W. (2024). Deep reinforcement learning for one-warehouse multi-retailer inventory management. *International Journal of Production Economics, 267*, Article 109088.

Kellogg, K. C., Valentine, M. A., & Christin, A. (2020). Algorithms at work: The new contested terrain of control. *Academy of Management Annals, 14*(1), 366–410.

Lee, H. L., Padmanabhan, V., & Whang, S. (1997). The bullwhip effect in supply chains. *Sloan Management Review, 38*(3), 93–102.

Li, M., Li, T., & Yu, L. (2026). Retail platform analytics: Practice, literature, and future research. *Production and Operations Management, 35*(1), 69–86.

Liu, Y., Jia, R., Ye, J., & Qu, X. (2022). How machine learning informs ride-hailing services: A survey. *Communications in Transportation Research, 2*, Article 100075.

Luo, X., Lim, W. M., Cheah, J. H., Lim, X. J., & Dwivedi, Y. K. (2025). Live streaming commerce: A review and research agenda. *Journal of Computer Information Systems, 65*(3), 376–399.

McIntyre, D. P., & Srinivasan, A. (2017). Networks, platforms, and strategy: Emerging views and next steps. *Strategic Management Journal, 38*(1), 141–160.

Nam, J., Kim, E., Loza Mencía, E., Gurevych, I., & Fürnkranz, J. (2014). Large-scale multi-label text classification—revisiting neural networks. In *Joint European Conference on Machine Learning and Knowledge Discovery in Databases* (pp. 437–452). Springer.

Ohno, T. (2019). *Toyota production system: Beyond large-scale production*. Productivity Press.

Özkan, E., & Ward, A. R. (2020). Dynamic matching for real-time ride sharing. *Stochastic Systems, 10*(1), 29–70.

Parker, G. G., Van Alstyne, M. W., & Choudary, S. P. (2016). *Platform revolution: How networked markets are transforming the economy—and how to make them work for you*. WW Norton & Company.

Parker, G., & Van Alstyne, M. (2018). Innovation, openness, and platform control. *Management Science, 64*(7), 3015–3032.

Rochet, J. C., & Tirole, J. (2003). Platform competition in two-sided markets. *Journal of the European Economic Association, 1*(4), 990–1029.

Schafer, J. B., Konstan, J. A., & Riedl, J. (2001). E-commerce recommendation applications. *Data Mining and Knowledge Discovery, 5*(1), 115–153.

Shapiro, A., Dentcheva, D., & Ruszczynski, A. (2021). *Lectures on stochastic programming: Modeling and theory*. SIAM.

Simchi-Levi, D., Kaminsky, P., & Simchi-Levi, E. (1999). *Designing and managing the supply chain: Concepts, strategies, and cases*. McGraw-Hill .

Sutton, R. S., & Barto, A. G. (1998). *Reinforcement learning: An introduction*. MIT Press.

Talluri, K. T., & Van Ryzin, G. J. (2004). *The theory and practice of revenue management* (Vol. 68). Springer Science & Business Media.

Tiwana, A., Konsynski, B., & Bush, A. A. (2010). Research commentary—platform evolution: Coevolution of platform architecture, governance, and environmental dynamics. *Information Systems Research, 21*(4), 675–687.

Van Alstyne, M. W., Parker, G. G., & Choudary, S. P. (2016). Pipelines, platforms, and the new rules of strategy. *Harvard Business Review, 94*(4), 54–62.

Wang, P., Du, S., Hu, L., & Tang, W. (2023). Logistics choices in a platform supply chain: A co-opetitive perspective. *Journal of the Operational Research Society, 74*(1), 93–111.

Wilder, B., Dilkina, B., & Tambe, M. (2019). Melding the data-decisions pipeline: Decision-focused learning for combinatorial optimization. *Proceedings of the AAAI Conference on Artificial Intelligence, 33*, 1658–1665.

Xia, L., Li, K., Wang, J., Xia, Y., & Qin, J. (2024). Carbon emission reduction and precision marketing decisions of a platform supply chain. *International Journal of Production Economics, 268*, Article 109104.

Yin, C., & Dai, Q. (2022). A deep multivariate time series multistep forecasting network. *Applied Intelligence, 52*(8), 8956–8974.
Zhang, Z., Xu, H., Chen, K., Zhao, Y., & Liu, Z. (2023). Channel mode selection for an e-platform supply chain in the presence of a secondary marketplace. *European Journal of Operational Research, 305*(3), 1215–1235.
Zhang, X., Chen, H., & Liu, Z. (2024). Operation strategy in an e-commerce platform supply chain: Whether and how to introduce live streaming services? *International Transactions in Operational Research, 31*(2), 1093–1121.
Zhao, X., Zhang, L., Xia, L., Ding, Z., Yin, D., & Tang, J. (2018). Deep reinforcement learning for page-wise recommendations. *Proceedings of the 12th ACM Conference on Recommender Systems* (pp. 95–103).
Zhao, B., Tan, H., Zhou, C., & Feng, H. (2023). Optimal delivery time and subsidy for it-enabled food delivery platforms considering negative externality and social welfare. *Industrial Management & Data Systems, 123*(5), 1336–1358.
Zhu, F., & Liu, Q. (2018). Competing with complementors: An empirical look at amazon.com. *Strategic Management Journal, 39*(10), 2618–2642.
Zuboff, S. (2019). *The age of surveillance capitalism: The fight for a human future at the new frontier of power*. Public Affairs.

Chapter 2
Data-Driven Product Design and Assortment Optimization for Online Retail Platform

Abstract Our study focuses on how real-world data can inform and enhance firms' decisions around product design and assortment, which is critical in logistics, automotive, fast fashion and other industries. This article presents a data-driven analytics study on the challenges of new product design and product assortment. We first implement predictive analytics, utilizing a Multinomial Logit (MNL) model to estimate consumer preferences for both existing and newly designed products. Subsequently, we proceed with assortment optimization, including a deterministic model and a robust model. By applying our data-driven method in the case study based on the historical data of a fast fashion e-retailer, we find that the robust assortment model balances revenue and stability, while performing significantly better in the worst-case than the deterministic assortment model. This demonstrates that the robust assortment model, which accounts for parameter uncertainty, may be more suitable for real-world applications. Furthermore, the numerical results indicate that our data-driven new product design and robust assortment approaches can help the firm achieve a 31% expected revenue improvement. Interestingly, our robust assortment methods based on the MNL model outperform machine learning based assortment methods, despite the latter's more accurate predictive abilities regarding consumer purchasing patterns. These results indicate that accurate predictions of consumer purchasing patterns alone are not sufficient to guarantee good assortment decisions. Firms are advised to adopt the simpler and more comprehensible MNL model as their predictive tool when making assortment decisions.

Keywords Data-driven · Product design · Assortment · Fast fashion

2.1 Introduction

Firms frequently design new products and update product line to attract customers' interest in purchasing and consuming products. New product design and product

---

Previously published in Transportation Research Part E: Logistics and Transportation Review, vol. 182 (2024): 103413. Reproduced with permission from Elsevier.

Y. Yu et al., *Platform Supply Chains 1*, Platform Supply Chains in the AI Era,
https://doi.org/10.1007/978-981-95-9965-3_2

assortment problems are prevalent among various industries (Lin & Pekkarinen, 2011; Resta et al., 2017; Umpfenbach et al., 2018; Liu et al., 2019b; Hong et al., 2020; Li et al., 2020; Zhang & Huang, 2021). For example, in the logistics industry, logistics service providers (e.g., SF Express) are faced with the new logistics service product design problems (Liu et al., 2019a) and the subsequent optimization problems for service product line, including old and new service products; it is critical for Scania, an automobile manufacturer mainly producing trucks, to set attribute values for truck core components (such as engine, axle, chassis, cargo capacity) at the design stage and update the product line after the launch of new products; in the fast fashion industry, Zara implements quick response to refresh its assortment with new designs for fashion (Kowsmann, 2016). Well designed new products largely stimulate consumer interest and significantly enhance market performance (Jindal et al., 2016; Liu et al., 2017). Subsequent informed product set selection can reduce product cannibalization between existing and new products and guide consumers to purchase products more profitable, further enhancing firm revenues (Rooderkerk et al., 2013). Product design and assortment play an increasingly role in boosting firms' competitiveness and achieving operational success.

However, the decision-making process for product design and assortment is challenging in reality. According to market survey results, despite significant investments, more than 50% of products launches fail to hit business targets (Alessandro et al., 2017). Less than 5% of firms surveyed think they can make appropriate product design decisions (Benedict et al., 2018). Unwise product design and assortment may cause the company to encounter operational difficulties. For instance, Volkswagen Phaeton's inefficient design and infrequent lineup updates resulted in a loss of $31,715 per Phaeton sold (Cremer, 2015), fast fashion company Gap has suffered a decline in market share as its products struggle to captivate consumers, furniture and decor retailer Pier 1 Imports went bankrupt in part owing to the lack of competitive design and assortment strategies for its diverse products. Thus, it is essential to investigate effective methods for tackling challenges in product design and assortment.

In practice, a product is comprised of diverse attributes. For example, a fast fashion dress includes attributes such as fabric, length, dress type, collar, decorations; a car consists of gearbox, fuel tank, alternator, body structure, tyres, etc. Moreover, new product design ideas are often thought of as the new combinations of existing attributes (Kumar et al., 2020). New product design and assortment phenomenon motivated by industry practices raises the following questions: (1) How to use real-world data including existing attributes to design new products? (2) How to estimate consumer preferences for the existing and newly designed products based on transaction data? (3) How to optimize the product assortment considering the design of new products?

To address these questions, we propose a new data-driven framework that integrates new product design, consumer preference prediction, and assortment optimization. Here, we develop deterministic and robust assortment models depending on whether to account for the uncertainty of estimates. When decision makers are faced with the design and assortment of products consisting of multiple attributes, the nature of new product design and assortment problems is similar across various

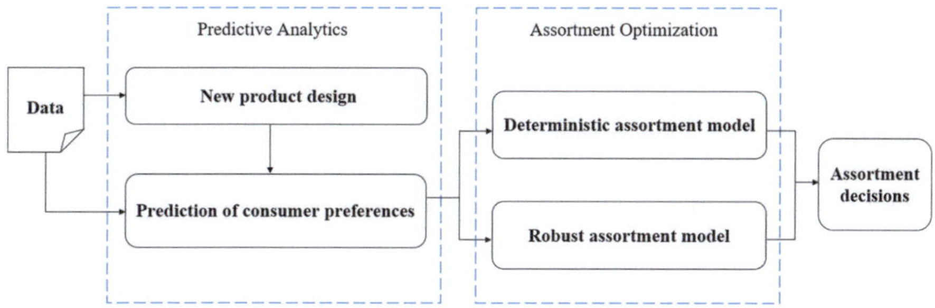

Fig. 2.1 The framework for our approach

industries. Therefore, our approach has the potential to provide guidance not only in the logistics, automotive, and fast fashion industry but also in other industries such as home furnishing, fast-moving consumer goods industries where products are composed of multiple attributes. Furthermore, we test our proposed data-driven framework using real-world data from a fast fashion e-retailer *Babyonlinedress* (BO).

Overview of Our Approach

The approach is built on a framework incorporating predictive analytics and assortment optimization, depicted in Fig. 2.1. During the initial stage of predictive analytics, we apply an attribute-compatible approach to design new products and aim to generate new product design schemes that are feasible in terms of technical practicality and marketing potential in an efficient manner. In the second stage, we estimate consumer preferences for the existing and newly designed products, which enables us to obtain partial information about the consumer preference distributions from the real data.

Building on the predictive analytics results, we develop deterministic and robust models to optimize assortment decisions for the existing and new products. We propose two approaches to the optimization problem, depending on whether the uncertainty of the choice parameters is taken into account. First. we develop a deterministic model by ignoring the consumer preference uncertainty and treating the estimated mean as the true value. Second, we construct a robust model by viewing the consumer preference for each product as a distribution with known partial information. Both models have the property of revenue-order under certain conditions, which enables us to solve the assortment problem efficiently.

Findings and Contributions

By applying the proposed framework to tackle product operation dilemma, we have obtained results for predictive analytics and assortment optimization. Moreover, we evaluate the efficacy of our approaches through a numerical analysis utilizing the historical data from BO. A concise overview of our findings and contributions is presented below.

- Our research proposes a practical data-driven framework for integrating new product design and product assortment optimization. This approach comprises three main components: new product design, consumer preference estimation, and assortment optimization. To connect the first two components, we utilize an attribute-based technique, whereby both the product design and parameter estimation processes are based on existing product attribute values. This approach allows us to fully leverage the available data and enables us to predict consumer preferences for newly designed products that have no historical sales data because new product ideas are treated as new combinations of existing attributes. To connect the last two components, we employ a bootstrap procedure and estimate the attribute coefficients of the consumer utility function under the choice model using maximum likelihood estimation for each sampling. According to the estimation results, we calculate the first- and second-order moments of the exponentially transformed consumer utility. Hence, the parameter values in the later deterministic and robust assortment optimization models are estimated from the real data. Utilizing the results of our predictive and prescriptive analysis in a case study with BO's data, we observe that our data-driven product design and assortment approaches can lead to a 31% improvement in expected revenue compared with BO's current solutions.
- Numerical experiments based on real-world data provide valuable and interesting managerial insights. After designing new products and estimating parameter values from BO's historical sales data, we solve the deterministic model and robust assortment models. Our results demonstrate that the degree of conservatism of decision-makers affects the optimal assortment decision. Besides this, we find that while assortment decisions obtained from the deterministic model may lead to higher expected revenue, they also exhibit greater revenue volatility. In contrast, the robust assortment decision strikes a balance between expected revenue and revenue stability. Although it may result in a slight loss of revenue, it is still very close to the optimal revenue. These findings suggest that the robust model yields superior assortment solutions for the firm by ensuring that worst-case revenue is not too unfavorable, while also obtaining almost optimal revenue with lower variance in the general case. Furthermore, our approaches, which employ the Multinomial Logit (MNL) model to predict consumer purchasing patterns, outperform machine learning based approaches that rely on machine learning as prediction tools, despite the latter's stronger prediction abilities. Our results suggest that better forecasting does not necessarily guarantee better decisions, especially when using machine

learning tools. Therefore, it is advisable for firms to use the MNL model as the prediction tool when making assortment decisions.

The rest of the paper is organized as follows. We review the relevant literature in Sect. 2.2. Section 2.3 shows the new product design and consumer preference predictive analytical approaches based on data. Section 2.4 presents the deterministic assortment model with known parameters, and the robust assortment optimization model with parameter uncertainty. Section 2.5 discusses our numerical experiments with model parameters estimated from BO's real transaction data and compares the performance of different methods. Lastly, the paper concludes in Sect. 2.6.

2.2 Literature Review

This study draws upon several streams of prior research: data-driven analytics, product design, consumer behavior modeling and estimation, and product assortment. In this section, we provide an overview of these research streams and highlight our contribution.

Our work first belongs to the growing literature on data-driven analytics. Data-driven analytics are progressively assuming a pivotal role in operations management (OM). With the proliferation of data and advances in data processing technologies, OM researchers seek to solve product operation challenges by leveraging data and optimization techniques to their full potential (Liu et al., 2020; Zhi et al., 2022). Bernstein et al. (2019) present a dynamic clustering policy for estimating the preferences of heterogeneous consumers and optimize the assortment based on the resulting mapping. Shi et al. (2020) develop predictions utilizing machine learning techniques based on historical data and propose models for optimizing inventory decisions. Zhang et al. (2022) extend the generalized Bass model to model new product adoption and study a price optimization problem in which the parameters can be learned from real-time demand data. Chen et al. (2022) devise machine learning methods to tackle the challenge of demand estimation and assortment through data-driven approaches, which account for cross-selling and substitution effects. In this paper, we introduce a data-driven framework that combines new product design and product assortment optimization, where the parameters modeling consumer preferences of existing and new products in the assortment optimization problem are estimated using the MNL choice model.

This work also relates to the literature on product design. Recognized as a pivotal activity, product design has a substantial impact on the performance of firms (Balakrishnan & Jacob, 1996; Li et al., 2020; Burnap et al., 2023). An essential aspect frequently mentioned in the extant product design literature is designing new products that cater to market preferences based on attribute reorganization methods (Singhal & Katz, 1990; Singhal & Singhal, 2002; Kumar et al., 2020; Pantourakis et al., 2022). Aligned with this premise, this paper focuses on the challenges of new product design as well as subsequent assortment optimization. A salient feature that sets this paper apart from prior works is that we offer newly designed products and assortment solutions through a data-driven framework derived from real-world data.

Our paper is also connected to the stream of literature on consumer behavior modeling and estimation. The majority of assortment optimization models rely on discrete choice models that capture customers' buying behavior (Jena et al., 2020). Fader & Hardie (1996) suggest modeling consumer preferences over product attributes rather than the products themselves; their approach can estimate the demand for new products. Guadagni and Little (1983) study a brand choice MNL model using scanner data calibration and show that the model predicts the share of purchases remarkably well. Fader and Hardie (2012) employ the efficient expectation-maximization method combined with an MNL model to estimate the model parameters. Moreover, Train (2008) provides methods for calculating the variance of the estimates in the discrete choice model. Similarly, we also employ an MNL model to describe consumer behavior, but unlike the literature, based on the estimated choice parameters, we focus on estimating first- and second-order moments of the exponentially transformed consumer utility through bootstrapping.

In addition, our research topic also contributes to the literature on product assortment. In that literature, Talluri and Van Ryzin (2004) demonstrate that the optimal solution of the assortment problem under the MNL model is revenue-ordered, while some other papers investigate the assortment optimization problem under different choice models (Feldman & Topaloglu, 2015; El Housni & Topaloglu, 2022; Chen et al., 2023). Moreover, the application of robust decision-making is widespread in the field of operations analytics due to the challenges of deriving full distribution information from data. There exist various methods to integrate robustness into decision optimization models (Delage & Ye, 2010; Rusmevichientong & Topaloglu, 2012; Hamdan & Diabat, 2020).

In this stream of literature, our work is closely related to the study of Li and Ke (2019), which analyze robust assortment optimization problems considering customer class under the MNL model with known moment information of parameters. However, this work differs from Li and Ke (2019) in the following three aspects. First, Li and Ke (2019) focus on robust assortment problems, whereas we take new product design into account and then optimize the assortment of existing and new products with deterministic and robust models based on the predictions of consumer purchasing patterns. Second, their models require prior knowledge of parameters that are simply obtained from random simulation; unlike them, we consider the MNL choice model to estimate the parameters from historical sales data. Finally, our new product design, parameter estimation, and product assortment process is attribute-based, a facet not studied by Li and Ke (2019).

2.3 Predictive Analytics

This section shows the predictive analytics conducted on data. The first step of predictive analytics is to design new products with compatible attributes and potential feasibility based on existing product attributes. Based on the transaction-level data, the second step of predictive analytics involves estimating the utility weight of each attribute and developing predictions for the consumer preference for existing and new products.

2.3.1 New Product Design

Given existing products and corresponding attribute values, we aim to design potentially marketable new products through combinations of previously used attributes. Generating new product idea based on existing products is straightforward to implement using the attribute data. A product idea can be represented as a combination of attributes, where each attribute has an impact on the product's overall appeal and interacts with other attributes. A product design is considered *feasible* if it does not have any pair of incompatible attributes, otherwise it is not feasible. Due to the limitations of production technology, public preference and other factors, there exist incompatible attributes that cannot simultaneously appear on a product in reality. For example, in the automotive industry, cars with different payload exert different pressures on tires, and heavily loaded cars frequently do not employ soft-material tires, so these attributes are incompatible; in the fast fast fashion industry, the mid-length mermaid dress requires a relatively stiffer fabric, thus the attribute values tulle and mermaid typically cannot coexist on a producible dress, and can be treated as incompatible attributes. More specifically, the attribute pairs that already appear in existing products are regarded as *compatible*. New feasible product designs are generated based on the attribute compatibility relationship of existing products, where each attribute pair in the new design is required to already exist in at least one product previously produced by firms.

Following Kumar et al. (2020), we construct the compatibility matrix for identifying feasible new product designs based on product attribute data. If a product has J attributes and if the attribute $j (j = 1, 2, ..., J)$ has a set of attribute values numbered $1, 2, ..., M(j)$, then the number of all possible designs generated by these attribute value combinations is $\prod_{j=1}^{J} M(j)$. An attribute value p for attribute j is denoted by (j, p). The compatibility matrix X of order $\sum_{j=1}^{J} M(j) \times \sum_{j=1}^{J} M(j)$ can be constructed, where each entry $x[(j, p), (k, q)]$ is 1 if the attribute pair (j, p) and (k, q) are compatible, and 0 if they are not ($j, k = 1, 2, ..., J$; $j \neq k$; $p = 1, 2, ..., M(j)$; $q = 1, 2, ..., M(k)$; and $M(j), M(k) \geq 1$). The concept of compatibility between two attribute values for the same attribute is not defined, as each product design includes only one attribute value for each attribute. Since compatibility is mutual, the matrix is symmetrical along the main diagonal, so $x[(j, p), (k, q)] = x[(k, q), (j, p)]$.

Based on the compatibility matrix generated from real data, the potential number of designs can be very large. Singhal and Katz (1990) devised a **branch-and-fathom algorithm** for effectively identifying designs without any incompatible attribute pairs. The main procedure of the algorithm consists of selecting the attribute as the branching operation and fathoming candidate matrices available to generate designs. Using existing product attribute data, we apply their algorithm to yield feasible product designs, and in what follows, we predict consumer preferences for the existing and newly designed products.

2.3.2 Prediction of Consumer Preferences

In this section, we formally introduce the approach used to estimate consumers' preferences for the existing products and newly designed products. The consumers' choice process is described by the MNL model, which is widely used in the literature (Lo & Topaloglu, 2019; Pichka et al., 2022). Our approach fits the MNL choice model to the historical transaction-level data. Consumers are assumed to be rational utility maximizers and derive purchase behavior choices. Then, the MNL choice model computes the probability of choosing a product as a function of the attributes available, where attribute coefficients are obtained using maximum likelihood estimation.

Consider a homogeneous consumer confronted with a choice from a product set S, containing N existing products. The consumer chooses the one with the largest utility after assessing attribute-based utilities for all products (including the no-purchase option). Denote the no-purchase option by 0, and set all of its corresponding attribute values to 0. Each customer browsing the website assigns a utility U_i to each product $i \in S \cup \{0\}$. The utility consists of two components, a deterministic component u_i and a random component ε_i, i.e., $U_i = u_i + \varepsilon_i$. The deterministic component of a consumer's utility for product i is modeled as a linear function of observed attribute variables. It is commonly assumed to be an additive utility function that implies $u_i = \sum_t \alpha_t x_{it}$ (Guadagni & Little, 1983; Fader & Hardie, 1996; Feldman et al., 2022), where x_{it} represents observed value of attribute t of product i, including the selling price and product attributes (e.g., fabric, collar, and dress type), and α_t represents utility weight of attribute t. According to the celebrated MNL model, the random utility part ε_i for each product i follows the i.i.d. Gumbel or type I generalized extreme value (GEV) distribution. The probability of a consumer selecting product i from $S \cup \{0\}$ is:

$$q_i = \Pr(U_i = \max_{k \in S \cup \{0\}} U_k) = \frac{\exp(u_i)}{\sum_{k \in S \cup \{0\}} \exp(u_k)} \tag{2.1}$$

The parameters of the MNL model are estimated using historical transaction data in which the purchase decisions of consumers are recorded. Let H denote the number of times choices are made, which we call choice occasions in the data, and I_i^h, the purchase indicator, equals 1 if product i is chosen on choice occasion h, and 0 otherwise. Given u_i, Eq. (2.1) can be used to calculate the choice probabilities. For obtaining the maximum likelihood estimate (MLE) for the attribute coefficient

α_t, we can write the log of the likelihood function that multiplies the probability of observing the purchase decision across all h:

$$LL(\boldsymbol{\alpha}) = \sum_{h=1}^{H} \sum_{i \in S \cup \{0\}} I_i^h (\textstyle\sum_t \alpha_t x_{it} - \ln \sum_{k \in S \cup \{0\}} \exp(\sum_t \alpha_t x_{kt})) \qquad (2.2)$$

McFadden (1974) demonstrates that the log-likelihood function (2.2) exhibits concavity, which enables the utilization of nonlinear optimization techniques, such as BFGS, to find the MLE estimate of $\boldsymbol{\alpha}$. Once attribute coefficient $\boldsymbol{\alpha}$ is estimated, the consumer utility u_i of each product i can be calculated based on attribute values. In order to solve the assortment problem with deterministic and robust optimization under the MNL model in the following section, it is necessary to estimate the first- and second-order moments of exponentially transformed consumer preferences, i.e., the mean and covariance matrix of $\mathbf{v}$, where $\mathbf{v} = (\exp(u_1), \exp(u_2), ..., \exp(u_N))^T$. Applying the exponential transformation to u_i, we estimate the mean of $\exp(u_i)$. Then, we use the method described below to estimate covariance matrix $\Sigma \in \mathbb{R}^{N \times N}$ of $\mathbf{v}$.

By definition, the sampling covariance of an estimator is a measure of the amount by which the estimates change when different samples are taken from the population. The original sample is a sample from the population, so if this sample is large enough, then drawing from the original sample, with replacement, is a proxy for drawing from the population itself, which is the logic of bootstrapping. The estimates obtained on the bootstrapped samples provide information on the distribution of parameter estimates. Therefore, to obtain the covariance matrix of $\mathbf{v}$, we re-estimate attribute coefficient $\boldsymbol{\alpha}$ numerous times on different samples through bootstrapping and calculate the covariance of $\mathbf{v}$ based on resulting estimates of each sample (Train, 2008).

Let the original sample consist of H choice occasions that are indexed by $h = 1, 2, ..., H$ from the data. The estimate that is obtained on the original sample is $\hat{\boldsymbol{\alpha}}$, and the exponentially transformed consumer preference calculated on this estimation is denoted by $\hat{\mathbf{v}}$. Randomly sample with replacement H choice occasions from the original sample, where some occasions might be represented more than once and others might not be included at all, and the new sample is the same size as the original. Re-estimate using the model on this new sample, and label the estimate $\boldsymbol{\alpha}_r$ with $r = 1$ for this first new sample. Then, repeat the random sampling numerous times, and obtain estimates $\boldsymbol{\alpha}_r$ for $r = 1, 2, ..., R$, where R is the number of times the estimation is repeated. According to estimates $\boldsymbol{\alpha}_r$ for each bootstrapped sample, the corresponding R exponentially transformed consumer utilities, denoted by $\mathbf{v}_1, \mathbf{v}_2, ..., \mathbf{v}_R$, can be calculated individually. After that, we calculate the covariance of the resulting estimates around the original estimate: $\Sigma_{ij} = \frac{1}{R} \sum_{r=1}^{R} (v_{ri} - \hat{v}_i)(v_{rj} - \hat{v}_j)$, where Σ_{ij} is the element in the ith row and jth column of covariance matrix Σ, and Σ is a symmetric positive semidefinite matrix. By the above methods, we can straightforwardly conceptually estimate the mean and covariance matrix of $\mathbf{v}$.

2.4 Assortment Optimization

Taking into account the newly designed feasible products, we consider an assortment of optimization problems to improve product assortment decisions. In this section, we develop a deterministic model that treats predictions of consumer preference as true values. Moreover, considering estimation uncertainty, a robust model using the moment information is developed.

2.4.1 *Deterministic Assortment Model*

In our problem formulation, we aim to maximize the total expected revenue by selecting an assortment D from a set of existing and new products $P = \{1, 2, ..., n\}$, where $D \subseteq P$. The revenue is r_i for product $i \in P$, which is an exogenous variable that can be determined based on product attributes and operational experience in advance. Under the MNL model described in Sect. 2.3.2, the probability of a customer purchasing product i is $\frac{\exp(u_i)}{1+\sum_{i \in D}\exp(u_i)}$ for $i \in D$. The assortment optimization under the MNL model can be formulated as follows:

$$\max_{D \subseteq P \cup \{0\}} \sum_{i \in D} \frac{r_i \exp(u_i)}{1 + \sum_{i \in D} \exp(u_i)} \tag{2.3}$$

where parameter $\exp(u_i)$ for each product i is considered as a deterministic value that we take to be the mean calculated from the data.

Without loss of generality, the products are assumed to be ranked in order of their revenue: $r_1 \geq r_2 \geq ... \geq r_n > 0$. Each offer set $D_k := \{1, 2, ..., k\}$ is referred to as a revenue-ordered assortment for $k = 0, ..., n$. Talluri and Van Ryzin (2004) show that the optimal solution for the assortment problem must be a *revenue-ordered* assortment. Therefore, we can find the optimal assortment of problem (2.3) by searching among all the revenue-ordered assortments and comparing their total revenues. With this efficient property, the search space is reduced from the number of all possible assortments 2^n to $n + 1$.

2.4.2 *Robust Optimization Using Worst-Case CVaR*

Although the assortment model that treats parameter estimates as deterministic is efficient to solve, the parameters are not deterministic values we can precisely estimate. To tackle this issue, it is common practice to model the parameter as a probability distribution. However, the estimation of the distribution of exponentially transformed consumer utility $\mathbf{v} = (\exp(u_1), \exp(u_2), ..., \exp(u_n))^T$ based on historical data is typically subject to uncertainty, while having partial information about the true distribution is typical. From our predictive analytics in Sect. 2.3.2, we find that estimating the mean $\boldsymbol{\mu} = (\mu_1, \mu_2, .., \mu_n)^T \in \mathbb{R}^n$ and covariance matrix $\Sigma \in \mathbb{R}^{n\times n}$ of $\mathbf{v}$ is more feasible. Let $\mathcal{F}$ denote the set of possible distributions with known first- and second-order moments. Instead of maximizing the expected revenue, we consider the problem of finding an optimal assortment that guarantees a probability of at least $1-\epsilon$ for achieving a maximum target t under a worst-case distribution from $\mathcal{F}(\mu, \Sigma)$, by incorporating a distributionally robust chance constraint:

$$\max_{\mathbf{x}\in\{0,1\}^n, t} \left\{ t : \inf_{F\in\mathcal{F}(\mu,\Sigma)} \Pr\left\{ \frac{\sum_{i=1}^n r_i v_i x_i}{1+\sum_{i=1}^n v_i x_i} \geq t \right\} \geq 1-\epsilon \right\} \tag{2.4}$$

where $\mathbf{x} = (x_1, x_2, ..., x_n)^T$, with $x_i \in \{0, 1\}$ denotes whether product i is chosen in the assortment decision D, and $\Pr\{\cdot\}$ is the probability of event "$\cdot$". Since $\mathbf{v}$ is positive, problem (2.4) can be equivalently expressed as:

$$\max_{\mathbf{x}\in\{0,1\}^n, t} \left\{ t : \inf_{F\in\mathcal{F}(\mu,\Sigma)} \Pr\left\{ \sum_{i=1}^n (t-r_i) v_i x_i + t \leq 0 \right\} \geq 1-\epsilon \right\} \tag{2.5}$$

The optimization problem involving a distributionally robust chance constraint is typically nonconvex and computationally challenging, so we adopt the worst-case CVaR convex conservative approximation method proposed by Zymler et al. (2013). Let $h(\mathbf{x}, \mathbf{v}) = \sum_{i=1}^n (t-r_i)v_i x_i + t$ be a function, and consider the corresponding CVaR of $h(\mathbf{x}, \mathbf{v})$, denoted as $\mathrm{CVaR}_\epsilon[h(\mathbf{x}, \mathbf{v})]$, which evaluates the conditional expectation of $h(\mathbf{x}, \mathbf{v})$ above the $(1-\epsilon)$-quantile of the distribution of $h(\mathbf{x}, \mathbf{v})$. Using the method proposed by Rockafellar and Uryasev (2002), we can compute $\mathrm{CVaR}_\epsilon[h(\mathbf{x}, \mathbf{v})]$ by the following equation:

$$\mathrm{CVaR}_\epsilon[h(\mathbf{x}, \mathbf{v})] := \min_\beta \left\{ \beta + \frac{1}{\epsilon}\mathbb{E}_F\left[\left(\sum_{i=1}^n (t-r_i)v_i x_i + t - \beta \right)^+ \right] \right\}$$

where $(\cdot)^+$ denotes $\max\{\cdot, 0\}$. Therefore, problem (2.5) can be reformulated in terms of the worst-case CVaR as a robust assortment optimization problem:

$$\max_{\mathbf{x}\in\{0,1\}^n} \max_t \left\{ t : \sup_{F\in\mathcal{F}(\mu,\Sigma)} \min_\beta \beta + \frac{1}{\epsilon}\mathbb{E}_F\left[((t\mathbf{x} - \mathbf{r_x})^T \mathbf{v} + t - \beta)^+ \right] \leq 0 \right\} \tag{2.6}$$

in which $\mathbf{r_x} = (r_1 x_1, ..., r_n x_n)^T$. Note that covariance matrix Σ is positive semidefinite, so a positive semidefinite matrix $\Sigma^{\frac{1}{2}} \in \mathbb{R}^{n\times n}$ implying $\Sigma = \Sigma^{\frac{1}{2}}\Sigma^{\frac{1}{2}}$ can be defined.

Given an assortment $\mathbf{x}$, the inner function $h(\mathbf{x}, \mathbf{v})$ is linear with respect to the random vector $\mathbf{v}$. In the case where the moments are known, Li and Ke (2019) prove that the distributionally robust chance constraint of program (2.5) is equivalent to problem (2.6). Moreover, the inner optimization problem of problem (2.6) for a known assortment plan $\mathbf{x}$ can be rephrased as a solvable second-order cone program (SOCP):

$$\max_t t$$
$$s.t. || - \left(\sqrt{\frac{1-\epsilon}{\epsilon}}\Sigma^{\frac{1}{2}}\mathbf{x}\right)t + \sqrt{\frac{1-\epsilon}{\epsilon}}\Sigma^{\frac{1}{2}}\mathbf{r_x}||_2 \leq -(1+\mathbf{x}^T\mu)t + \mathbf{r_x}^T\mu \tag{2.7}$$

Obtaining the optimal assortment requires solving SOCP (2.7) for all feasible assortments, which can be computationally challenging, especially when dealing with a large number of products. As mentioned by Li and Ke (2019), problem (2.6) given moment information is equivalent to the robust assortment optimization problem as follows:

$$\max_{\mathbf{x}\in\{0,1\}^n} \min_{\bar{\mathbf{v}}\in\mathcal{V}} \frac{\mathbf{r_x}^T\bar{\mathbf{v}}}{1+\mathbf{x}^T\bar{\mathbf{v}}}$$

where $\mathcal{V} = \left\{\bar{\mathbf{v}} : \bar{\mathbf{v}} = \mu + \sqrt{\frac{1-\epsilon}{\epsilon}}\Sigma^{\frac{1}{2}}\mathbf{z},\ 1+\mathbf{x}^T\bar{\mathbf{v}} \geq 0,\ ||\mathbf{z}|| \leq 1,\ \mathbf{z}\in\mathbb{R}^n\right\}$ denotes the uncertainty set. Rusmevichientong & Topaloglu (2012) demonstrate that for any $\mathcal{V} \subset \mathbb{R}^n_{++}$, the assortment ordered by revenue can be still optimal.

To ensure that the convex and compact uncertainty set $\mathcal{V}$ is positive, we need to impose a condition on ϵ:

$$\min_{i,\mathbf{z}} \left\{\bar{v}_i : \bar{v}_i = \mu_i + \sqrt{\frac{1-\epsilon}{\epsilon}}\sum_{j=1}^{n}\sigma_{ij}z_j,\ ||\mathbf{z}|| \leq 1,\ i = 1, ..., n\right\} > 0$$

which leads to $\epsilon > \max_i \frac{\sum_{j=1}^n \sigma_{ij}^2}{\mu_i^2 + \sum_{j=1}^n \sigma_{ij}^2}$, where σ_{ij} is the element in the ith row and jth column of $\Sigma^{\frac{1}{2}}$, and $\sum_{j=1}^n \sigma_{ij}^2 = \Sigma_{ii}$ denotes the variance of v_i. Li and Ke (2019) show that the *revenue-ordered* property of problem (2.6) still holds when ϵ satisfies a certain condition, which is indicated in Lemma 2.1.

Lemma 2.1 *(Theorem 1 in Li and Ke (2019)) If* $\epsilon > \underline{\epsilon} = \max_i \frac{\Sigma_{ii}}{\mu_i^2 + \Sigma_{ii}}$, *then the optimal assortment of the problem (2.6) given moment information is revenue-ordered.*

Lemma 2.1 implies that if $\epsilon > \underline{\epsilon}$, we can obtain the optimal assortment and its corresponding value by solving the SOCP (2.7) for only $n+1$ revenue-ordered assortments.

2.5 Case Study

This section investigates how to effectively apply our new product design and product assortment method using BO's real data. We first apply the branch-and-fathom algorithm shown in Sect. 2.3.1 to design new potential products. After designing new products, we estimate the attribute coefficients of consumer's utility and the first- and second-order moments of $\mathbf{v}$, where $\mathbf{v} = (\exp(u_1), \exp(u_2), ..., \exp(u_n))^T$. Based on the estimation results, we can optimize assortment decisions by the fitted deterministic and robust MNL model and then evaluate the performance of our approaches.

2.5.1 Data Set and Newly Designed Products

The case study is performed using a dataset provided by BO, including the attribute values of each basic dress and its corresponding price, revenue and sales over a selling season. Table 2.1 displays the descriptive statistics for the price, revenue and sales, as well as attribute values for all dress attributes. Our data includes nine attributes that are common and necessary to specify a dress, and any dress has a unique vector of these attribute values. Figure 2.2 illustrates BO's one dress and the corresponding attributes as a example.

The pricing strategies adopted by BO are cost-plus pricing, which is widely used in practice (Diamantopoulos, 1991; Noble & Gruca, 1999). Under cost-plus pricing, the prices for dresses are set at a point that gives BO a specified percentage profit margin over the costs, including production costs, shipping costs, platform commissions, and other factors. For example, the cost of one SKU is CNY 200 and the percentage profit margin is 40%, so the selling price for this SKU is CNY 280. In the following analysis, the new products' prices are calculated through the cost-plus pricing methods used by BO.

Table 2.1 Descriptive statistics of selling price, revenue, sales and attributes

Data	Mean	Min	Max	SD
Selling price	59.53	31.83	113.96	15.65
Revenue	27.94	2.92	44.90	10.62
Sales	26.40	1	343	65.03
Attributes	Values			
Collar	V-neck, bateau, scoop, square, crew, high neck, sweetheart			
Dress type	A-line, sheath, mermaid			
Fabric	Lace, satin, chiffon, spandex, sequins, tulle			
Shoulder type	Portrait, halter, off the shoulder, one-shoulder, strapless			
Skirt length	Floor-length, ankle-length, mini, asymmetrical			
Panel train	Sweep, a foot, no panel train			
Back design	Hollow, zipper, backless, button			
Sleeve type	Capped, illusion, natural			
Sleeve length	Sleeveless, short, $\frac{3}{4}$long, long			

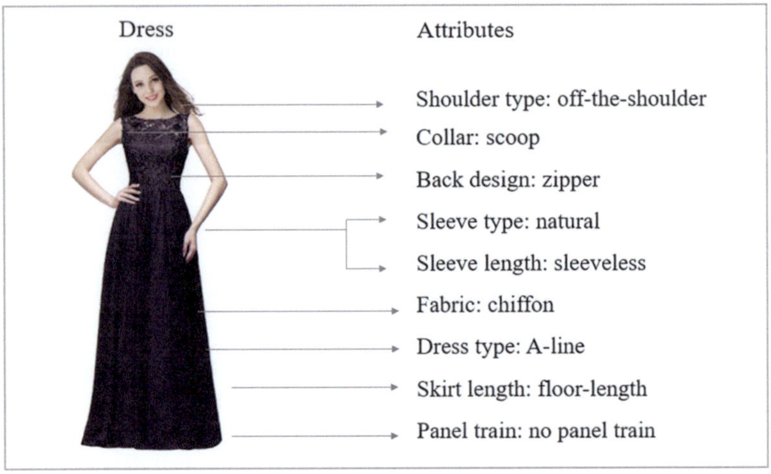

Fig. 2.2 An illustration of BO's one dress and corresponding attributes on its website

We collect 1,452 transaction records of 55 basic dresses over the selling season, from which the sales volume of each dress can be obtained. In addition, BO's website backend records the id and product browsing history of each consumer who clicks through. We observe that 30.02% of consumer ids that viewed the basic dress placed the purchase order, and an average of 22 clicks per dress results in one purchase.

Using the attribute value data for the 55 existing products, we first apply the branch-and-fathom algorithm shown in Sect. 2.3.1 to design 271 new potential products that do not contain any incompatible attribute pairs. In contrast, a full enumeration of attribute values without considering compatibility would generate 362,825 new products.

2.5.2 Parameter Estimation Results

Here, we show the resulting attribute coefficient estimates under our MNL model. Using the attribute data and transaction records obtained for existing products, we transform each dress attribute value into a dummy variable and use these, along with the price, to uniquely represent a dress. For the no-purchase option, the price and all attribute values are set to 0, and the utility is thus 0. Based on the MNL model utilizing the maximum likelihood estimation method shown in Sect. 2.3.2, we can obtain the estimates of attribute coefficients using the sales volume of each dress and the number of consumers who visited BO's website but did not purchase, which are shown in Table 2.2. There are 25 specific attribute values significant at the 0.05 level of significance, indicating that the majority of the attribute values of the 55 existing dresses significantly affect the consumer utility. Given the estimated significant

Table 2.2 MNL model parameter estimation results of attribute coefficients

	Coefficient	Std err.	z	p> |z|
Price	−0.0439***	0.004	−11.277	0.000
Sequins	−1.0906	0.732	−1.490	0.136
Spandex	1.8788***	0.387	4.856	0.000
Lace	1.1407*	0.522	2.185	0.029
Tulle	2.4391***	0.317	7.689	0.000
Chiffon	3.0336***	0.389	7.790	0.000
V-neck	−2.6126***	0.375	−6.966	0.000
Bateau	−4.9788***	1.077	−4.624	0.000
Scoop	−2.6021**	0.878	−2.965	0.003
Crew	−2.4445***	0.265	−9.213	0.000
Square	−1.7623***	0.275	−6.420	0.000
High neck	−3.4821***	0.472	−7.375	0.000
Portrait	0.8450*	0.382	2.211	0.027
One-shoulder	1.2995	0.763	1.703	0.089
Halter	1.0403*	0.426	2.444	0.015
Sheath	3.4489***	0.227	15.195	0.000
Mermaid	2.3338***	0.275	8.485	0.000
Mini	0.7724*	0.366	2.111	0.035
Ankle-length	−3.2455**	1.074	−3.021	0.003
Floor-length	−0.4739	0.308	−1.536	0.124
Sweep	0.9742**	0.332	2.934	0.003
No panel train	2.8196***	0.461	6.119	0.000
Zipper	0.2754	0.380	0.724	0.469
Button	1.9564***	0.573	3.412	0.001
Backless	2.2795***	0.363	6.281	0.000
Natural	−1.2244*	0.495	−2.473	0.013
Capped	0.5374	0.754	0.712	0.476
$\frac{3}{4}$long	2.4856***	0.433	5.737	0.000
Sleeveless	−1.3941***	0.388	−3.591	0.000
Long	−1.6175***	0.466	−3.471	0.001

Significance codes: *** $p < .001$; ** $p < .01$; * $p < .05$.

attribute coefficients and the attribute data for all existing and new dresses, we can calculate estimates of consumer utility, and by doing an exponential transformation on these, the estimates of the mean of exp (u_i) can be obtained, i.e., the first-order moment of $\exp(u_i)$.

The way to estimate the second-order moment of **v** is through bootstrapping as described in Sect. 2.3.2. Using the results of re-estimation, the consumer utility for each re-estimation of the existing and new products can be calculated. After the exponential transformation of the consumer utility for each re-estimation, the covariance matrix Σ of $\mathbf{v}$ is obtained by calculating the covariance of the numerous resulting estimates around the original estimate. Note that $\Sigma^{\frac{1}{2}}$ is a symmetric and positive semidefinite matrix, and $\underline{\epsilon} = \max_i \frac{\Sigma_{ii}}{\mu_i^2+\Sigma_{ii}}$ of $\Sigma^{\frac{1}{2}}$ is 0.86, which means that when the maximum revenue is guaranteed with at least a probability lower than 86%, i.e., $\epsilon > 0.14$, the optimal assortment of robust optimization is revenue-ordered.

2.5.3 Assortment Decisions and Performance Evaluation

Using the estimated first- and second-order moments of consumer preference $\mathbf{v}$, we can determine revenue-ordered product assortments using the deterministic and robust model. Figure 2.3 presents the variation of the number of categories in the optimal product assortments with the level of uncertainty (ϵ) regarding achieving the maximum revenue. We find that as ϵ increases, the category of products tends to decrease. Table 2.3 shows specifically the assortment decisions and corresponding expected revenues generated by the deterministic case and the robust cases with $\epsilon =$ 0.15, 0.2, 0.25, and 0.5. To guarantee the probability of obtaining maximum revenue (i.e., higher $1 - \epsilon$), decision-maker develops a more conservative revenue-ordered assortment decision with a greater number of existing and new products, yet it leads to a slight decrease in expected revenue. Besides, compared to the deterministic case where the realization of maximum revenue is not considered, robust assortments enhance the probability of obtaining the maximum revenue, despite a minor revenue sacrifice.

To evaluate the effectiveness of robust product assortment, we also conduct extensive numerical experiments by comparing the expected revenues of the deterministic and robust models. Given that the mean and covariance matrix of $\mathbf{v}$ estimated from

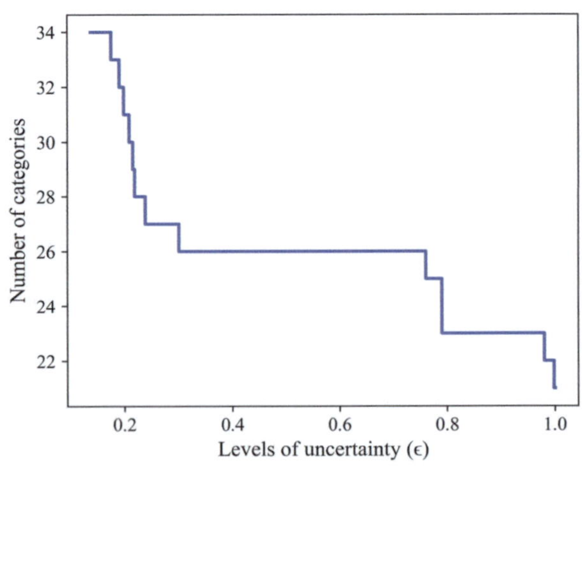

Fig. 2.3 The number of categories in product assortment under different levels of uncertainty (ϵ)

Table 2.3 Assortment decisions and expected revenue under deterministic and robust models

Policy	Assortment	Category	Expected revenue
Deterministic ($\epsilon = 1$)	C620 C487 C411 C519 N16 N100 C533 N193 N9 N24 C104 C551 C570 C384 C616 C361 C507 C504 N184 N234 N49	21	38.4787
Robust ($\epsilon = 0.15$)	C620 C487 C411 C519 N16 N100 C533 N193 N9 N24 C104 C551 C570 C384 C616 C361 C507 C504 N184 N234 N49 N246 N270 N156 C363 N70 N254 N176 N126 N34 N106 N111 N152 N72	34	38.0034
Robust ($\epsilon = 0.2$)	C620 C487 C411 C519 N16 N100 C533 N193 N9 N24 C104 C551 C570 C384 C616 C361 C507 C504 N184 N234 N49 N246 N270 N156 C363 N70 N254 N176 N126 N34 N106	31	38.0803
Robust ($\epsilon = 0.25$)	C620 C487 C411 C519 N16 N100 C533 N193 N9 N24 C104 C551 C570 C384 C616 C361 C507 C504 N184 N234 N49 N246 N270 N156 C363 N70 N254	27	38.1343
Robust ($\epsilon = 0.5$)	C620 C487 C411 C519 N16 N100 C533 N193 N9 N24 C104 C551 C570 C384 C616 C361 C507 C504 N184 N234 N49 N246 N270 N156 C363 N70	26	38.2896

Product numbers begin with C for existing products and with N for new products.

the real data, we randomly simulate a test group with 3,000 samples, each representing the actual $\mathbf{v}$ for all products, which cannot be known in advance. As mentioned previously, optimal assortment decisions for different ϵ, i.e., S_{ϵ}^{*}, can be obtained

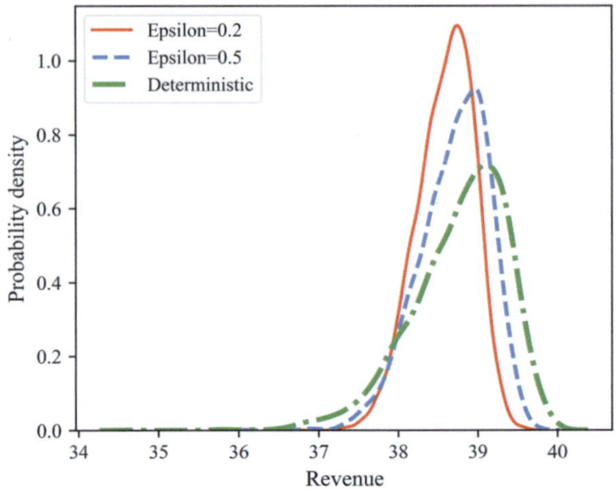

Fig. 2.4 Comparison of revenue distributions across different assortment policies

Table 2.4 Performance comparisons of deterministic and robust models

Policy	Category	Average revenue	Variance	Average gap (%)	Max gap (%)
Deterministic ($\epsilon = 1$)	21	38.7676	0.3631	0.4293	7.4807
Robust ($\epsilon = 0.2$)	31	38.5924	0.1288	0.8700	2.8625
Robust ($\epsilon = 0.5$)	26	38.7030	0.1945	0.5892	3.0443

using the results estimated from the data. We apply the optimal assortments under $\epsilon = 0.2, 0.5$, and 1 to each sample in the test group and display the revenue distributions $\frac{\sum_{i \in S_\epsilon^*} r_i \exp(u_i)}{1+\sum_{i \in S_\epsilon^*} \exp(u_i)}$ in Fig. 2.4. The values of average revenue of the sample, variance, and gap to optimal the revenue with known parameters are shown in detail in Table 2.4. We can see that the peak of the revenue distribution shifts to the left and the shape becomes narrower as ϵ decreases. A more conservative product assortment significantly lowers the volatility of obtaining the expected revenue but sacrifices about 0.45% of the revenue compared to the deterministic case. In particular, in the worst case, the gap between the revenues of the robust decision and the optimal revenue is only 2.86%, compared with 7.48% for the deterministic decision, which means that the robust decision can effectively reduce losses in the worst case.

Overall, a trade-off exists between high revenue and stability of revenue; decisions that may yield higher revenue often also mean taking greater risks. In practice, it is very difficult to precisely estimate consumer preferences from actual data; therefore, given our numerical results, robust product assortment taking uncertainty into account is likely to be better for enterprises.

After illustrating the effectiveness of robust assortment methods, we evaluate the performance of our data-driven new product design and assortment approaches and BO's approaches. Note that the actual new product design and assortment approaches adopted by BO are not available to us because such data is confidential business information. However, we can obtain BO's new product design and assortment decisions and calculate the revenue of BO's by analyzing the transactional data. From the transactional data, we find that the new products designed by BO contain some dress attributes that do not appear in the old products. It is likely that BO's designers generated these new product ideas from experts, a market survey, or the competitors' products. Since the attributes in our usage data are regular dress attributes with relatively few variations, in the next selling season, BO introduced only 3 dresses with new attributes (such as empire dress type and petal sleeve type) not present in the previous selling season, accounting for 2.21% of sales. To exclude the effect of the new attributes and fairly evaluate the performances of our approaches and BO's current solutions, we remove products containing the new attributes and re-normalize the market share to 1 when calculating the revenue of BO's approaches. We find that adopting our data-driven new product design and robust product assortment method can lead to a 31% expected revenue improvement compared with BO's current method. These results indicate that our data-driven new product design and assortment approaches can be useful for BO in practice.

Due to the limitation of the firm's data set, some important attributes (e.g., colours, patterns, and decorations) may be not considered in our work, which may affect the efficiency of generating potential new products and assortment optimization. To further investigate the impact of the absence of attributes, we extend numerical experiments using incomplete attribute data with several randomly deleted attributes. We randomly delete 1, 2, 3, 4, 5 attributes and test our proposed data-driven approach based on the incomplete attribute data. Table 2.5 shows performance comparisons of full and partial attribute data based on robust assortment optimization under $\epsilon = 0.2$, where the optimal robust assortments are all revenue-ordered. With an increase in the number of deleted attributes, the *feasible* new product designs decrease. Note that applying the consistent parameter estimation method, the vast majority of attribute values significantly influence consumer utility in all tests. We observe that product assortments based on the data with different numbers of available attributes lead to different numbers of categories, and the more absent product attributes, the lower the corresponding expected revenue. It implies that more complete attribute data a firm accumulates can strengthen the predicting capabilities for consumer purchasing decisions and enhance expected revenue. Moreover, our proposed data-driven approach can still perform well and lead to revenue improvement compared with the firm's current method when the missing attributes are relatively few.

Table 2.5 Performance comparisons of full and partial attribute data ($\epsilon = 0.2$)

Policy and available attributes	Feasible new designs	Number of categories	Expected revenue
Roubst with full attributes	271	31	38.0803
Roubst with 1 deleted attributes	193	23	37.9516
Roubst with 2 deleted attributes	106	18	36.4832
Roubst with 3 deleted attributes	101	17	36.4625
Roubst with 4 deleted attributes	76	20	35.2473
Roubst with 5 deleted attributes	22	23	31.4789
BO with full attributes	16	38	29.0689

2.5.4 *Performance Comparisons of Our Approaches and Machine Learning Based Approaches*

To further examine the effectiveness of assortment decisions under our data-driven method, we compare the performance of our approaches with the machine learning based assortment approaches, which use machine learning to predict consumers' purchase probabilities and then optimize the assortment decisions of existing and newly designed products. It is a consensus in the literature that the prediction ability of the black-box machine learning model is much higher than the interpretable statistical models with clear mathematical structure, such as the MNL choice model (e.g., Feldman et al., 2022; Filom et al., 2022; Sun & Shen, 2022). One may intuit that the machine learning based assortment approach should outperform the MNL based assortment approach due to the excellent prediction accuracy of machine learning. However, our results suggest this intuition can be wrong.

Using the same real dataset as our approaches, machine learning models are fitted based on product attributes and historical sales performance of existing products, where the attributes and price are the inputs, and product sales are the output. New products designed with compatible attribute pairs are combinations of existing attributes, so the trained machine learning model can be applied to make sales predictions for new products. After fitting the machine learning models, we can estimate consumers' purchase probabilities q_j^e for any product $j \in D$ given any assortment $D \subseteq P \cup \{0\}$, where P is the set of existing and new products. Then the assortment decisions are made by solving the following optimization problem:

$$\max_{D \subseteq P \cup \{0\}} \sum_{j \in D} r_j q_j^e.$$

In our testing, we employ six machine learning techniques: decision tree, random forest, gradient boosting decision tree (GBDT), XGBoost, support vector machines (SVM) and artificial neural network (ANN). When training machine learning models, we randomly split the full dataset, using 75% as the training set and 25% as the test set, and divide the training set into K folds with K set to 10. For each iteration, we use one fold as a validation set, and the remaining K-1 folds for training. Perform grid search on the training data and the Root Mean Square Error (RMSE) is used as a score for refit to find the optimal hyperparameters. Table 2.6 summarizes the details of hyperparameter tuning on each of the machine learning techniques. To compare the prediction power of different machine learning techniques and MNL model, we evaluate the performance of the fitted models on the test set using the selected evaluation metrics, as shown in Table 2.7. Obviously, the predictive accuracy of machine learning surpasses that of the MNL choice model. All the simulations are coded using Python 3.8 on a 3.20 GHz i7-8700 CPU Windows PC with 24GB RAM.

After obtaining assortments by the machine learning based methods, we similarly apply assortments to all samples in the test group previously considered and examine the performance. Table 2.8 summarizes the performance comparisons of different approaches. Assortment decisions based on machine learning methods contain different numbers of product categories. Interestingly, the numerical results show that the average revenue is obviously lower than that obtained by our robust and deterministic decision methods, and the machine learning technique solution losses in the worst case are worse compared to our robust decisions.

Figure 2.5a displays the expected revenue of different product assortment policies for each random simulation sample. Figure 2.5b displays the gaps of different assortments, relative to the optimal revenue with certain parameters. Clearly, compared to machine learning based assortment methods, our MNL based assortment approaches provide higher expected revenue, as well as better performance in the worst case. These results confirm that in contrast to the assortment decisions based on black-box machine learning prediction techniques, assortment optimization built on the interpretable MNL choice model can provide better decisions.

These results indicate that better forecasting does not always means better decisions, especially when using machine learning tools for prediction, which is consistent with the results presented in Feldman et al. (2022). The findings deliver an important message for fast fashion retailers: it is better to use the simpler and more interpretable MNL model than the black-box machine learning tools with higher prediction power to predict customer purchasing patterns when making assortment decisions.

2.6 Conclusion and Future Directions

In this study, we address the new product design and assortment problems widespread across a wide range of industries, including logistics, automotive, and fast fashion.

Table 2.6 Hyperparameter tuning with grid search for machine learning models

Model and hyperparamete	Tuning range of grid search	Optimal hyperparameter
Decision tree		
Tree depth	3, 5, 7, 9	5
Min number of samples required to split	2, 5, 10	2
Min number of samples required in a leaf node	1, 2, 4	1
Random forest		
Number of trees	50, 100, 150, 200, 250, 300	200
Tree depth	3, 5, 7, 9	7
Min number of samples required to split	2, 5, 10	2
Min number of samples required in a leaf node	1, 2, 4	1
GBDT		
Number of trees	50, 100, 150, 200, 250, 300	150
Tree depth	3, 5, 7, 9	7
Learning rate	0.01, 0.1, 0.2, 0.3, 0.4, 0.5	0.1
Subsample	0.6, 0.7, 0.8, 0.9	0.8
Min number of samples required to split	2, 5, 10	2
Min number of samples required in a leaf node	1, 2, 4	1
XGBoost		
Tree depth	3, 5, 7, 9	7
Learning rate	0.01, 0.1, 0.2, 0.3, 0.4, 0.5	0.1
Number of trees	50, 100, 150, 200, 250, 300	150
Subsample	0.6, 0.7, 0.8, 0.9	0.8
The proportion of features for training each tree	0.7, 0.75, 0.8, 0.85, 0.9	0.85
SVM		
Regularization parameter C	0.001, 0.01, 0.1, 1, 10, 100	0.1
Scale parameter gamma	0.001, 0.01, 0.1, 1, 10, 100	1
Kernel function	Linear, poly, rbf, sigmoid	rbf
ANN		
Learning rate	0.001 0.01, 0.1, 0.2, 0.3	0.01
Activation function	Logistic, tanh, relu	Relu
Max number of iterations	50, 100, 150, 200	100
Batch size	16, 32, 64, 128	16
Regularization term coefficient alpha	0.0001, 0.001, 0.01, 0.1, 1	0.001
Hidden layer sizes	number of layers: 1, 2, 3; neurons per layer: 5 to 20	2 layers with 15 and 10 neurons

Table 2.7 Prediction performance comparisons of different models on the test set

Model	RMSE	MAPE (%)	Kendall rank correlation
MNL	2.2864	28.9547	0.6112
Decision tree	1.8301	34.0580	0.6013
Random forest	0.2242	6.3156	0.8545
GBDT	0.1202	5.0896	0.9045
XGBoost	0.1001	4.7383	0.9745
SVM	1.0579	24.4126	0.6914
ANN	0.1016	4.9944	0.9240

Note Root Mean Square Error (RMSE) is calculated as $RMSE = \sqrt{\frac{1}{n}\sum_{i=1}^{n}(\hat{y}_i - y_i)^2}$, Mean Absolute Percentage Error (MAPE) is calculated as $MAPE = \frac{100\%}{n}\sum_{i=1}^{n}\left|\frac{\hat{y}_i - y_i}{y_i}\right|$, where $\hat{y}_i$ and y_i are the predicted and true values of the purchase probability, respectively. Kendall rank correlation coefficient is used to assess the strength and direction of the correlation between predicted and true product rankings in order of purchase probability.

Table 2.8 Performance comparisons of our approaches and machine learning based approaches

Policy	Category	Average revenue	Average gap (%)	Max gap (%)
Deterministic ($\epsilon = 1$)	21	38.7676	0.4293	7.4807
Robust ($\epsilon = 0.2$)	31	38.5924	0.8700	2.8625
Decision tree	57	37.2263	4.3668	7.8392
Random forest	50	37.8053	2.8823	6.1248
GBDT	41	38.3051	1.6039	4.1430
XGBoost	44	37.9204	2.5874	5.8003
SVM	53	37.2305	4.3559	7.8343
ANN	46	37.8972	2.6469	5.8315

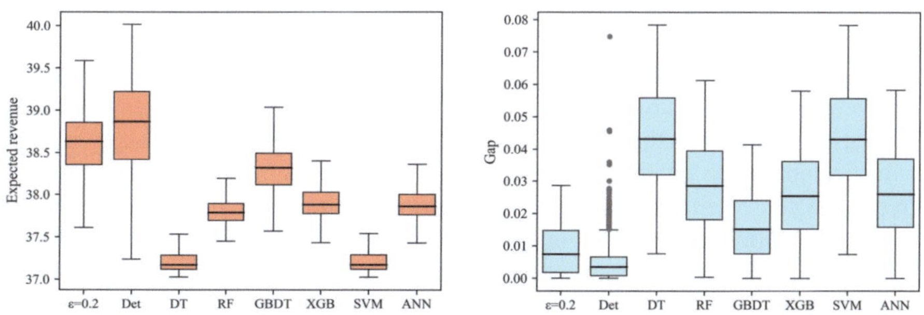

(a) Expected revenue (b) Gap to optimal revenue

Fig. 2.5 Performance of different product assortment policies

To accomplish this, we present a data-driven framework comprising both predictive analytics and assortment optimization, and assess the framework with the real-world data from a fast-fashion e-tailer. In the predictive analytics part, we first apply branch-and-fathom algorithm to design new products. Under attribute compatibility constraints, the number of potential new products is significantly reduced compared to full enumeration. Then, we employ the MNL model to describe consumer behavior and estimate model parameters by assuming that utility is a linear function of attribute variables. Using real-world data, we find that the parameter estimates for the vast majority of the attribute coefficients are significant, which indicates that the estimation method is effective for real data. Third, we calculate the moment information (mean and covariance matrix) of the consumer preferences based on the estimated results of each bootstrapped sampling. From this, we obtain partial information about the true consumer preference distribution for each product and consider the estimation uncertainty.

Using these predictive estimations, we move on to the assortment optimization phase to solve the assortment decisions for existing and new products. We develop a deterministic model and a robust model. The deterministic model simply views consumer preferences as deterministic values expressed by the estimated mean values, which can be solved efficiently using the revenue-ordered property. In contrast, the robust model treats consumer preferences as distributions with known means and covariance matrices, and we can still use the revenue-ordered property to solve the problem under certain conditions.

Combining the estimation and optimization results, we perform a case study employing our data-driven new product design and assortment approaches. The performance comparison between our deterministic and robust models reveals that using robust assortments results in more consistent revenue and less worst-case loss, albeit with a slight decline in revenue. Our findings suggest that robust assortment can lead to better decisions in practice. Importantly, our data-driven new product design and robust assortment approaches would have resulted in a 31% expected revenue increase compared with BO's current solutions. Furthermore, we compare our MNL-based assortment approaches with machine learning based assortment approaches, finding that our method outperforms in terms of both expected revenue and worst-case loss, even though machine learning tools have stronger predictive capability.

Several potential future research directions exist based on our work. In this work, we focus exclusively on the MNL model, but it would be worthwhile to explore other sophisticated choice models, for example, the Nested Logit (NL) model. Another direction is considering the impact of cardinality constraints on product assortments in our optimization framework. Finally, we focus on assortment optimization without taking price into account because firms usually use the cost-plus pricing strategy. In practice, firms may need to jointly optimize assortment and price. Incorporating pricing decisions into the data-driven assortment problem with new product design will be an interesting future direction.

References

Alessandro, B., Alice, d. A., Volker, G., & Alex, K. (2017, October 13). How to make sure your next product or service launch drives growth. *McKinsey & Company*. https://www.mckinsey.com/capabilities/growth-marketing-and-sales/our-insights/how-to-make-sure-your-next-product-or-service-launch-drives-growth

Balakrishnan, P., & Jacob, V. S. (1996). Genetic algorithms for product design. *Management Science, 42*(8), 1105–1117.

Benedict, S., Hugo, S., Garen, K., & Fabricio, D. (2018, October 25). The business value of design. *McKinsey & Company*. https://www.mckinsey.com/capabilities/mckinsey-design/our-insights/the-business-value-of-design.

Bernstein, F., Modaresi, S., & Sauré, D. (2019). A dynamic clustering approach to data-driven assortment personalization. *Management Science, 65*(5), 2095–2115.

Burnap, A., Hauser, J. R., & Timoshenko, A. (2023). Product aesthetic design: A machine learning augmentation. *Marketing Science*.

Chen, J., Feng, X., Kou, G., & Mu, M. (2023). Multiproduct newsvendor with cross-selling and narrow-bracketing behavior using data mining methods. *Transportation Research Part E: Logistics and Transportation Review, 169*, Article 102985.

Chen, Z. Y., Fan, Z. P., & Sun, M. (2022). Machine learning methods for data-driven demand estimation and assortment planning considering cross-selling and substitutions. *INFORMS Journal on Computing*.

Cremer, A. (2015, January 28). Cost-cutting VW bets big to revamp loss-making luxury phaeton. *Reuters*. https://www.reuters.com/article/us-volkswagen-strategy/cost-cutting-vw-bets-big-to-revamp-loss-making-luxury-phaeton-idUKKBN0L11RH20150128

Delage, E., & Ye, Y. (2010). Distributionally robust optimization under moment uncertainty with application to data-driven problems. *Operations Research, 58*(3), 595–612.

Diamantopoulos, A. (1991). Pricing: theory and evidence-a literature review. *Perspectives on Marketing Management, 1*, 63–192.

El Housni, O., & Topaloglu, H. (2022). Joint assortment optimization and customization under a mixture of multinomial logit models: On the value of personalized assortments. *Operations Research*.

Fader, P. S., & Hardie, B. G. (1996). Modeling consumer choice among SKUs. *Journal of Marketing Research, 33*(4), 442–452.

Feldman, J., Zhang, D. J., Liu, X., & Zhang, N. (2022). Customer choice models vs. machine learning: Finding optimal product displays on Alibaba. *Operations Research, 70*(1), 309–328.

Feldman, J. B., & Topaloglu, H. (2015). Capacity constraints across nests in assortment optimization under the nested logit model. *Operations Research, 63*(4), 812–822.

Filom, S., Amiri, A. M., & Razavi, S. (2022). Applications of machine learning methods in port operations-a systematic literature review. *Transportation Research Part E: Logistics and Transportation Review, 161*, Article 102722.

Guadagni, P. M., & Little, J. D. (1983). A logit model of brand choice calibrated on scanner data. *Marketing Science, 2*(3), 203–238.

Hamdan, B., & Diabat, A. (2020). Robust design of blood supply chains under risk of disruptions using Lagrangian relaxation. *Transportation Research Part E: Logistics and Transportation Review, 134*, Article 101764.

Hong, Z., Li, M., Han, X., & He, X. (2020). Innovative green product diffusion through word of mouth. *Transportation Research Part E: Logistics and Transportation Review, 134*, Article 101833.

Jena, S. D., Lodi, A., Palmer, H., & Sole, C. (2020). A partially ranked choice model for large-scale data-driven assortment optimization. *Informs Journal on Optimization, 2*(4), 297–319.

Jindal, R. P., Sarangee, K. R., Echambadi, R., & Lee, S. (2016). Designed to succeed: Dimensions of product design and their impact on market share. *Journal of Marketing, 80*(4), 72–89.

Kowsmann, P. (2016, December 6). Fast fashion: How a ZARA coat went from design to fifth avenue in 25 days. *The Wall Street Journal.* https://www.wsj.com/articles/fast-fashion-how-a-zara-coat-went-from-design-to-fifth-avenue-in-25-days-1481020203

Kumar, S., Singhal, J., & Singhal, K. (2020). A programmed method for generating new product ideas from an existing product line. *Decision Sciences, 53*(4), 771–776.

Li, H., Webster, S., & Yu, G. (2020). Product design under multinomial logit choices: Optimization of quality and prices in an evolving product line. *Manufacturing & Service Operations Management, 22*(5), 1011–1025.

Li, X., & Ke, J. (2019). Robust assortment optimization using worst-case CVaR under the multinomial logit model. *Operations Research Letters, 47*(5), 452–457.

Lin, Y., & Pekkarinen, S. (2011). QFD-based modular logistics service design. *Journal of Business & Industrial Marketing, 26*(5), 344–356.

Liu, W., Wang, D., Zhao, X., Si, C., & Tang, O. (2019). The framework for designing new logistics service product: A multi-case investigation in china. *Asia Pacific Journal of Marketing and Logistics, 31*(4), 898–924.

Liu, W., Yan, X., Li, X., & Wei, W. (2020). The impacts of market size and data-driven marketing on the sales mode selection in an internet platform based supply chain. *Transportation Research Part E: Logistics and Transportation Review, 136*, Article 101914.

Liu, Y., Li, K. J., Chen, H., & Balachander, S. (2017). The effects of products' aesthetic design on demand and marketing-mix effectiveness: The role of segment prototypicality and brand consistency. *Journal of Marketing, 81*(1), 83–102.

Liu, Z., Li, K. W., Li, B. Y., Huang, J., & Tang, J. (2019). Impact of product-design strategies on the operations of a closed-loop supply chain. *Transportation Research Part E: Logistics and Transportation Review, 124*, 75–91.

Lo, V., & Topaloglu, H. (2019). Assortment optimization under the multinomial logit model with product synergies. *Operations Research Letters, 47*(6), 546–552.

McFadden, D. (1974). Conditional logit analysis of discrete choice behavior. *Frontiers of Econometrics*.

Noble, P. M., & Gruca, T. S. (1999). Industrial pricing: Theory and managerial practice. *Marketing Science, 18*(3), 435–454.

Pantourakis, M., Tsafarakis, S., Zervoudakis, K., Altsitsiadis, E., Andronikidis, A., & Ntamadaki, V. (2022). Clonal selection algorithms for optimal product line design: A comparative study. *European Journal of Operational Research, 298*(2), 585–595.

Pichka, K., Alwan, L. C., & Yue, X. (2022). Fulfillment and pricing optimization for omni-channel retailers considering shipment of in-store demand. *Transportation Research Part E: Logistics and Transportation Review, 167*, Article 102912.

Resta, B., Gaiardelli, P., Cavalieri, S., & Dotti, S. (2017). Enhancing the design and management of the product-service system supply chain: an application to the automotive sector. *Service Science, 9*(4), 302–314.

Rockafellar, R. T., & Uryasev, S. (2002). Conditional value-at-risk for general loss distributions. *Journal of Banking & Finance, 26*(7), 1443–1471.

Rooderkerk, R. P., Van Heerde, H. J., & Bijmolt, T. H. (2013). Optimizing retail assortments. *Marketing Science, 32*(5), 699–715.

Rusmevichientong, P., & Topaloglu, H. (2012). Robust assortment optimization in revenue management under the multinomial logit choice model. *Operations Research, 60*(4), 865–882.

Shi, Y., Wang, T., & Alwan, L. C. (2020). Analytics for cross-border e-commerce: inventory risk management of an online fashion retailer. *Decision Sciences, 51*(6), 1347–1376.

Singhal, J., & Katz, J. L. (1990). Note—A branch-and-fathom algorithm for the long range process design problem. *Management Science, 36*(4), 513–516.

Singhal, J., & Singhal, K. (2002). Supply chains and compatibility among components in product design. *Journal of Operations Management, 20*(3), 289–302.

Sun, Y., & Shen, Z. J. M. (2022). Improving accuracy without losing interpretability: A machine learning approach for time series forecasting. Available at SSRN 4263186

Talluri, K., & Van Ryzin, G. (2004). Revenue management under a general discrete choice model of consumer behavior. *Management Science, 50*(1), 15–33.

Train, K. E. (2008). *Discrete choice methods with simulation*. Cambridge University Press.

Umpfenbach, E. L., Dalkiran, E., Chinnam, R. B., & Murat, A. E. (2018). Promoting sustainability of automotive products through strategic assortment planning. *European Journal of Operational Research, 269*(1), 272–285.

Vulcano, G., Van Ryzin, G., & Ratliff, R. (2012). Estimating primary demand for substitutable products from sales transaction data. *Operations Research, 60*(2), 313–334.

Zhang, J., & Huang, J. (2021). Vehicle product-line strategy under government subsidy programs for electric/hybrid vehicles. *Transportation Research Part E: Logistics and Transportation Review, 146*, Article 102221.

Zhang, M., Ahn, H. S., & Uichanco, J. (2022). Data-driven pricing for a new product. *Operations Research, 70*(2), 847–866.

Zhi, B., Wang, X., & Xu, F. (2022). Managing inventory financing in a volatile market: A novel data-driven copula model. *Transportation Research Part E: Logistics and Transportation Review, 165*, Article 102854.

Zymler, S., Daniel, K., & Berc, R. (2013). Distributionally robust joint chance constraints with second-order moment information. *Mathematical Programming, 137*(1), 167–198.

Chapter 3
Analytics for Multi-period Risk-Averse Newsvendor Under Nonstationary Demands

Abstract Based on the practice of a Chinese food manufacturer, this paper presents a predictive-prescriptive analytics framework for the multi-period risk-averse newsvendor problem with nonstationary demands. We commence with predictive analysis aimed at converting nonstationary demand series into predictable stationary ones, then develop inventory models to derive prescriptive decisions based on the transformed stationary data. For demand transformation, we examine three widely adopted techniques—detrending (DET), differencing (DIT), and percentage change transformation (PCT)—all of which reliably render nonstationary demand stationary. These methods not only offer desirable simplicity and interpretability but also outperform the ARIMA methodology in predictive accuracy. Moreover, we propose an ensemble of the three transformations via a model averaging approach, achieving predictive performance comparable to state-of-the-art machine learning methods. For prescriptive inventory decisions, we formulate tailored dynamic risk-averse newsvendor models to align with the distinct structures of the three transformations. Our analysis reveals that optimal order quantities under DET and DIT exhibit monotonicity with increasing risk aversion of the newsvendor, while those under PCT do not necessarily follow this pattern. Similarly, we develop a heuristic ensemble of inventory decisions from the three methods, which delivers superior profit performance. Extensive numerical simulations using the manufacturer's historical dataset demonstrate that the heuristic ensemble decision outperforms individual decisions derived from each transformation method, achieving an average performance improvement of up to 92.25%. Several extensions are also considered to validate the robustness of our results.

Keywords Nonstationary demand series · Risk-averse · Transformation methods · Newsvendor · Analytics

Previously published in Decision Sciences, vol. 54, no. 5 (2023): 554–572. Reproduced with permission from Wiley Online Library.

Y. Yu et al., *Platform Supply Chains 1*, Platform Supply Chains in the AI Era,
https://doi.org/10.1007/978-981-95-9965-3_3

3.1 Introduction

Decision makers facing heightened market volatility exhibit varying attitudes towards risk and base their operational decisions on their individual level of risk aversion. Motivated by this observation, researchers have systematically incorporated risk aversion into operations management (OM), particularly in the domain of inventory control. Over past decades, a substantial body of literature has addressed risk-averse inventory management and provided valuable insights into how risk preferences affect optimal ordering decisions. However, a notable limitation persists in this literature stream: the majority of studies assume that the demand series exhibits *weak* stationarity over time (Bradley, 2004; Decroix & Arreolarisa, 1998; Eeckhoudt et al., 1995; Shi et al., 2019).

Stationarity, as formally defined by Yang and Zurbenko (2010), requires that a demand series satisfies two key conditions: (a) the series maintains constant mean and variance, and (b) its covariance function depends only on the time difference between observations. This statistical property endows stationary demand series with stable characteristics that remain invariant over time, allowing for reliable inference from any sampled subset of the data. Furthermore, these stable statistical properties enable OM researchers to develop precise predictive models for future demand and construct tractable inventory optimization frameworks. The stationary demand assumption frequently fails to align with practical realities across numerous industries. A demand series violating either condition (a) or (b) is properly classified as nonstationary. The inherent instability of statistical properties in nonstationary series presents two fundamental challenges: they become significantly less predictable, and they introduce substantial difficulties in formulating and solving risk-averse inventory management models. A natural methodological approach to overcome these challenges involves transforming the original nonstationary series into a stationary counterpart, thereby enabling the application of well-established prediction methods designed for stationary data.

The literature identifies several approaches for achieving such transformations, with the simplest and most widely applied being mapping-based methods (Salles et al., 2019). These methods operate by generating a new demand series through mathematical transformations applied to each observation of the original series. The transformed series typically exhibits stationarity, allowing the application of standard time series prediction techniques. Importantly, for any such transformation method, the parameters derived during the forward transformation process can be subsequently used to reverse the transformation, thereby recovering demand forecasts in the original scale.

Among mapping-based methods, three approaches have gained particular prominence in both theoretical and applied work (Salles et al., 2019): (i) *detrending* (DET), which estimates an observable trend using a deterministic functional form and incorporates it as a fixed component within the demand pattern; (ii) *differencing* (DIT), which generates a new series by computing differences between demands in adjacent periods; and (iii) *percentage change transformation* (PCT), which applies logarithmic transformation to the relative percentage changes between consecutive demand observations to mitigate fluctuations in the original series. Each transformation method imposes a distinct structural assumption on the underlying demand process, and consequently, varying choices in data preprocessing may lead to meaningfully different decisions regarding inventory replenishment. This differential impact is particularly pronounced when decision makers exhibit risk aversion, creating a critical yet underexplored intersection between statistical preprocessing and operational decision-making under uncertainty.

This research addresses three interconnected questions that bridge predictive analytics and prescriptive decision-making under risk aversion. Specifically, we investigate: (i) which transformation method (DET, DIT, or PCT) most effectively handles nonstationarity for demand forecasting; (ii) how optimal inventory policies differ across transformation methods and interact with decision makers' risk tolerance; and (iii) how these policies perform empirically under varying risk attitudes in practical settings.

Our analysis yields several important findings. First, we demonstrate that an ensemble approach combining forecasts from all three transformation methods achieves predictive accuracy comparable to sophisticated machine learning benchmarks while maintaining superior interpretability. Second, we derive closed-form optimal policies for a dynamic risk-averse newsvendor under each transformed demand structure, revealing that while risk aversion monotonically decreases order quantities in additive models (DET, DIT), it can have nonmonotonic effects in the multiplicative model (PCT) due to shifting dominance between overage and underage risks. Third, our empirical case study shows that no single model dominates across risk attitudes, but a weighted ensemble of decisions improves performance by approximately 92.25% relative to individual model approaches.

This paper contributes to two established literature streams: risk-averse inventory management and nonstationary time series transformation methods. Relative to the risk-averse inventory literature, we extend beyond the conventional stationary demand assumption that characterizes much prior work (Ahmed et al., 2007; Bradley, 2004; Decroix & Arreolarisa, 1998). Relative to the transformation literature, to the best of our knowledge, this represents the first comprehensive study examining these nonstationarity transformation methods within an explicitly risk-averse decision framework while proposing an ensemble learning methodology.

Most specifically, our work connects closely with Shi et al. (2019), who analyze a risk-averse newsvendor with additive AR(1) demand. Our research extends this foundation by considering both additive and multiplicative structures arising from different transformation approaches. We demonstrate that multiplicative demand structure can induce nonmonotonic relationships between optimal order quantity and risk attitude—a novel theoretical insight that extends beyond Shi et al. (2019)'s findings. Additionally, our model incorporates practical elements such as lost-sale costs, enhancing its relevance to real-world inventory management contexts.

This paper is organized as follows. Section 3.2 presents the practical problem and the solution framework. Section 3.3 presents an empirical analysis of different nonstationary transformation methods and their ensemble using the food company's demand

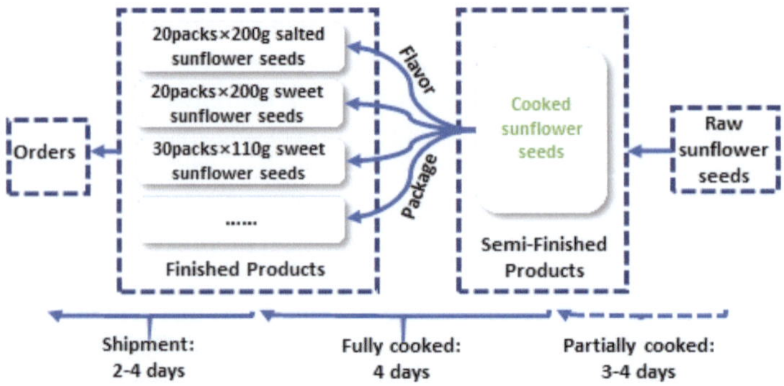

Fig. 3.1 Illustration for the snack production process

data. In Sect. 3.4, we construct our multi-period risk-averse inventory model and theoretically compare these transformation methods in terms of inventory decision and the impact of the risk parameter on the optimal inventory solution. Besides, we propose a heuristic ensemble of these transformation methods for efficient inventory decision-making. Section 3.5 conducts a case study to evaluate these transformation methods and their ensemble for the food company's risk-adjusted profit realization. To examine the robustness of our findings, Sect. 3.6 considers extensions of the base model. Finally, we provide concluding remarks in Sect. 3.7.

3.2 Risk-Averse Newsvendor

Our research is grounded in a consulting engagement with a major food manufacturer in China,[1] specializing in snack products including sunflower seeds and peanuts. The company employs a two-stage production process (illustrated in Fig. 3.1). In the initial stage, raw materials undergo preprocessing and partial cooking to become semi-finished products (SFPs), requiring approximately three to four days. The subsequent stage involves final cooking with flavor enhancers and packaging, transforming SFPs into finished products (FPs) over an additional four days. These FPs are then distributed to downstream partners including retailers and distributors.

Historically operating under a make-to-order paradigm, the manufacturer produced both SFPs and FPs only upon receiving downstream orders. This approach resulted in substantial lead times of ten to twelve days,[2] frequently causing order delays, partner complaints, and occasional order cancellations. To mitigate these operational challenges, the manufacturer strategically implemented an SFP inven-

[1] For confidentiality reasons, specific details regarding the manufacturer are omitted.

[2] The total order lead time comprises the eight-day production lead time plus two to four days for delivery.

tory buffer, produced in anticipation of downstream orders.[3] This initiative reduces the time required for SFP preparation, thereby shortening total order lead time to six to eight days. However, managing SFP inventory presents a complex trade-off: excessive inventory leads to waste due to the perishable nature of SFPs, while insufficient inventory undermines lead time reduction objectives.

Our detailed analysis revealed two particularly challenging aspects of this inventory management problem. First, statistical testing confirms that the SFP demand series is nonstationary (see Table 3.2 and Appendix 1 for stationarity test results), rendering conventional forecasting approaches potentially unreliable. Second, decision-makers within the organization exhibit pronounced risk aversion in their inventory decision-making, influenced by the inherent uncertainty and nonstationarity of downstream demand patterns. Consequently, effectively managing SFP inventory necessitates simultaneous consideration of nonstationary demand characteristics and decision-maker risk preferences—precisely the intersection addressed by our research framework.

To address the practical challenges described above, we develop an integrated analytical framework that combines predictive analytics for demand forecasting with prescriptive analytics for inventory optimization under risk aversion. Our approach proceeds through three systematic phases corresponding to the research questions outlined in Sect. 3.1.

First, for demand forecasting, we implement and compare three transformation methods (DET, DIT, and PCT) to convert the nonstationary SFP demand series into stationary formats. We evaluate their performance against sophisticated benchmarks including ARIMA models, random forests, and neural networks. Recognizing that no single transformation may be universally optimal, we further develop an ensemble approach employing model averaging, where each transformation method serves as a weak learner with assigned positive weights summing to unity.

Second, for inventory optimization, we formulate a dynamic risk-averse newsvendor model that explicitly incorporates the transformed demand structures. A key analytical insight enables decomposition of this multi-period problem into a sequence of single-period risk-averse subproblems, facilitated by the linear structure of the optimal value function. We derive three distinct dynamic newsvendor models corresponding to the structural properties induced by each transformation: DET and DIT models exhibit additive structures (with independent and autocorrelated demands, respectively), while the PCT model follows a multiplicative autocorrelated structure. Each model yields closed-form optimal inventory policies, allowing for analytical examination of how risk aversion affects ordering decisions across different demand structures.

Third, for empirical validation, we conduct a comprehensive case study utilizing the manufacturer's actual demand data and the optimal policies derived above. We evaluate performance across varying risk tolerance levels using risk-adjusted profit

---

[3] The choice of SFP rather than FP inventory aligns with the company's commitment to maintain a make-to-order mode for finished goods, minimizing inventory risks while benefiting from the cost-effectiveness of holding semi-finished versus finished inventory.

(CVaR) metrics. Building upon the ensemble concept from predictive analytics, we further develop a weighted combination of optimal decisions from all three models, testing whether this integrated approach can leverage complementary strengths to achieve superior practical performance.

While our analytical framework emerges from a specific industrial context, the underlying challenges—managing perishable inventory under nonstationary demand with risk-averse decision-making—arise across numerous sectors including pharmaceuticals, fresh produce, fashion retail, and high-technology products. The transformation methods we examine represent fundamental approaches to handling nonstationarity that extend beyond inventory management to diverse forecasting applications. Similarly, the risk-averse newsvendor framework provides a foundational model for decision-making under uncertainty applicable across operational contexts.

Our integrated approach, combining multiple transformation methods within an ensemble framework and connecting forecasting directly to optimization outcomes, offers methodological insights that transcend the specific case study. By systematically examining how different structural assumptions (additive versus multiplicative) interact with risk preferences to influence optimal decisions, we contribute to a deeper theoretical understanding of risk-averse operations management under realistic demand conditions. The empirical demonstration that ensemble approaches can significantly outperform individual models provides practical guidance for managers facing similar challenges in other industries and contexts.

3.3 Predictive Analytics: Nonstationary Transformation Methods

In this section, we respectively apply the three transformation methods discussed previously (DET, DIT and PCT) to deal with the nonstationary demand series of the food company. This allows an empirical analysis to examine the fitting effect of the three methods' corresponding nonstationary demand patterns. The details of implementing the three methods are as follows.

3.3.1 Dataset

We collected a dataset provided by the food company, including all their FP sales records for the year 2017. A sample record is "2017-03-16/salted sunflower seeds/20 packs × 200 g/50/finished", where "2017-03-16" is the order time, "salted sunflower seeds" is the product type (simple recipe stating the composition of the FP, e.g., it is easy to infer that the salted sunflower seeds are obtained by adding flavors to tasteless cooked sunflower seeds and the latter is corresponding SFP), "20 packs × 200 g" is the packaging specification and indicates the final product is packed in a box of 20

Table 3.1 Descriptive statistics of the data

Field	Values				
SFP	Sunflower seeds, peanuts, almonds, cashews				
Flavor	Sweet, salty, spiced, honey, spicy				
Package	30 packs × 110 g, 20 packs × 200 g, 10 packs × 450 g				
	10 packs × 500 g, 1 pack × 5000 g				
Order status	Finished, prepared, canceled				
Dataset	Demand				
	Mean (kg)	Max (kg)	Min (kg)	Standard deviation	CV
All SFPs	144126	453077	24386	97977	0.694
Best-selling SFP	10421	38437	1070	8178	0.785

small bags containing 200 g of salty sunflower seeds (i.e., one unit of this FP requires 4 kg of cooked sunflower seeds), "50" is the sales volume, "finished" represents the status of this order. Various values of these fields are showed in Table 3.1.

To obtain the real demand of FPs, we take orders in all states including canceled into account. Since the company follows a make-to-order strategy for their FPs, the FP order volume can be regarded as its demand quantity. We can, therefore, easily obtain the real demands for corresponding SFP by simple transformation according to the recipes. Based on sales records from February 12, 2017 to December 30, 2017, we calculated the products' weekly demands, which are measured in terms of weight (kg). Table 3.1 provides the descriptive statistics for the weekly demand series for all of the company's SFPs and the best-selling SFP. In particular, the Coefficient of Variance (CV) of the 46 weeks' demands for all SFPs and the best-selling SFP are both around 70.00%, which again implies great demand fluctuation. Since the best-selling SFP is a typical representative of all SFPs and is a key product that affects the company's revenue, we take the demand series of the best-selling SFP as an example. In addition to the significant nonstationarity, with the rapid expansion of the entire industry, the SFP's demand series also shows a polynomial growth trend.

3.3.2 Forecasting Methods

In this section, we empirically demonstrate the effectiveness of three transformation methods (DET, DIT and PCT) using the food company's data. We report two widely used metrics, MAPE (mean absolute percentage error) and relative RMSE (root mean square error), to measure the forecasting performance.[4] The outline of three transformation methods is as follows:

3.3.2.1 Detrending Transformation

DET involves the determination and removal of an inherent trend observed in a time series behavior (Shumway & Stoffer, 2017). Generally, a DET can be formulated as $\hat{x}_t = x_t - \gamma_t$, where γ_t represents a determined trend component, and $\hat{x}_t$ is the detrended demand series. Note that the nonstationary demand series as a whole shows a polynomial growth trend; we therefore estimate the trend term as a polynomial function of period t (generally a polynomial of degree 3 is sufficient to achieve a good fit). Since the p-value of the Augmented Dickey-Fuller (ADF) test on the detrended demand series is less than 0.01 (<0.05), the detrended demand series is stationary. Moreover, the Ljung-Box (L-B) test confirms its randomness. Therefore, the residual term can be regarded as an independent and identically distributed (i.i.d.) random variable and the demand process can be modeled as follows:

$$\hat{D}_t^{DET} = \gamma_t + \tau^{DET} + \varepsilon_t^{DET}, \tag{3.1}$$

where τ^{DET} is the mean of the detrended demand and ε_t^{DET} is a noise term with zero mean and variance σ_{DET}^2.

3.3.2.2 Differencing Transformation

DIT does not demand a parameter estimation process and is capable of generating a stationary demand series when the original series presents stationary behavior around a deterministic or stochastic trend (Shumway & Stoffer, 2017). The DIT method can generally be formulated as $\hat{x}_t = x_t - x_{t-1}$. As Table 3.2 shows, the demand series transformed with a first difference is already stationary and has no lag correlation, thus, we determine the order of DIT to be 1 and depict the demand process as follows:

$$\hat{D}_t^{DIT} = D_{t-1} + \tau^{DIT} + \varepsilon_t^{DIT}, \tag{3.2}$$

where D_{t-1} is the realized demand of period $t - 1$. Similarly, τ^{DIT} is the mean of the transformed demand series, while ε_t^{DIT} is a noise term with zero mean and variance σ_{DIT}^2.

---

[4] Given the demand forecast $\hat{D}_t$, the out-of-sample MAPE is given by MAPE $= \frac{1}{T}\sum_{t=1}^{T} \left|D_t - \hat{D}_t\right| \Big/ D_t$, measuring the absolute error relative to the mean, and the out-of-sample relative RMSE is given by relative RMSE $= \sqrt{\frac{1}{T}\sum_{t=1}^{T} (D_t - \hat{D}_t)^2} \Big/ \frac{1}{T}\sum_{t=1}^{T} D_t$.

Table 3.2 Stationarity and randomness tests of demand series transformed with different methods

Transformation method	p-value of ADF test	p-value of L-B test
Original data	0.223	0.035
DET	<0.01	0.519
DIT	<0.01	0.158
PCT	<0.01	0.179

Note For the ADF test, a p-value less than 0.05 suggests stationarity. While for the L-B test, a p-value over 0.05 suggests randomness

3.3.2.3 Percentage Change Transformation

PCT is one of the simplest and most applied methods of mathematical transformation. It assumes that there is considerable stability in the relative percentage of change between two adjacent observations of a demand series (Cryer & Chan, 2010), that is, $\hat{x}_t = \ln(x_t/x_{t-1})$. This method is only applicable when the percentage change is within an interval $[-100\rho, 100\rho](0 \leq |\rho| < 1)$, which is easily satisfied for our original demand data. As shown in Table 3.2, the transformed demand series is also stationary, and $\hat{x}_t$ is an i.i.d. random variable. After backstepping, the demand pattern corresponding to this transformation method is obtained, as seen in Equation (3.3).

$$\hat{D}_t^{PCT} = D_{t-1} \cdot e^{\tau^{PCT}} \cdot \xi_t^{PCT}, \tag{3.3}$$

Note that demand series (3.3) can be transformed into an additive structure by taking the logarithm of (3.3):

$$\ln(\hat{D}_t^{PCT}) = \ln(D_{t-1}) + \tau^{PCT} + \varepsilon_t^{PCT}. \tag{3.4}$$

Here, D_{t-1} is the realized demand of period $t-1$, τ^{PCT} is the mean of the transformed demand series, and $\varepsilon_t^{PCT} = \ln(\xi_t^{PCT})$ is a noise term with zero mean and variance σ_{PCT}^2.

A summary of the stationarity and randomness tests of the transformed series is shown in Table 3.2. We have used two other statistical methods, the Kwiatkowski-Phillips-Schmidt-Shin (KPSS) test and Unit-Root test, to estimate the stationarity of transformed demand series, and they lead to similar results. In addition, we give a brief examination of seasonality and exclude the existence of seasonal effect on the series before and after the nonstationary transformation. The specific processes of the two additional stationarity tests and the seasonality examination are provided in Appendix A.2.1 and A.2.2.

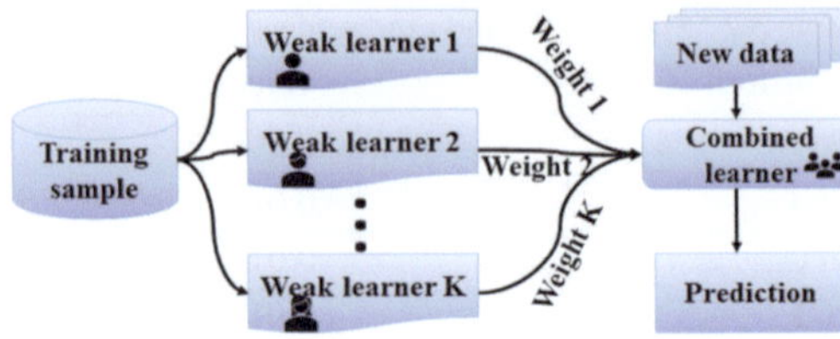

Fig. 3.2 Illustration for ensemble learning

3.3.2.4 Ensemble of Transformation Methods

To further improve the predictive power of the transformation methods, we treat DET, DIT and PCT as three weak learners and follow the well-known ensemble learning approach, *model averaging* (Hansen, 2007; Zhang et al., 2019), to obtain enhanced predictions. Ensemble learning uses the base models' outputs as the input features and the predicted variable remains the same as in the original dataset. A test instance is first predicted by each of the individual week learners. These predictions are then fed into a combined learner which provides the final output. The main idea of ensemble learning is that by combining multiple models, the errors of a single inducer will likely be compensated by other inducers, and as a result, the overall prediction performance of the ensemble would be better than that of a single inducer (Sagi & Rokach, 2018) (Fig. 3.2).

Specifically, we assign three positive weights $(\lambda^{DET}, \lambda^{DIT}, \lambda^{PCT})$ to the three methods and output the following weighted sum as the ensemble prediction of the three methods:

$$\lambda^{DET}\hat{D}_t^{DET} + \lambda^{DIT}\hat{D}_t^{DIT} + \lambda^{PCT}\hat{D}_t^{PCT}, \tag{3.5}$$

where $(\hat{D}_t^{DET}, \hat{D}_t^{DIT}, \hat{D}_t^{PCT})$ are predictions of the three methods, and $\lambda^{DET} + \lambda^{DIT} + \lambda^{PCT} = 1$. Following the literature (Hansen, 2007), the weights can be estimated using a Mallows criterion (Mallows, 2000), which aims to minimize the average squared error from the model average fit. By weighting the average we can communicate how confident we are in each individual model's view of the nonstationary demand series. Thus, the single demand pattern (in the DET, DIT or PCT) closer to the original demand process is assigned a lager weight. When the original demand process completely conforms to one of the above three nonstationary demand patterns, the corresponding weight tends to be 1 and the ensemble learning is simplified to forecasting with this sole demand pattern.

To evaluate the effectiveness of the three transformation methods and their ensemble, we also apply three benchmark methods for demand forecasting. One is the ARIMA(p,d,q) model, another commonly used approach dealing with nonstationary series by differentiating the original data first. The other two are the most widely used machine learning approaches: random forest and neural network. The former uses multiple regression trees to train and predict samples and then averages the prediction results of these trees. The latter uses multiple hidden layers to introduce more nonlinearities at each layer node with the help of activation functions to improve the generalization ability of the trained model. Both approaches have been proven to be the most effective in literature and in practical operations. In particular, the result of ARIMA is considered to be the lower bound and the result of random forest and neural network is considered as the upper bound of the forecasting performance available. Specifically, when applying ARIMA, we draw support from the function of automatically selecting the optimal value of p, d and q in the statistical software R (Hyndman & Khandakar, 2008). Thus, a best-selected ARIMA(p,d,q) model can be determined in each of the 20 periods. We find that ARIMA(0,1,0), which equals the demand pattern in the DIT, dominates in 13 of the periods. When applying the machine learning methods, note that the product attributes such as flavor and packaging specifications in the FPs no longer exist in the SFP; the only factors that contribute to the demand forecasting are the historical demands of the same year and the demand data of the same week in other years. We also integrate the nonstationary trends by including lagged polynomial trend terms to be predictive factors in the machine learning setup. Moreover, the machine learning forecasting is conducted with k-fold ($k = 8$ after many tests) cross-validation so as to avoid overfitting.

3.3.3 *Predictive Performances*

For each forecasting method, we employ a rolling-horizon validation approach to assess predictive performance. Specifically, to forecast demand $D_t (t \geq 27)$, we utilize data from the preceding 26 periods as the training set, applying the trained model to the current period's data. By iterating this procedure over the final 20 periods, we generate 20 distinct training models and corresponding in-sample forecasts, with the average performance across these iterations serving as the definitive evaluation metric for each method. Table 3.3 presents the Mean Absolute Percentage Error (MAPE) and relative Root Mean Squared Error (RMSE) metrics for all examined approaches. Percentage improvements relative to the ARIMA baseline—which serves as a conventional lower bound—are indicated parenthetically.

Three key observations emerge from this analysis. First, as anticipated, machine learning methodologies, specifically random forests and neural networks, achieve superior forecasting accuracy in both in-sample and out-of-sample contexts. However, these nonparametric approaches possess a significant limitation: they operate as "black-box" systems that fail to reveal the underlying structural characteristics of the demand process. This opacity restricts their utility in contexts where interpretability informs strategic decision-making, such as capacity planning or inventory policy formulation. Second, all three transformation-based methods (DET, DIT, and PCT) substantially reduce forecasting error relative to the ARIMA benchmark. Among these, DET demonstrates the strongest individual performance, suggesting that deterministic polynomial growth trends play a dominant role in the original demand series—an insight with direct managerial implications for production planning and inventory investment timing. Third, and most notably, the ensemble forecast that strategically combines predictions from all three transformation methods delivers out-of-sample

Table 3.3 Summary of demand forecast performance with different methods

Forecasting method	In-sample		Out-of-sample	
	MAPE (%)	Relative RMSE(%)	MAPE (%)	Relative RMSE(%)
ARIMA	61.8 (0.0%)	59.8 (0.0%)	82.4 (0.0%)	75.4 (0.0%)
DET	22.3 (63.8%)	19.6 (67.2%)	56.7 (31.2%)	54.0 (28.5%)
DIT	25.7 (53.4%)	23.1 (61.4%)	59.1 (28.3%)	61.3 (18.8%)
PCT	22.8 (63.1%)	25.4 (57.6%)	58.5 (29.0%)	64.5 (14.5%)
Ensemble	45.0 (27.1%)	44.0 (26.4%)	49.5 (40.0%)	53.0 (29.8%)
Random forest	16.3 (73.6%)	18.9 (68.5%)	32.2 (60.9%)	40.4 (46.5%)
Neural network	21.8 (64.8%)	24.4 (59.3%)	35.8 (56.5%)	45.7 (39.5%)

performance that not only surpasses any individual transformation method but also approaches the accuracy levels achieved by advanced machine learning techniques. This finding highlights the complementary nature of different transformation perspectives in capturing diverse aspects of nonstationary demand behavior.

To further explore forecasting alternatives, we examined an attribute-based indirect forecasting strategy: first predicting demand for individual finished products (FPs) using product-specific attributes (e.g., flavors, packaging specifications), then aggregating these forecasts to estimate requirements for the corresponding semi-finished product (SFP). While this approach improved accuracy at the individual FP level, its aggregated SFP forecasts proved inferior to our direct transformation-based methods. This counterintuitive outcome illustrates the “polling effect”, wherein direct aggregation of demand signals can yield more robust forecasts than piecewise bottom-up estimation—a phenomenon with practical implications for forecasting system design in multi-stage production environments. Collectively, these findings affirm that while each transformation method individually provides substantial improvement over conventional approaches, their strategic combination through ensemble methods yields forecasting performance comparable to sophisticated machine learning techniques while preserving full interpretability.

Our methodological choice to employ transformation-based predictive models rather than machine learning alternatives for inventory decision support is grounded in two critical considerations. First, despite recent advances in applying machine learning to inventory problems (Ban & Rudin, 2019; Bertsimas & Kallus, 2020), these applications remain largely confined to static decision contexts. As noted by Mišić and Perakis (2020), multi-period inventory optimization that fundamentally constitutes a dynamic programming problem requires explicit characterization of demand distributions to ensure analytical tractability and optimality guarantees. The opaque nature of machine learning models precludes such characterization, limiting their applicability to dynamic settings. Second, our ensemble approach not only mitigates the individual limitations of each transformation method but also achieves forecasting accuracy rivaling that of complex machine learning systems. This dual capability combining interpretability with competitive accuracy makes the ensemble methodology particularly suitable for inventory optimization contexts where both predictive performance and model transparency are essential for managerial adoption and implementation. Consequently, we proceed with the transformation-based framework for subsequent newsvendor modeling and inventory optimization.

Building upon these predictive insights, we now construct a multi-period risk-averse newsvendor model that explicitly incorporates the nonstationary demand patterns derived from our transformation methods. Prior research by Shi et al. (2019) has established that in stationary AR(1) demand settings, demand autocorrelation plays a decisive role in determining optimal order quantities and their relationship with the decision maker's risk tolerance. Our framework extends this understanding to nonstationary contexts while revealing an important nuance: although all three transformation methods successfully convert nonstationary demand into independently distributed residuals, they preserve fundamentally different temporal dependency structures. Specifically, the DET method yields demand patterns with no autocorrelation, DIT generates additively autocorrelated demands, and PCT produces multiplicatively autocorrelated demands. These structural distinctions—often obscured in purely predictive analyses—have profound implications for inventory policy design, safety stock determination, and replenishment rhythm optimization. The anticipated differences in optimal inventory decisions arising from these distinct nonstationary demand patterns constitute a central focus of our subsequent prescriptive analysis.

3.4 Prescriptive Analytics: Model and Theoretical Results

Taking into account the decision maker's risk-averse behavior, we consider a multi-period single-item newsvendor problem under nonstationary demand patterns corresponding to each of the three transformation methods.

3.4.1 Model Setup

At the beginning of period t (=1, ..., T), the newsvendor infers the demand distribution of $D_t|d_{t-1}$ from her observation of realized demand d_{t-1} and determines the product's stocking quantity Y_t with a cost w per unit. During period t, the demand D_t is realized and the newsvendor satisfies the demand using on-hand inventory as much as possible. At the end of period t, the newsvendor collects the revenue $p \cdot \min\{D_t, Y_t\}$ and pays an inventory cost $c \cdot (D_t - Y_t)^+ + h \cdot (Y_t - D_t)^+$, where h is the holding cost per unit, and b is the shortage cost per unit. Therefore, the newsvendor's profit function in period t is

$$\begin{aligned}\Pi_t(Y_t, D_t|d_{t-1}) =& p \cdot \min(D_t|d_{t-1}, Y_t) - b \cdot (D_t|d_{t-1} - Y_t)^+ \\ & - h \cdot (Y_t - D_t|d_{t-1})^+ - w \cdot Y_t,\end{aligned} \tag{3.6}$$

Since the profit-and-loss performance of an investment for our problem can be correlated over time, we employ a dynamic CVaR, which has been proved to be time-consistent by Ruszczyński (2010), as the risk measure. CVaR for an uncertain "gain", random variable X, can be computed by solving a simple optimization problem:

$$R(X) = \max_{z \in \mathbb{R}} \left\{ z - \frac{E\,[z - X]^+}{\eta} \right\}, \tag{3.7}$$

where η is the degree of risk aversion. Hence, a smaller η is associated with greater risk aversion. The expression of CVaR given in (3.7) is concave in X and continuous in η. Owing to these strong properties, a multi-period inventory problem using a dynamic CVaR approach can be formulated as a dynamic programming problem. We, therefore, use the dynamic CVaR to measure the newsvendor's utility $R_{t|d_{t-1}}$ for the random profit from period t to period T conditioned on realized demand d_{t-1}. The problem can then be formulated as the following dynamic programming problem:

$$\begin{aligned}V_t(d_{t-1}) &= \max_{Y_t \geq 0} \; R_{t|d_{t-1}} \left[\Pi_t(Y_t, D_t|d_{t-1}) + \beta V_{t+1}(D_t|d_{t-1})\right] \\ &= \max_{z \in \mathbb{R}} \left\{ z - \frac{E\left[z - \Pi_t(Y_t, D_t|d_{t-1}) - \beta V_{t+1}(D_t|d_{t-1})\right]^+}{\eta} \right\}.\end{aligned} \tag{3.8}$$

where β is a constant discount factor, η is the newsvendor's risk tolerance level, and the newsvendor becomes more risk-averse as η decreases ($\eta = 1$ refers to the risk-neutral case). $V_t(d_{t-1})$ is the optimal value function that represents the optimal value obtained by the newsvendor from period t to period T after observing realized demand d_{t-1}, and by definition, $V_{T+1}() \equiv 0$.

Before further analyzing Problem (3.8), we first show definitions of some parameters and functions in Table 3.4 for ease of exposition. Note that S is the well-known critical quantile that points to the optimal inventory level of a single-period risk-neutral newsvendor problem combined with a given demand distribution. Based on this critical quantile, we can define the overage and underage risk factors υ^+ and υ^-, which reflect the decision maker's attitude to risk with regard to overstock and understock. Additionally, parameters υ and $\overline{\upsilon}$, and function $I(X)$, B_t^{DIT} and B_t^{PCT} are also embedded into the newsvendor's optimal inventory decisions.

Table 3.4 Notation and definitions of some of the parameters and functions

Notation	Interpretation
$S := \frac{p+b-w}{p+b+h}$	Critical quantile
$F(\cdot)$	CDF of the noise term ε_t^{DET}, ε_t^{DIT} and ξ_t^{PCT}
$v^+ := F^{-1}(S\eta)$	Overage risk factor (increasing in η)
$v^- := F^{-1}(1-(1-S)\eta)$	Underage risk factor (decreasing in η)
$v := F^{-1}(\eta)$	$v^+ \leq v^-$ and $v^+ = v^- = F^{-1}(S)$ when $\eta = 1$
$\overline{v} := F^{-1}(1-\eta)$	$\overline{v} = v$ when $E(\varepsilon_t^i) = 0$ and $f(\varepsilon_t^i) = f(-\varepsilon_t^i)$
	$(i \in \{DET, DIT, PCT\})$
$I(X) := \int_{\underline{\varepsilon}}^{X} F(z)dz$	$X \in \{v^+, v^-, v, \overline{v}\}$

$$B_t^{DIT} := \begin{cases} p - w + \beta B_{t+1}^{DIT} - \frac{b-\beta B_{t+1}^{DIT}}{\eta}, & if \quad t < T+1,\ B_{t+1}^{DIT} \leq \frac{b}{\beta}, \\ p - w + \beta B_{t+1}^{DIT}, & if \quad t < T+1,\ B_{t+1}^{DIT} > \frac{b}{\beta}, \\ 0, & if \quad t = T+1. \end{cases}$$

$$B_t^{PCT} := \begin{cases} e^{\tau^{PCT}}\Bigg[(p+h+\beta B_{t+1}^{PCT})\overline{v} - (h+w)v^- & if \quad t < T+1, \\ -\frac{(p+b+h)(\overline{v}-v^-)+(b-\beta B_{t+1}^{PCT})\left(I(\overline{v})-\overline{v}+E(e^{\varepsilon_t^{PCT}})\right)}{\eta}\Bigg], & B_{t+1}^{PCT} \leq -\frac{p+h}{\beta}, \\ e^{\tau^{PCT}}\Bigg[(p+h+\beta B_{t+1}^{PCT})Sv^+ - (b-\beta B_{t+1}^{PCT})(1-S)v^- & if \quad t < T+1, \\ -\frac{(p+h+\beta B_{t+1}^{PCT})I(v^+)+(b-\beta B_{t+1}^{PCT})\left(I(v^-)-v^-+E(e^{\varepsilon_t^{PCT}})\right)}{\eta}\Bigg], & -\frac{p+h}{\beta} \leq B_{t+1}^{PCT} \leq \frac{b}{\beta}, \\ e^{\tau^{PCT}}\Bigg[(p+b-w)v^+ + (\beta B_{t+1}^{PCT} - b)v & if \quad t < T+1, \\ -\frac{(p+b+h)I(v^+)+(\beta B_{t+1}^{PCT}-b)I(v)}{\eta}\Bigg], & B_{t+1}^{PCT} > \frac{b}{\beta}, \\ 0, & if \quad t = T+1. \end{cases}$$

3.4.2 *Optimal Inventory Decision*

Starting from period T, we use mathematical induction to exploit the mathematical structure of the optimal value function $V_t(d_{t-1})$ and find it can be simplified to a linear function of d_{t-1}. Lemma 3.1 gives a detailed description of the linear structure under different nonstationary demand patterns, especially focusing on the parameter $B_t^i (i \in \{DET, DIT, PCT\})$, which measures the extent to which $V_t(d_{t-1})$ depends on the observed demand d_{t-1}. For DET, since there is no demand autocorrelation in the demand process, the optimal value function is independent of d_{t-1} (i.e., $B_t^{DET} = 0$ for $t = 1, 2, ..., T+1$), which helps to simplify the inventory decision. For DIT and PCT, although their demand processes are both autocorrelated demand patterns, the dependence of $V_t(d_{t-1})$ on d_{t-1} is additive for DIT but multiplicative for PCT. Correspondingly, the former $V_t(d_{t-1})$ is a polynomial of d_{t-1}, while the latter $V_t(d_{t-1})$

is a monomial of d_{t-1} (i.e., $A_t^{PCT} = 0$). Moreover, as shown in Table 3.4, the transition paradigm of B_t^i is determined by comparing B_{t+1}^i with $-\frac{p+h}{\beta}$ and $\frac{b}{\beta}$.

Lemma 3.1 *For any $t = 1, ..., T$, the optimal value function $V_t(d_{t-1})$ under a demand series with nonstationarity processed with different transformation methods can be simplified to the following:*
(i) with DET, $V_t(d_{t-1}) = A_t^{DET}$ and is independent of the observed demand d_{t-1};
(ii) with DIT, $V_t(d_{t-1}) = A_t^{DIT} + B_t^{DIT} \cdot d_{t-1}$;
(iii) with PCT, $V_t(d_{t-1}) = B_t^{PCT} \cdot d_{t-1}$.

Proof Proofs are provided in Appendix A.2.3.

With the help of the simple linear form of the optimal value function, dynamic program (3.8) can be transformed into a sequence of single-period risk-averse problems that depend on d_{t-1} and B_{t+1}^i. We present the optimal order quantities and their properties under the additive pattern (in the DET and DIT) and multiplicative one (in the PCT) in Sects. 3.3.2.1 and 3.3.2.2, respectively.

3.4.2.1 Additive Demand Pattern

For additive demand patterns, because the minimum mean square error (MSE) forecast for demand in period t is given by $E(D_t|d_{t-1})$, the optimal inventory decision equals the expected demand $E(D_t|d_{t-1})$ plus a risk-adjusted safety stock y_t^* that depends on the error term $\varepsilon_t^i (i \in \{DET, DIT\})$.

Proposition 3.1 *The optimal solution Y_t^* for Problem (3.8) under additive demand patterns (in the DET and DIT) are summarized as follows:*
(i) in the DET, $Y_t^* = \gamma_t + \tau^{DET} + y_t^*$, where

$$y_t^* = \frac{(p+h)\upsilon^+ + b\upsilon^-}{p+b+h}, \tag{3.9}$$

(ii) in the DIT, $Y_t^* = D_{t-1} + \tau^{DIT} + y_t^*$, where

$$y_t^* = \begin{cases} \upsilon^-, & B_{t+1}^{DIT} \leq -\frac{p+h}{\beta} \\ \frac{(p+h)\upsilon^+ + b\upsilon^-}{p+b+h}, & -\frac{p+h}{\beta} < B_{t+1}^{DIT} < \frac{b}{\beta} \\ \upsilon^+. & B_{t+1}^{DIT} \geq \frac{b}{\beta} \end{cases} \tag{3.10}$$

Proof Proofs are provided in Appendix A.2.3.

According to Proposition 3.1, the determination of optimal inventory level relies on the dependence of V_{t+1} on the observed demand d_t. If V_{t+1} is strongly and positively correlated with d_t (i.e., $B_{t+1}^i > \frac{b}{\beta}$), then the optimal safety stock y_t^* equals the overage risk factor υ^+, which is increasing with η. If V_{t+1} is strongly and negatively correlated with d_t (i.e., $B_{t+1}^i < -\frac{p+h}{\beta}$), then the underage risk factor υ^- is the optimal safety stock and makes it possible for a more risk-averse newsvendor to optimally stock more inventory (i.e., Y_t^* is decreasing with η). Otherwise, if B_{t+1}^i is within the range of $(-\frac{p+h}{\beta}, \frac{b}{\beta})$, the optimal safety stock is a weighted sum of the risk factors $\frac{p+h}{p+b+h}\upsilon^+ + \frac{b}{p+b+h}\upsilon^-$, and there is a joint influence of υ^+ and υ^- on the optimal inventory decision. Since demand pattern generated by DET has independent demands over time, the long-term expected return is not considered when making a single-period inventory decision for DET model, thus the inventory solution is simplified to always the weighted sum of risk factors. In particular, the risk-adjusted safety stock reduces to the classic newsvendor solution when the decision maker is risk-neutral, that is, when $\eta = 1$, we have $y_t^* = \upsilon^- = \frac{(p+h)\upsilon^+ + b\upsilon^-}{p+b+h} = \upsilon^+ = F^{-1}(S)$.

Corollary 3.1 *With additive demand patterns (in the DET and DIT), the impact of risk tolerance level η on the optimal inventory level Y_t^* in period t given in Proposition 3.1 can be summarized as follows:*

(i) if $y_t^* = \upsilon^+$, then Y_t^* is always increasing with η;

(ii) if $y_t^* = \upsilon^-$, then Y_t^* is always decreasing with η;

(iii) if $y_t^* = \frac{(p+h)\upsilon^+ + b\upsilon^-}{p+b+h}$ and if $\varepsilon_t^i \sim N(0, \sigma_i^2)(i \in \{DET, DIT\})$, then Y_t^* is always increasing with η.

Proof Proofs are provided in Appendix A.2.4.

Given the optimal inventory solution, we further study the impact of the degree of risk aversion η on the optimal solution Y_t^*. Since the optimal inventory decision equals the expected demand $E(D_t|d_{t-1})$ plus the optimal safety stock, the relationship between Y_t^* and η is the same as that between y_t^* and η. First, it is easy to verify that $y_t^* = \upsilon^+$ is increasing with η and $y_t^* = \upsilon^-$ is decreasing with η. Second, if $y_t^* = \frac{(p+h)\upsilon^+ + b\upsilon^-}{p+b+h}$, there is a trade-off between the overstock risk and understock risk, which is separately captured by the overage risk factor υ^+ and the underage risk factor υ^-. On the one hand, the overage risk factor υ^+ drives the newsvendor to stock less as she becomes more risk-averse. On the other hand, the underage risk factor υ^- induces the newsvendor to stock more as she becomes more risk-averse. Set $\varepsilon_t^i(i \in \{DET, DIT\})$ following the normal distribution as an example. Then, Corollary 3.1 states that for additive demand patterns, the influence of overage risk factor on the optimal inventory decision dominates, such that the optimal inventory level is always increasing with η.

3.4.2.2 Multiplicative Demand Pattern

Different from additive demand patterns, the multiplicative demand pattern's corresponding optimal inventory decision is equal to the forecast scalar $d_{t-1} \cdot e^{\tau^{PCT}}$ multiplied by (rather than added to) the risk-adjusted safety stock y_t^* that is determined by the noise term $e^{\varepsilon_t^{PCT}}$.

Proposition 3.2 *The optimal solution Y_t^* for Problem (3.8) under multiplicative demand pattern (in the PCT) is $Y_t^* = D_{t-1} \cdot e^{\tau^{PCT}} \cdot y_t^*$, where*

$$y_t^* = \begin{cases} v^-, & B_{t+1}^{PCT} \leq -\frac{p+h}{\beta} \\ \frac{(p+h)v^+ + bv^-}{p+b+h}, & -\frac{p+h}{\beta} < B_{t+1}^{PCT} < \frac{b}{\beta} \\ v^+. & B_{t+1}^{PCT} \geq \frac{b}{\beta} \end{cases} \tag{3.11}$$

Proof Proofs are provided in Appendix A.2.3.

Based on the fact that demand pattern generated from PCT is autocorrelated, the optimal inventory solution corresponding to PCT model is also determined by the dependence of V_{t+1} on the observed demand d_t. The specific decision rules of y_t^* shown in Proposition 3.2 look similar to that of DIT model, but with an exponentially transformed distribution for F. That is, if ε_t^i is normally distributed, then F is the CDF of normal distribution in Proposition 3.1 but is the CDF of lognormal distribution in Proposition 3.2. Similarly, the risk-adjusted safety stock reduces to the classic newsvendor solution when the decision maker is risk-neutral, that is, when $\eta = 1$, $y_t^* = v^- = \frac{(p+h)v^+ + bv^-}{p+b+h} = v^+ = F^{-1}(S)$.

Corollary 3.2 *With a multiplicative demand pattern (in the PCT), the impact of the risk tolerance level η on the optimal inventory level Y_t^* in period t given in Proposition 3.2 can be summarized as follows:*

(i) if $y_t^* = v^+$, then Y_t^* is always increasing with η;

(ii) if $y_t^* = v^-$, then Y_t^* is always decreasing with η;

(iii) if $y_t^* = \frac{(p+h)v^+ + bv^-}{p+b+h}$ and if $\varepsilon_t^{PCT} \sim N(0, \sigma_i^2)$, then

(a) if $\frac{(p+h)S}{b(1-S)} \geq \frac{F^{-1'}(1-\eta+S\eta)}{F^{-1'}(S\eta)}$, Y_t^* is increasing with η;

(b) if $\frac{(p+h)S}{b(1-S)} < \frac{F^{-1'}(1-\eta+S\eta)}{F^{-1'}(S\eta)}$, Y_t^* is first decreasing with η for $\eta \in [0, \tilde{\eta}]$ and then increasing with η for $\eta \in [\tilde{\eta}, 1]$, where $\tilde{\eta}$ solves $\frac{(p+h)S}{b(1-S)} = \frac{F^{-1'}(1-\eta+S\eta)}{F^{-1'}(S\eta)}$.

Proof Proofs are provided in Appendix A.2.4.

We summarize the impact of the risk tolerance level η on the optimal inventory level Y_t^* under multiplicative demand pattern in Corollary 3.2. Given that the optimal inventory decision in Proposition 3.2 equals a positive constant multiplied by y_t^*, the property of Y_t^* is also decided by the property of the optimal safety stock. In view of the definitions of v^+ and v^- in Table 3.4, the monotonicity of overage risk factor or underage risk factor with respect to η is independent of the demand pattern and is the same as in Corollary 3.1. However, when the optimal safety stock is decided as the weighted sum of risk factors $\frac{(p+h)v^+ + bv^-}{p+b+h}$, the relationship between Y_t^* and η can be nonmonotonic under certain conditions for normal distributed ε_t^{PCT}. That is, a newsvendor may stock more inventory as she becomes more risk-averse, which never happens for the same weighted sum of risk factors under additive demand patterns.

To show the relationship between Y_t^* and η under different demand patterns more intuitively, we conduct a numerical experiment. The solutions of Y_t^* changing with

η are presented in Fig. 3.3. First, no matter what η is, the optimal safety stock of DET model is the weighted sum of risk factors, and the y_t^* corresponding to DIT model and PCT model changes from v^- to the weighted sum of risk factors and then to v^+ as η increases from 0 to 1. This is because the pattern generated by DET has independent demands over time, while those generated by DIT and PCT have autocorrelated demands. Second, when focusing on the weighted sum of risk factors, it is clear from the three plots that $\frac{(p+h)v^+ + bv^-}{p+b+h}$ is monotonically increasing with η for DET model and DIT model, but is first decreasing and then increasing with η for PCT model. This is mainly because the patterns generated by DET and DIT follow an additive structure, while that generated by PCT follows a multiplicative structure.

Proposition 3.3 *For any $i \in \{DET, DIT, PCT\}$, if $\varepsilon_t^i \sim N(0, \sigma_i^2)$, the impact of variance σ_i on the optimal inventory level Y_t^* in period t given in Propositions 3.1 and 3.2 can be summarized as follows:*

(i) if $S\eta > 0.5$, then Y_t^* is always increasing with σ_i;

(ii) if $1 - \eta + S\eta < 0.5$, then Y_t^* is always decreasing with σ_i.

As shown in Proposition 3.3, whether the impact of the variance parameter $\sigma_i (i \in \{DET, DIT, PCT\})$ on the optimal inventory level is positive or negative can be judged by comparing the risk-adjusted critical quantile $S\eta$ or $1 - \eta + S\eta$ with the threshold 0.5 for normally distributed noise terms. If the quantile of overage risk factor exceeds the threshold, no matter which optimal inventory policy the vendor chooses, she will maintain a larger inventory level when faced with greater demand uncertainty. If the quantile of underage risk factor is less than the threshold, the vendor is more likely to make conservative inventory decision when facing a more volatile demand process. In addition, these two properties hold for all three demand models with nonstationarity handled by DET, DIT and PCT (Fig. 3.4).

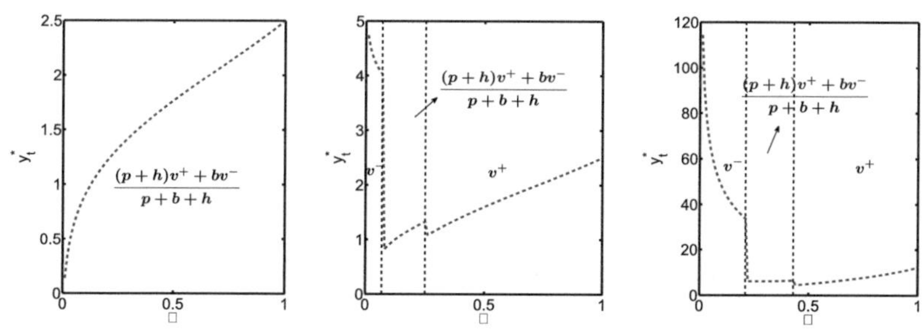

(a) DET model (b) DIT model (c) PCT model

Fig. 3.3 Monotonicity of Y_t^* with respect to η ($\tau^i = 2$, $\sigma_i = 1$, $p = 20$, $b = 3$, $h = 3$, $w = 5$, $\beta = 0.9$)

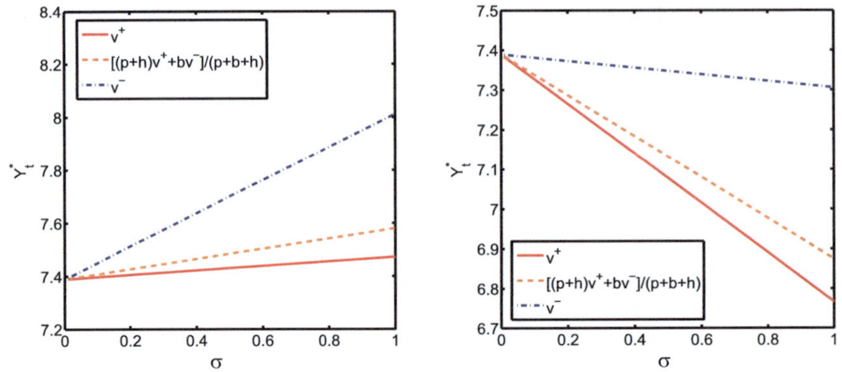

(a) $S\eta > 0.5$ (b) $1-\eta+S\eta < 0.5$

Fig. 3.4 Monotonicity of Y_t^* with respect to σ_i ($\tau^i = e^2, p = 10, b = 3, h = 2, \beta = 0.9, \eta = 0.8$)

3.4.2.3 Heuristic of Ensemble Inventory Decisions

Inspired by the improvement of ensemble predictions in Sect. 3.2, we also propose a heuristic ensemble of the inventory decisions under the three methods. Set Y_t^{DET}, Y_t^{DIT} and Y_t^{PCT} as the optimal inventory levels recommended under the DET, DIT and PCT demand patterns, respectively. We decide the ensemble inventory decision as a weighted linear combination of Y_t^{DET}, Y_t^{DIT} and Y_t^{PCT} in (3.12).

$$\lambda^{DET} Y_t^{DET} + \lambda^{DIT} Y_t^{DIT} + \lambda^{PCT} Y_t^{PCT}, \tag{3.12}$$

where λ^i is the weight assigned to $Y_t^i (i \in \{DET, DIT, PCT\})$, representing the contribution of Y_t^i to the ensemble inventory level. Noting that there are often cases where all Y_t^i are less than or greater than the optimal inventory level, we relax the assumption about the value range of λ^i in this heuristic ensemble so as to allow the ensemble inventory decision to be closer to the optimal value than each individual decision. The intuitive explanation for the ensemble methodology stems from human nature and the tendency to gather different opinions and weigh and combine them to make a complex decision, which is just in line with the manufacturer's inventory problem. Thus, weighing and aggregating several individual opinions could be better than choosing the opinion of one individual.

Algorithm 3.1 Algorithm for the heuristic of ensemble inventory decisions

---

Input: Historical demands $d_1, d_2, ..., d_{t-1}$; planning horizon T, and risk tolerance level η; price and various cost parameters
Output: Ensemble inventory decision in period t
for each t in $t_1 (t_1 > n_1), ..., T$ **do**
  Decide Y_t^i using $d_{t-n_1}, d_{t-n_1+1}, ..., d_{t-1}$ and distribution D_t^i for $i \in \{DET, DIT, PCT\}$
end for
for each t in $t_2 (t_2 - t_1 = n_2 > 0), ..., T$ **do**
  Estimate weights $(\lambda^{DET}, \lambda^{DIT}, \lambda^{PCT})$ using $d_{t-n_2}, d_{t-n_2+1}, ..., d_{t-1}$ and $Y_{t-n_2}^i, Y_{t-n_2+1}^i, ..., Y_{t-1}^i (i \in \{DET, DIT, PCT\})$
  Decide the ensemble inventory solution as $\lambda^{DET} Y_t^{DET} + \lambda^{DIT} Y_t^{DIT} + \lambda^{PCT} Y_t^{PCT}$
end for
End

In this heuristic algorithm, we do not directly apply the weights estimated in ensemble predictions to calculate ensemble inventory decisions. This is because the mapping from demands to CVaR is not in a simple linear pattern, and the demand model with a higher weight may not always play a more important role in determining a better inventory decision. The procedures of the algorithm are summarized in Algorithm 3.1. Using the training sample, we re-estimate weights $(\lambda^{DET}, \lambda^{DIT}, \lambda^{PCT})$ based on realized demands and individual inventory decisions Y_t^{DET}, Y_t^{DIT} and Y_t^{PCT}, and then apply these estimated weights to calculate the ensemble inventory decision in period t.

3.5 Application

In this section, we investigate how to effectively apply the nonstationary transformation method to help the food manufacturer make better SFP inventory decisions under different risk tolerance levels. The possible demand patterns (in the DET, DIT, PCT and their ensemble) shown in Sect. 3.2 are estimated from the food company's real data. Figure 3.5 demonstrates the framework of our case study. At the beginning of each period t, we first apply DET, DIT or PCT to remove the nonstationarity in the original demand series. In this process, we separately fit the historical demand series $d_{t-n_1}^{t-1} (= d_{t-n_1}, d_{t-n_1+1}, ..., d_{t-1})$ to the demand patterns in (3.1), (3.2) and (3.3) to estimate the mean and variance of the transformed demand series, that is, the values of τ^i and $\sigma_i (i \in \{DET, DIT, PCT\})$. For DET, there is an extra estimation of a polynomial of period t to be the trend term. For the model averaging ensemble of DET, DIT and PCT, we additionally estimate these weights $\lambda^i (i \in \{DET, DIT, PCT\})$ based on the realized demands and predicted demands with DET, DIT and PCT methods in the training periods. The results of demand forecasting and the resulting demand patterns corresponding to three transformation methods and their ensemble have been shown in Sect. 3.2. Also, we can infer p and w from the sales records,

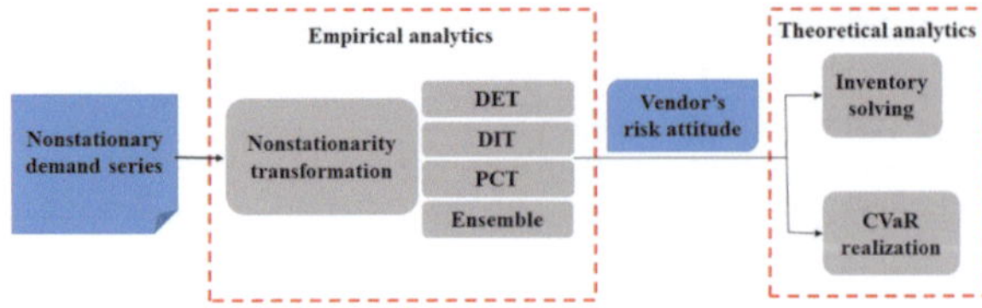

Fig. 3.5 The framework for our case study

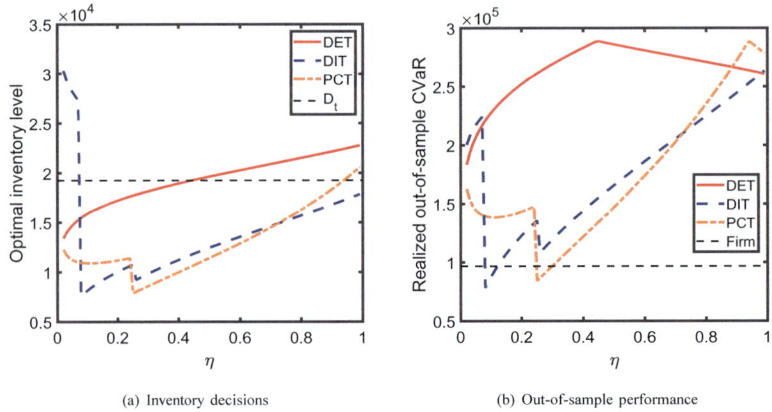

Fig. 3.6 Inventory decisions and out-of-sample performance with different nonstationary demand patterns calculated from real demand data

and h and b are estimated as proportions of the price by the manager (based on experience).

Based on these fitted demand processes, a given planning horizon T, and a given risk tolerance level η, we are able to decide the optimal inventory levels according to Propositions 3.1 and 3.2, and then obtain the out-of-sample CVaR. In period $t+1$, these steps are repeated in a rolling horizon, that is, the optimal inventory decision Y_{t+1}^* is calculated from the demand process derived from the historical demand series $d_{t-n_1+1}^t (= d_{t-n_1+1}, d_{t-n_1+2}, ..., d_t)$. Figure 3.6b reports the realized out-of-sample CVaR with different risk tolerance levels η. In the case of this SFP, the optimal inventory level is almost always less than the realized demand in period t, so that the increase (decrease) in inventory decision suggests that the newsvendor sets a larger (smaller) inventory level that is closer to (farther from) the real demand, which finally results in an increase (a decrease) in realized profit as well as in the risk-adjusted profit, CVaR.

First of all, almost all the realized out-of-sample CVaRs generated by DET, DIT and PCT are greater than those obtained from the firm's original inventory decision. When the nonstationarity in the demand series is handled with DET, as Fig. 3.7a shows, the inventory decision changes smoothly with η. Besides, due to the better fitting efficiency, DET does achieve a higher out-of-sample CVaR than the other two nonstationary demand patterns in most cases. However, for this SFP, DIT achieves a higher out-of-sample CVaR than DET and PCT when the newsvendor is highly

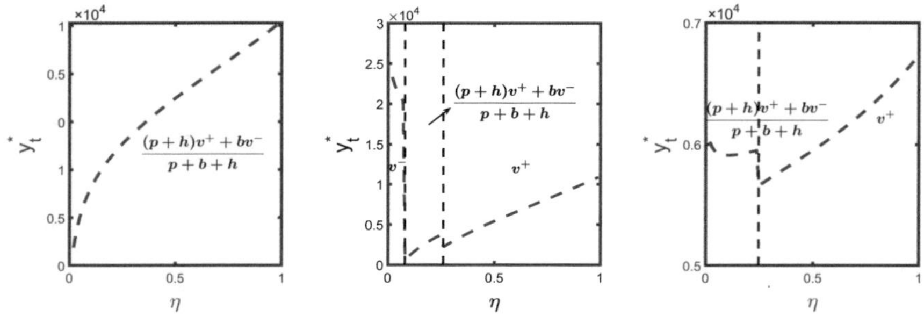

(a) DET model (b) DIT model (c) PCT model

Fig. 3.7 Risk parameter's impact on the choice of optimal safety stock

risk-averse, and PCT outperforms DET and DIT when the newsvendor is nearly risk-neutral. This result shows that regardless of fitting power, each transformation method has its own advantages when faced with different risk tolerance levels of decision makers.

In our case study, with the increasing of η, the optimal safety stock for DIT model changes from v^- to $\frac{(p+h)v^+ + bv^-}{p+b+h}$ and then to v^+, which is shown in Fig. 3.7b. Similarly, when PCT is used to deal with nonstationarity in the demand series, as Fig. 3.7c shows, the optimal safety stock in our case study is first $\frac{(p+h)v^+ + bv^-}{p+b+h}$ and then changes to v^+ as η increases from 0 to 1. Consequently, there are some abrupt changes in the process of out-of-sample CVaR variation with η in Fig. 3.6b. If the newsvendor is highly risk-averse, the optimal safety stock v^- tends to increase sharply when η is very close to 0; then, the choice of DIT or PCT as the nonstationarity transformation method corresponds to a higher Y_t^* than in the case of DET. When the newsvendor is nearly risk-neutral, the optimal safety stock of DIT and PCT models are both v^+. However, as shown in Fig. 3.6b, the optimal safety stock with PCT model increases much faster than that with DIT model. This is because the multiplicative demand structure amplifies the influence of a change in the optimal safety stock y_t^* on the optimal inventory level Y_t^*. Once the optimal safety stock formula is selected, it is obvious that the safety stock in Fig. 3.7a or b either increases or decreases with η while the safety stock $\frac{(p+h)v^+ + bv^-}{p+b+h}$ in Fig. 3.7c is nonmonotonically related to η.

Combining the above analyses, although there is always a statistically superior transformation method in terms of nonstationary demand series fitting, the method sometimes is not the optimal choice for a risk-averse newsvendor to help with her multi-period operational decision, especially when the decision maker is risk-averse. To take full advantages of all the transformation methods, we calculate the ensemble inventory decisions using the model averaging idea and test their effectiveness under different risk tolerance levels.

Table 3.5 Percentage improvement in out-of-sample CVaR for ensemble inventory decisions

Ex	Compared with DET (%)			Compared with DIT(%)			Compared with PCT(%)		
	η			η			η		
	0.1	0.5	1.0	0.1	0.5	1.0	0.1	0.5	1.0
1	16.15	1.00	8.97	199.79	74.07	7.85	91.17	96.13	2.14
2	49.36	10.33	22.18	50.96	11.52	21.34	20.51	10.97	37.21
3	36.43	17.19	0.54	97.03	156.67	208.30	87.17	143.81	192.86
4	44.78	7.08	24.31	83.78	90.36	92.79	65.49	41.94	22.32
5	14.13	3.25	13.78	408.27	470.69	409.55	106.58	148.42	107.44
6	28.27	11.22	45.59	100.13	100.19	100.30	145.86	70.18	4.29
7	36.60	3.50	40.71	56.83	10.78	31.93	12.72	20.37	51.07
8	319.27	10.86	309.02	45.64	88.44	127.10	50.83	89.55	124.51
9	14.65	7.73	2.30	200.67	227.06	215.23	264.53	360.12	317.27
Ave	62.18	8.02	51.93	138.12	136.64	134.93	93.87	109.05	95.46

For any period $t - k(k = 1, ..., n_2)$ on the training data set,[5] we calculate the hindsight optimal inventory level with realized demand known in advance. Then, the values of weights $\lambda^i (i \in \{DET, DIT, PCT\})$ can be estimated from the training data so as to minimize the average squared error. We next apply the estimated weights to transform $Y_t^i (i \in \{DET, DIT, PCT\})$ into ensemble inventory decision in period t. We repeat this procedure for the last 9 periods and calculate the out-of-sample CVaR resulted from ensemble inventory decision, which is then compared with the out-of-sample CVaR caused by separate application of Y_t^{DET}, Y_t^{DIT} or Y_t^{PCT}. The percentage improvement from ensemble learning in the last 9 periods is summarized in Table 3.5. We perform this comparison under different risk tolerance levels ($\eta \in \{0.1, 0.5, 1.0\}$) and it is shown that the out-of-sample CVaR of ensemble inventory decision is always greater than that achieved with individual inventory decision for all the testing periods and regardless of the decision makers' risk tolerance level. Besides, the improvement compared with DET is on a whole much less than the improvement compared with DIT or PCT. Overall, ensemble inventory decision in our case study achieves an average 92.25% increase in CVaR realization than individual inventory decision, which again verifies the effectiveness of the weighted ensemble of transformation methods.

In addition, taking the first experiment in Table 3.5 as an example, we show the inventory decisions and out-of-sample performance of all the four techniques in Fig. 3.8. According to Fig. 3.8a, it is obvious that the ensemble is a tractor that

[5] The total length of the original nonstationary demand series is 46 periods. As we use the data for the previous 26 periods as training set for demand forecasting (i.e., $n_1 = 26$), the separate inventory decision Y_t^{DET}, Y_t^{DIT} and Y_t^{PCT} of the last 20 periods can be obtained in a rolling-horizon pattern. Then the ensemble forecast is based on this 20 periods data. Regarding the data for the previous 11 periods as training set (i.e., $n_2 = 11$), we finally obtain the ensemble inventory decisions of the last 9 periods in a rolling-horizon pattern.

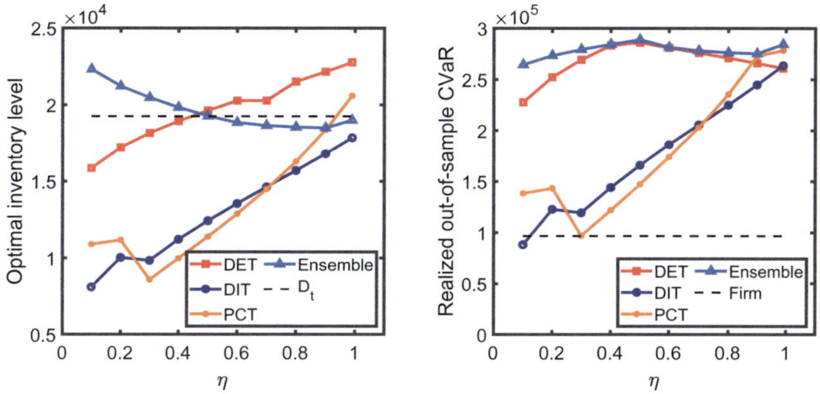

(a) Inventory decisions

(b) Out-of-sample performance

Fig. 3.8 Inventory decisions and out-of-sample performance with different nonstationary demand patterns and their ensemble

guides individual decisions to approach the optimal inventory level. In the left half of the figure, the decision maker is more risk-averse and all the individual decisions fall below the realized demand. Then the estimated weights result in much larger ensemble inventory decisions, which cause holding cost but still output better profit performance compared with individual inventory decisions in Fig. 3.8b. In the right half of Fig. 3.8a, where the risk tolerance level is higher, inventory decisions using DET and PCT demand patterns can be larger than the realized demand. Thus, the estimated weights lead the ensemble inventory decision to a more compromised position, which is also more beneficial for out-of-sample CVaR.

3.6 Extensions

We explore several extensions of the base model and examine the robustness of the previous findings.

3.6.1 Utility-Based Dynamic Inventory Model

First, we consider our results' robustness to the risk measure used in the dynamic risk-averse newsvendor problem. In static newsvendor settings, many optional risk measures can be applied to model the risk-aversion of decision makers, such as utility functions (Eeckhoudt et al., 1995; Choi & Ruszczyński, 2011), mean-variance (Wu et al., 2009), semi-deviation (Choi & Chiu, 2012), VaR (Gan et al., 2005; Wu et al., 2013) and static CVaR (Chen et al., 2009). However, when the profit-and-loss performance of an investment is correlated with time, a static risk measure is time-inconsistent, leading to inconsistent investment decisions over time. Therefore, Ahmed et al. (2007) propose a dynamic CVaR approach that is a recursive composition of static CVaR, which is used in our dynamic problem (3.8). Besides this, Chen et al. (2007) extend the application of utility-based risk measure to a multiperiod inventory problem. They prove the optimality of a base-stock policy based on the additive utility functions and especially the additive exponential utility model. In this section, we examine whether the impact of risk aversion on inventory decision and risk-adjusted profit realization still holds when using the additive exponential utility model.

Following Chen et al. (2007), for a decision maker with risk-tolerance ρ and an exponential utility function, the amount of money she feels indifferent to a gamble with random payoff X can be expressed as the following certainty equivalent:

$$\mathcal{R}^{\rho}[X] = -\rho \ln E\left[e^{-X/\rho}\right], \tag{3.13}$$

where ρ is the "effective risk tolerance" per period and is defined as:

$$\rho_t = \sum_{\tau=t}^{T} \frac{\eta}{(1+r)^{\tau-t}}, \tag{3.14}$$

Here, r is the risk-free saving and borrowing interest rate and η is the risk tolerance factor. Then the inventory decisions in the dynamic risk-averse inventory control model can be calculated through the following dynamic programming recursion:

$$\begin{aligned} V_t(d_{t-1}) &= \max_{Y_t \geq 0} \ \mathcal{R}^{\rho_t}\left[\Pi_t(Y_t, D_t|d_{t-1}) + \frac{1}{1+r} V_{t+1}(D_t|d_{t-1})\right] \\ &= \max_{Y_t \geq 0} \ -\rho_t \ln E\left\{e^{-[\Pi_t(Y_t, D_t|d_{t-1}) + \frac{1}{1+r} V_{t+1}(D_t|d_{t-1})]/\rho_t}\right\}. \end{aligned} \tag{3.15}$$

It has been proved that a base-stock inventory policy is optimal under exponential utility risk criterion; see Chen et al. (2007). Since there is no inventory solution of analytical form under utility-based risk measure, we present the results of a numerical study based on the food company's real data to see how the decision maker's risk aversion can affect the optimal inventory level. The computational results are summarized in Fig. 3.9. Under the exponential utility risk criterion, we do not observe any abrupt change of inventory decisions as η increases, and the optimal inventory levels with the three nonstationary transformation methods all increase monotonically with η. That is, a more risk-averse newsvendor always stocks less inventory. However, we still find that there is no method that is always dominant in prescriptive decisions. In particular, the best-performing method is PCT when the decision maker is highly risk-averse and is DET when η exceeds a certain threshold. This finding is in line with our results under dynamic CVaR risk measure.

Table 3.6 The behavior of y_t^* under different distribution of demand noise term

Distribution	Method	The formula for possible y_t^*	The property of possible y_t^*
Uniform	DET or DIT	$v^+ = (2S\eta - 1)\sqrt{3}\sigma_i$ $v^- = (1 - 2(1 - S)\eta)\sqrt{3}\sigma_i$ $\frac{(p+h)v^+ + bv^-}{p+b+h} = \frac{2(p-w)\eta - (p-b+h)}{p+b+h}\sqrt{3}\sigma_i$	$y_t^* \uparrow \eta$ $y_t^* \downarrow \eta$ $y_t^* \uparrow \eta$
Uniform	PCT	$v^+ = e^{(2S\eta-1)\sqrt{3}\sigma_i}$ $v^- = e^{(1-2(1-S)\eta)\sqrt{3}\sigma_i}$ $\frac{(p+h)v^+ + bv^-}{p+b+h} = \frac{(p+h)e^{(2S\eta-1)\sqrt{3}\sigma_i} + be^{(1-2(1-S)\eta)\sqrt{3}\sigma_i}}{p+b+h}$	$y_t^* \uparrow \eta$ $y_t^* \downarrow \eta$ $y_t^* \searrow\nearrow \eta$
Logistic	DET or DIT	$v^+ = -\ln\left(\frac{1}{S\eta} - 1\right)\frac{\sqrt{3}\sigma_i}{\pi}$ $v^- = -\ln\left(\frac{1}{1-(1-S)\eta} - 1\right)\frac{\sqrt{3}\sigma_i}{\pi}$ $\frac{(p+h)v^+ + bv^-}{p+b+h} = -\frac{(p+h)\ln\left(\frac{1}{S\eta} - 1\right) + b\ln\left(\frac{1}{1-(1-S)\eta} - 1\right)}{p+b+h}\frac{\sqrt{3}\sigma_i}{\pi}$	$y_t^* \uparrow \eta$ $y_t^* \downarrow \eta$ $y_t^* \uparrow \eta$

(continued)

Table 3.6 (continued)

Distribution	Method	The formula for possible y_t^*	The property of possible y_t^*
Logistic	PCT	$v^+ = \left(\frac{1}{S\eta} - 1\right)^{-\frac{\sqrt{3}\sigma_i}{\pi}}$ $v^- = \left(\frac{1}{1-(1-S)\eta} - 1\right)^{-\frac{\sqrt{3}\sigma_i}{\pi}}$ $\frac{(p+h)v^+ + bv^-}{p+b+h} = \frac{(p+h)\left(\frac{1}{S\eta}-1\right)^{-\frac{\sqrt{3}\sigma_i}{\pi}} + b\left(\frac{1}{1-(1-S)\eta}-1\right)^{-\frac{\sqrt{3}\sigma_i}{\pi}}}{p+b+h}$	$y_t^* \uparrow \eta$ $y_t^* \downarrow \eta$ $y_t^* \searrow\nearrow \eta$

Proof. Proofs are provided in Appendix A.2.5

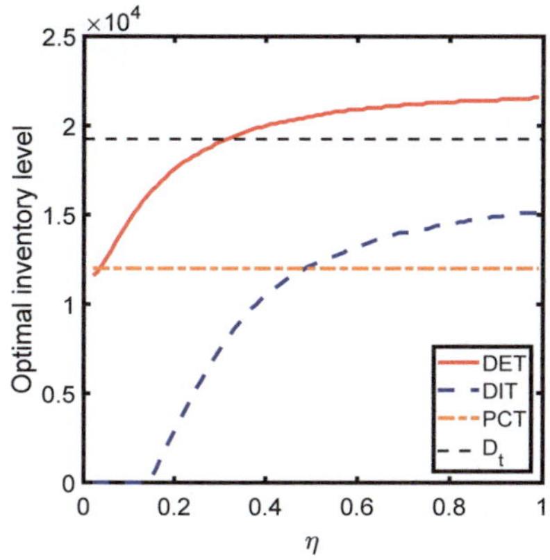

(a) Inventory decisions

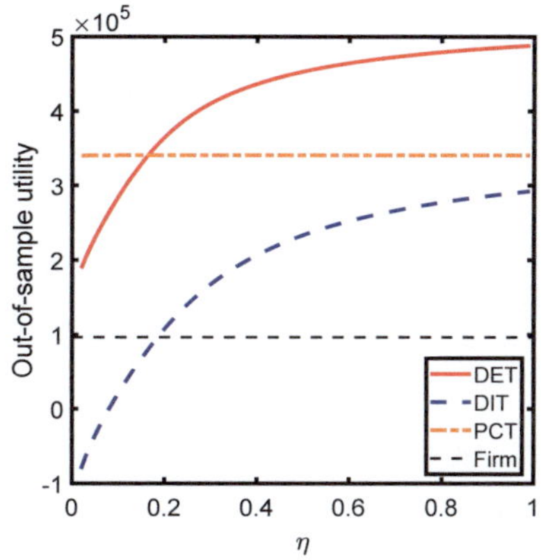

(b) Out-of-sample performance

Fig. 3.9 Inventory decisions and out-of-sample utility with exponential utility risk measure

3.6.2 Other Noise Distributions

Second, we examine whether the previous results continue to hold if noise terms $\varepsilon_t^i (i \in \{DET, DIT, PCT\})$ do not follow normal distributions. We assess the property of possible y_t^* for the other two most commonly used distributions: the uniform and logistic distributions. Table 3.6 summarizes the analytical results. The relationship between the risk tolerance factor η and the optimal inventory level is identical to the findings under the normal distribution summarized in Corollaries 3.1 and 3.2. Regardless of the transformation method the demand process derived from, y_t^* is increasing with η when the optimal safety stock is υ^+ and is decreasing with η when the optimal safety stock is υ^-. Moreover, if the optimal safety stock is decided as $\frac{(p+h)\upsilon^+ + b\upsilon^-}{p+b+h}$, then y_t^* is increasing with η under additive demand patterns (in the DET and DIT) and is nonmonotonically related to η under a multiplicative demand pattern (in the PCT).

In addition to the analytical results, we also perform case studies using the same data and the same framework as in Sect. 3.4 but change the noise term to reflect a uniform distribution and logistic distribution, respectively. Figure 3.10 clearly shows that for a given risk tolerance level η, the optimal inventory decisions under the three distributions of the noise term are almost coincident, no matter which nonstationary transformation method is chosen. The only exception is that the absolute value of Y_t^* with the multiplicative demand pattern differs between different distributions, but the change pattern of Y_t^* still varies with η in the same way. Consequently, the out-of-sample CVaR under the uniform distribution and logistic distribution, as shown in Fig. 3.11, is in line with all our findings under the normal distribution. The relative advantages of each method at different risk tolerance levels are not affected by the distribution of noise term.

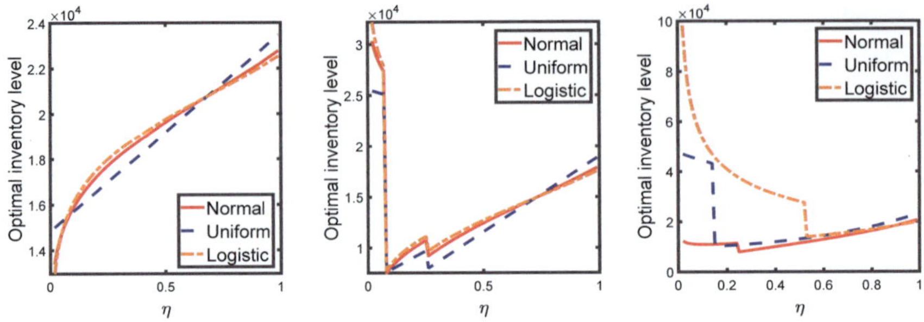

(a) DET model (b) DIT model (c) PCT model

Fig. 3.10 Inventory decisions under different noise term distributions

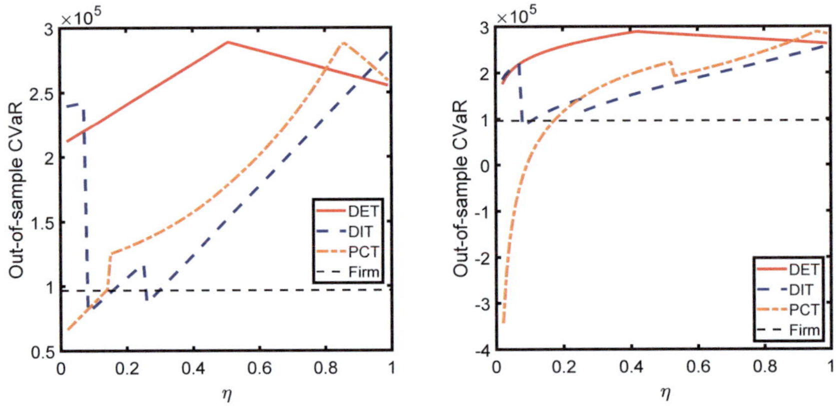

(a) Uniform noise term (b) Logistic noise term

Fig. 3.11 Out-of-sample CVaR under different noise term distributions

3.6.3 Other SFPs

Third, to test the robustness of findings on the best-selling products, we perform the two-step analytics on the demand series of other SFPs. The results of predictive and prescriptive analytics for two of these SFPs (one fast-moving SFP and one slow-moving SFP) are separately shown in Table 3.7 and Fig. 3.12. DET shows a great advantage over DIT and PCT in forecasting nonstationary demand series for this food company. While for the inventory decision and out-of-sample CVaR realization, there are always cases where DIT or PCT, which perform poorly in predictive analytics, outperforms DET. These results are consistent with our main findings for the best-selling SFP.

Table 3.7 Summary of demand forecast performance with two other SFPs

	Forecasting method	In-sample		Out-of-sample	
		MAPE (%)	Relative RMSE(%)	MAPE (%)	Relative RMSE(%)
SFP1	ARIMA	43.7 (0.0%)	50.2 (0.0%)	53.0 (0.0%)	56.6 (0.0%)
	DET	32.3 (26.1%)	32.4 (35.6%)	38.5(27.2%)	59.1 (-4.4%)
	DIT	36.4 (16.6%)	35.1 (30.1%)	49.4 (6.8%)	65.3 (-15.3%)
	PCT	32.8 (24.9%)	42.6 (15.2%)	50.6 (4.4%)	62.4 (-10.2%)
	Ensemble	32.7 (25.1%)	37.9 (24.5%)	37.7 (28.9%)	56.3 (0.7%)
	Random forest	14.0 (68.0%)	16.0 (68.2%)	30.3 (42.7%)	35.3 (37.7%)
	Neural network	55.1 (-26.3%)	54.7 (-8.8%)	53.7 (-1.4%)	64.6 (-14.1%)
SFP2	ARIMA	81.7 (0.0%)	55.6 (0.0%)	72.4 (0.0%)	57.2 (0.0%)
	DET	45.3 (44.6%)	44.9 (19.3%)	77.4 (-6.8%)	61.1 (-6.8%)
	DIT	29.1 (64.4%)	47.6 (14.4%)	96.2 (-32.8%)	61.7 (-8.0%)
	PCT	48.6 (40.6%)	47.2 (15.1%)	92.4 (-27.6%)	75.4 (-31.8%)
	Ensemble	27.9 (65.8%)	22.5 (59.5%)	76.6 (-5.7%)	59.7 (-4.5%)
	Random forest	23.4 (71.3%)	15.6 (72.0%)	70.4 (2.8%)	47.4 (17.0%)
	Neural network	35.6 (56.4%)	30.2 (45.7%)	96.3 (-33.0%)	94.3 (-64.8%)

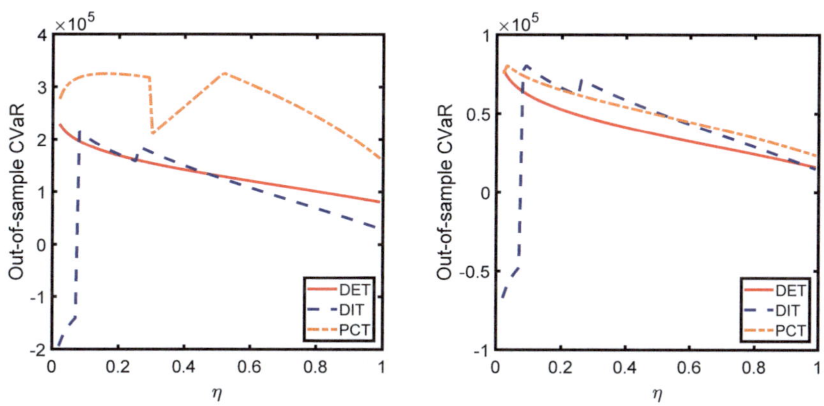

(a) Out-of-sample performance of SFP1 (b) Out-of-sample performance of SFP2

Fig. 3.12 Inventory decisions and out-of-sample performance for two other products

3.7 Concluding Remarks

This paper examines the multi-period inventory management challenge faced by risk-averse decision makers operating under nonstationary demand conditions. To address this complex problem, we systematically implement three prevalent transformation methodologies—detrending (DET), differencing (DIT), and percentage change transformation (PCT)—to derive distinct nonstationary demand patterns. Utilizing empirical demand data from a food manufacturing enterprise, we conduct an integrated investigation that bridges predictive analytics with prescriptive decision-making, thereby evaluating both the statistical efficacy and operational implications of these transformation approaches.

From a predictive analytics perspective, our analysis reveals that all three transformation methods significantly enhance forecasting accuracy relative to conventional ARIMA modeling. Notably, the DET method demonstrates particular effectiveness in our empirical context, yielding superior predictive performance compared to its counterparts. Most importantly, we establish that an ensemble forecasting framework, which strategically synthesizes predictions from all three transformation methods, achieves accuracy levels comparable to sophisticated machine learning algorithms while offering substantially greater interpretability and computational efficiency. This finding carries important managerial implications: organizations can achieve state-of-the-art forecasting performance without resorting to opaque"black-box" algorithms, thereby maintaining decision transparency and facilitating organizational adoption.

Transitioning to prescriptive analytics, we incorporate the derived demand patterns into a formal multi-period risk-averse inventory model. Our theoretical analysis uncovers fundamental structural differences in how inventory policies respond to risk aversion across transformation methods. For additive demand structures (generated by DET and DIT), increased risk aversion systematically reduces optimal safety stock levels as decision makers prioritize avoidance of overstocking costs. Conversely, for the multiplicative structure (generated by PCT), the relationship proves nonmonotonic—under certain conditions, heightened risk aversion may paradoxically increase optimal inventory levels as understocking risks become dominant. This counterintuitive finding challenges conventional inventory management wisdom and underscores the critical importance of aligning transformation choices with both demand characteristics and organizational risk profiles.

Integrating these predictive and prescriptive insights, our empirical case study addressing the company's semi-finished product inventory problem yields several operationally significant findings. First, we demonstrate that no single transformation method dominates across all decision contexts; rather, optimal performance depends systematically on the decision maker's risk attitude. The DIT method proves most effective under high risk aversion, PCT excels in near risk-neutral environments, while DET performs optimally at intermediate risk levels. This contingency perspective offers managers a nuanced framework for method selection based on their organizational risk posture.

Most substantively, we develop and validate an ensemble decision-making heuristic that strategically combines inventory policies derived from all three transformation methods. This integrated approach achieves performance improvements exceeding 90% compared to individual method applications, demonstrating remarkable robustness across varying risk tolerances and temporal contexts. From a managerial standpoint, this ensemble strategy offers a practical, implementable solution to a pervasive operational challenge: how to make robust inventory decisions under nonstationary demand without requiring precise identification of the "correct" demand structure. The approach effectively hedges against model misspecification while leveraging the complementary strengths of different transformation perspectives.

Our research contributions extend beyond methodological developments to offer several important managerial insights. First, we demonstrate that the choice of data transformation method is not merely a statistical preliminary but constitutes a strategic decision with material operational consequences. Second, we provide empirical evidence that relatively simple, interpretable methods can effectively address complex nonstationary demand patterns when deployed within an appropriate analytical framework. Third, we establish that explicitly modeling decision makers' risk attitudes fundamentally alters optimal inventory policies, highlighting the importance of incorporating behavioral considerations into operational models. Finally, we offer a practical implementation pathway through our ensemble heuristic, which balances sophistication with practicality—a crucial consideration for real-world adoption.

While this study advances both theory and practice, several limitations suggest promising directions for future inquiry. The transformation methods examined, though widely applicable, represent parametric approaches with specific structural assumptions. Future research could productively explore nonparametric alternatives that offer greater flexibility in capturing complex nonstationary patterns. Additionally, extending the current framework to incorporate dynamic risk preferences—where decision makers' risk attitudes evolve in response to market conditions or organizational performance—would enhance model realism. From an implementation perspective, developing decision support systems that automate the ensemble approach while providing intuitive visualizations of risk-inventory trade-offs would facilitate managerial adoption. Finally, examining how these methods scale in multi-product, multi-echelon supply chain contexts would further enhance their practical utility.

In conclusion, this research demonstrates that effectively managing inventory under nonstationary demand requires more than sophisticated forecasting—it demands an integrated approach that thoughtfully connects data transformation choices with decision models attuned to organizational risk preferences. By bridging predictive accuracy with prescriptive relevance, we offer both theoretical insights and practical tools for navigating one of operations management's most persistent challenges.

References

Ahmed, S., Cakmak, U., & Shapiro, A. (2007). Coherent risk measures in inventory problems. *European Journal of Operational Research, 182*(1), 226–238.

Aviv, Y. (2002). A time-series framework for supply-chain inventory management. *Operations Research, 51*(2), 210–227.

Ban, G. Y., & Rudin, C. (2019). The big data newsvendor: Practical insights from machine learning. *Operations Research, 67*(1), 90–108.

Bertsimas, D., & Kallus, N. (2020). From predictive to prescriptive analytics. *Management Science, 66*(3), 1025–1044.

Bradley, J. (2004). A Brownian approximation of a production-inventory system with a manufacturer that subcontracts. *Operations Research, 52*(5), 765–784.

Chen, X., Sim, M., Simchi-Levi, D., & Sun, P. (2007). Risk aversion in inventory management. *Operations Research, 55*(5), 828–842.

Chen, Y., Xu, M. H., & Zhang, Z. G. (2009). Technical note: A risk-averse newsvendor model under the CVaR criterion. *Operations Research, 57*(4), 1040–1044.

Choi, T. M., & Chiu, C. H. (2012). Mean-downside-risk and mean-variance newsvendor models: Implications for sustainable fashion retailing. *International Journal of Production Economics, 135*(2), 552–560.

Choi, S., & Ruszczyński, A. (2011). A multi-product risk-averse newsvendor with exponential utility function. *European Journal of Operational Research, 214*(5), 78–84.

Cryer, J. D., & Chan, K. S. (2010). *Time series analysis: With applications in R* (2nd ed.). Springer.

Decroix, G. A., & Arreolarisa, A. (1998). Optimal production and inventory policy for multiple products under resource constraints. *Management Science, 44*(7), 950–961.

Eeckhoudt, L., Gollier, C., & Schlesinger, H. (1995). The risk-averse (and prudent) newsboy. *Management Science, 41*(5), 786–794.

Fan, S., & Hyndman, R. J. (2011). The price elasticity of electricity demand in South Australia. *Energy Policy, 39*(6), 3709–3719.

Franses, P. H. (1991). Seasonality, non-stationarity and the forecasting of monthly time series. *International Journal of Forecasting, 7*(2), 199–208.

Franses, P. H. (1992). Testing for seasonality. *Economics Letters, 38*(3), 259–262.

Gaalman, G. (2006). Bullwhip reduction for ARMA demand: The proportional order-up-to policy versus the full-state-feedback policy. *Automatica, 42*(8), 1283–1290.

Gan, X., Suresh, S. P., & Yan, H. (2005). Channel coordination with a risk-neutral supplier and a downside-risk-averse retailer. *Production and Operations Management, 14*(1), 80–89.

Gilbert, K. (2005). An ARIMA supply chain model. *Management Science, 51*(2), 305–310.

Graves, S. C. (1999). A single-item inventory model for a nonstationary demand process. *Manufacturing & Service Operations Management, 1*(1), 50–61.

Haefen, R. H. V. (2002). A complete characterization of the linear, log-linear, and semi-log incomplete demand system models. *Journal of Agricultural and Resource Economics*, 27(2).

Hansen, B. E. (2007). Least squares model averaging. *Econometrica, 75*(4), 1175–1189.

Hyndman, R. J., & Khandakar, Y. (2008). Automatic time series forecasting: The forecast package for R. *Journal of Statixtical Software, 27*(3), 1–22.

Kamath, K. R., & Pakkala, T. P. M. (2002). A Bayesian approach to a dynamic inventory model under an unknown demand distribution. *Computers & Operations Research, 29*(4), 403–422.

Levin, Y., Mcgill, J., & Nediak, M. (2008). Risk in revenue management and dynamic pricing. *Operations Research, 56*(2), 326–343.

Mallows, C. L. (2000). Some comments on C_p. *Technometrics, 42*(1), 87–94.

Mišić, V. V., & Perakis, G. (2020). Data analytics in operations management: A review. *Manufacturing & Service Operations Management, 22*(1), 158–169.

Neale, J. J., & Willems, S. P. (2009). Managing inventory in supply chains with nonstationary demand. *Interfaces, 39*(5), 388–399.

Ruszczyński, A. (2010). Risk-averse dynamic programming for Markov decision processes. *Mathematical Programming, 125*(2), 235–261.
Sagi, O., & Rokach, L. (2018). Ensemble learning: A survey. *Wiley Interdisciplinary Reviews: Data Mining and Knowledge Discovery, 8*(4), Article e1249.
Salles, R., Belloze, K. T., Porto, F., Gonzalez, P. H., & Ogasawara, E. (2019). Nonstationary time series transformation methods: An experimental review. *Knowledge Based Systems*, 274-291.
Shi, Y., Alwan, L. C., Tang, C., & Yue, X. (2019). A newsvendor model with autocorrelated demand under a time-consistent dynamic CVaR measure. *IISE Transactions, 51*(6), 653–671.
Shumway, R. H., & Stoffer, D. S. (2017). *Time series analysis and its applications: With R examples* (4th ed.). Springer.
Taylor, J. W. (2003). Short-term electricity demand forecasting using double seasonal exponential smoothing. *Journal of the Operational Research Society, 54*(8), 799–805.
Wu, J., Li, J., Wang, S., & Cheng, T. C. E. (2009). Mean-variance analysis of the newsvendor model with stockout cost. *Omega, 37*(3), 724–730.
Wu, M., Zhu, S. X., & Teunter, R. H. (2013). The risk-averse newsvendor problem with random capacity. *European Journal of Operational Research, 231*(2), 328–336.
Yang, W., & Zurbenko, I. (2010). Nonstationarity. *Wiley Interdisciplinary Reviews: Computational Statistics, 2*(1), 107–115.
Zhang, X., Ma, Y., & Carroll, R. J. (2019). MALMEM: model averaging in linear measurement error models. *Journal of The Royal Statistical Society Series B-Statistical Methodology, 81*(4), 763–779.

Chapter 4
Analytics for Cross-Border e-Commerce: Inventory Risk Management of an Online Fashion Retailer

Abstract This study presents a data-driven analytics framework applied to a Chinese fashion retailer engaged in cross-border e-commerce. While the retailer successfully fulfills overseas orders through online platforms, it faces significant inventory management challenges in its overseas warehouses due to operational complexities such as extensive product assortments and high demand uncertainty. Traditional model-driven approaches often prove inadequate in addressing these dynamic challenges. Therefore, this research proposes a novel data-driven methodology for inventory management in overseas warehousing operations. We implement a two-stage predictive analytics approach. First, we classify all products into two categories: $\mathcal{A}$-items, which are profitable to store in overseas warehouses, and $\mathcal{B}$-items, which are not. Second, we predict demand for SKUs within each $\mathcal{A}$-item. Building on these predictions, we develop prescriptive models for optimizing inventory decisions. These include a deterministic model that treats predicted demand as certain, and a stochastic model that explicitly incorporates demand uncertainty through maximum entropy distributions. (1) Comparative analysis of machine learning techniques demonstrates that random forest outperforms other methods in both classification and demand prediction tasks. (2) The deterministic model can be efficiently solved as a linear program, while the stochastic model with maximum entropy distributions is solved using Karush-Kuhn-Tucker conditions. (3) Empirical application shows that predictive classification yields substantial cost reductions (up to 20% on average) by preventing $\mathcal{B}$-items from being shipped to overseas warehouses. Furthermore, the stochastic model provides near-optimal inventory solutions for $\mathcal{A}$-items, with performance losses as low as 0.00% compared to perfect foresight benchmarks.

Keywords Analytics · Inventory · Cross-border e-commerce · Predictive analytics · Prescriptive analytics · Machine learning techniques · Maximum entropy

---

Previously published in Decision Sciences, vol. 51, no. 6 (2020): 1347–1376. Reproduced with permission from Wiley Online Library.

Y. Yu et al., *Platform Supply Chains 1*, Platform Supply Chains in the AI Era,
https://doi.org/10.1007/978-981-95-9965-3_4

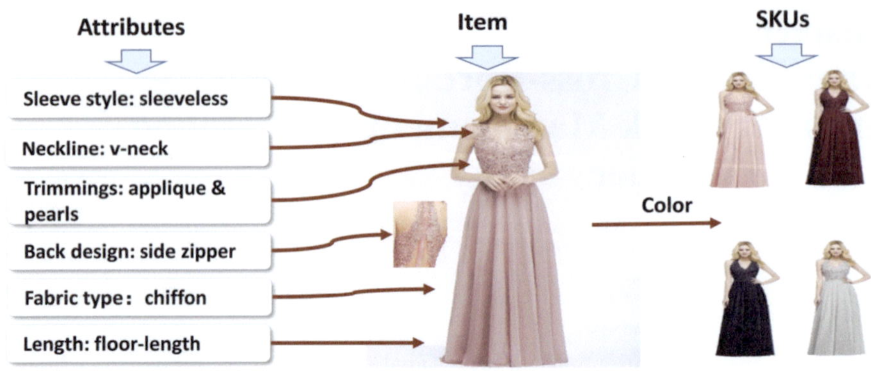

Fig. 4.1 An example of BO's dress attributes, item, and SKUs

4.1 Introduction

With increasingly advanced online technologies and global logistics networks, cross-border e-commerce has expanded rapidly over the past five years (van Heel et al., 2014). China, as one of the leading countries in this sector, is expected to reach total cross-border e-commerce sales of US$144 billion by 2021.[1] Many Chinese enterprises, particularly small and medium-sized ones, have begun selling goods in foreign markets via business-to-business (B2B) and business-to-consumer (B2C) platforms, thereby significantly expanding their operations. However, alongside these business opportunities, cross-border e-commerce introduces substantial operational complexities.

This study focuses on inventory management challenges within cross-border e-commerce, based on a research collaboration with a Chinese fashion apparel retailer that sells to overseas consumers through online platforms such as Amazon.com, DHgate.com, and Aliexpress.com. For privacy, the retailer is referred to as "BO" throughout this paper. BO's product line includes thousands of women's dress items (e.g., evening, prom, and cocktail dresses), which vary by fabric, design, and length. Each dress item is further differentiated by color and size, with each unique combination constituting a distinct stock keeping unit (SKU) (see Fig. 4.1). Currently, BO fulfills approximately 1.3 million overseas orders annually from 150 countries, making it one of the largest cross-border fashion retailers in China.

The high operational complexity of cross-border e-commerce means that traditional model-driven approaches often fail to provide effective solutions for inventory problems in overseas warehouses. Therefore, this study aims to develop a new data-driven approach that integrates predictive analytics and prescriptive analytics. Predictive analytics are used to reduce risks through reliable forecasts, while prescriptive analytics establish data-driven models to optimize inventory decisions and better accommodate risks inherent to cross-border e-commerce. Our approach offers

[1] Source: https://www.chinainternetwatch.com/24363/cross-border-ecommerce-retail-2021/.

insights for managing operational risks in other complex settings similar to cross-border e-commerce, from both theoretical modeling and empirical research perspectives.

4.1.1 Relevant Literature

In recent years, cross-border e-commerce has become a prominent topic in e-commerce research, attracting significant attention from both practitioners and researchers (van Heel et al., 2014). A growing body of literature discusses the benefits and barriers of developing cross-border e-commerce and provides strategic-level suggestions for companies and policymakers (Gomez-Herrera et al., 2014; Gessner & Snodgrass, 2015; Xue et al., 2016; Valarezo et al., 2018). A recurring theme is the critical role of logistics operations, including offshore sourcing, international freight shipment, and overseas warehouse management (Liu et al., 2015; Giuffrida et al., 2017). Aligning with this focus, our paper concentrates on the inventory problem for overseas warehouses of a cross-border e-commerce retailer. A key distinction is our aim to provide operational solutions within an operations analytics paradigm, grounded in real-life data.

Data-driven analytics is increasingly influential in operations management (OM). With greater data availability, OM researchers are leveraging data and machine learning techniques to address operational challenges. Levi et al. (2015) analyze the sample average approximation approach for the data-driven newsvendor problem. Saghafian and Tomlin Saghafian & Tomlin (2016) study the newsvendor problem by combining data with moment and tail information. Ferreira et al. (2015) present a case study of an online apparel retailer (RueLaLa.com) that uses machine learning to predict future demand for new products and optimize pricing decisions. Ban and Rudin Ban & Rudin (2018) propose algorithms for solving the newsvendor problem via single-step machine learning algorithms following the empirical risk minimization principle.

Our work shares similarities with Ferreira et al. (2015) in employing machine learning techniques for prediction based on historical data. However, there are important differences. First, we focus on inventory decisions rather than pricing. Second, in predictive analytics, we introduce an additional step of classifying items (as $\mathcal{A}$ or $\mathcal{B}$) before predicting demand, which helps optimize assortments in overseas warehouses. Finally, due to demand prediction imprecision, we incorporate robustness into the inventory model during the prescriptive analytics phase. Robust decision-making is common in operations analytics due to the difficulty of obtaining full distribution information. Various approaches exist, such as minimax regret over ambiguity sets (Ben-Tal et al., 2006; Bertsimas & Thiele, 2006; Bertsimas et al., 2011; Natarajan et al., 2017) and entropy maximization (Andersson et al., 2013; Fleischhacker & Fok, 2015a, b; Maglaras & Eren, 2015). In this paper, we adopt the principle of maximum entropy (ME) to regenerate demand distributions based on moment information.

From a warehouse design perspective, our paper relates to literature on two-echelon warehouse systems with a central warehouse and multiple sub-warehouses (Hartely, 1976; Jönsson & SILVER, 1987; Sarma, 1987; Pakkala & Achary, 1992; Zhou, 2003). Recent studies have examined such systems in cross-border e-commerce contexts (Wu, 2016). For example, Shuyan and Lisi Shuyan & Lisi (2013) consider the problem of building overseas warehouses to balance logistics costs and profit performance, while Hou et al. (2019) study overseas warehouse location in the context of globalization and the new Silk Road. Unlike these works, which often simplify demand assumptions, we consider stochastic demand and use nonparametric approaches to capture nonlinear relationships between demand, time, and product attributes.

Additionally, our paper connects to vendor-managed inventory (VMI) literature, widely used in cross-border trade to control inventory costs under high demand uncertainty (Rabah & Mahmassani, 2002; Disney & Towill, 2003; Choudhary & Shankar, 2015; Zhan et al., 2018). Recent studies have begun applying data-driven approaches to VMI; for instance, Bertsimas et al. (2016) use machine learning to manage video entertainment product inventories in VMI settings. Similarly, we employ data-driven analytics to manage inventory allocation for BO's overseas warehouses, but we enhance robustness by regenerating demand distributions based on predictive moment information using the ME principle.

4.1.2 Findings and Contributions

Following the proposed framework, we derive both predictive and prescriptive results to address BO's inventory challenges. In the predictive phase, we evaluate multiple data-driven methods—including machine learning techniques—and select the best performer based on out-of-sample validation. Subsequently, we develop deterministic and stochastic optimization models for inventory decision-making and assess their effectiveness using BO's historical data. The key findings and contributions are summarized below.

We first formulate predictive classification as a supervised learning problem. Based on historical sales records, items are first classified as $\mathcal{A}$ (profitable to store overseas) or $\mathcal{B}$ (not profitable). We then apply machine learning methods, including logistic regression and random forest (classification tree), to learn a mapping from item attributes to class labels.[2] For BO's data, random forest achieves higher classification accuracy than logistic regression, consistent with findings by Ferreira et al. (2015). For demand prediction of $\mathcal{A}$-item SKUs, we compare moving-average forecasting with supervised regression techniques such as linear regression and random forest (regression tree). Again, random forest yields the most accurate predictions.

[2] BO maintains a library of apparel attributes; designers compose new items by selecting from this library in accordance with seasonal trends.

We then first propose a deterministic model that treats predicted demand as certain; this model can be solved efficiently as a linear program. However, its performance is highly sensitive to forecast accuracy. To address this limitation, we develop a stochastic model that explicitly incorporates demand uncertainty. Although full demand distributions are difficult to estimate, we find that moment information (mean and variance) can be reliably extracted from historical data. We therefore regenerate demand distributions using the principle of maximum entropy (ME), which identifies the distribution with maximum entropy among all distributions consistent with the given moment information (Fleischhacker & Fok, 2015a, b; Maglaras & Eren, 2015). Using these ME distributions, we solve the stochastic model to obtain robust inventory decisions.

In numerical experiments, we further find that predictive classification enables average cost reductions of up to 20% by preventing unprofitable items from being shipped to overseas warehouses. For $\mathcal{A}$-items, we compare inventory decisions from the deterministic model (using point forecasts) and the stochastic model (using ME distributions) against the optimal solution derived under perfect demand hindsight. Results show that the stochastic model yields solutions with smaller performance losses than the deterministic model, indicating that the robust ME distributions effectively compensate for incomplete demand information.

4.2 Inventory Management of an Online Fashion Retailer

To fulfill its high volume of overseas orders, BO established a global warehousing system consisting of a domestic warehouse and over 20 overseas warehouses. The domestic warehouse is large and located close to suppliers in China. It is responsible for (a) replenishing overseas warehouses, (b) fulfilling orders for items not stored overseas, and (c) partially meeting backorders when stockouts occur overseas. In contrast, overseas warehouses are relatively small and located close to consumers to ensure timely delivery. Managing inventory in the domestic warehouse is relatively straightforward due to low warehousing costs and short lead times.[3] However, managing inventory in overseas warehouses is more complex. Before each selling season (e.g., Homecoming Day), BO must carefully plan inventories for overseas warehouses due to higher warehousing costs abroad. Additional challenges include:

First, BO must store and update diverse SKU assortments in overseas warehouses based on local consumers' dynamically changing preferences. Second, due to long lead times (30–40 days), BO has only one opportunity to replenish overseas inventories before the selling season begins. At this stage, demand is unknown and highly variable, leading to significant demand risks. Moreover, BO continuously designs and launches new items to follow fashion trends; planning inventories for these new items without historical data further increases demand risks.

[3] Most suppliers are located near the domestic warehouse, making lead times negligible. BO, as a dominant player, can also request expedited orders from suppliers within days.

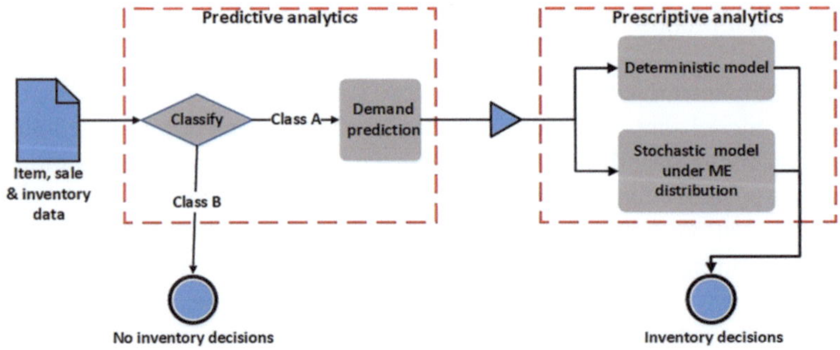

Fig. 4.2 The framework for solving BO's inventory issues in overseas warehouses

4.2.1 Overview of Our Approach

Our approach is based on a framework that integrates predictive analytics and prescriptive analytics (see Fig. 4.2). In the predictive analytics phase, we first classify all items into two classes, $\mathcal{A}$ and $\mathcal{B}$, based on profitability. It is profitable to store $\mathcal{A}$-items in overseas warehouses, but not $\mathcal{B}$-items. This classification helps optimize SKU assortments by avoiding shipping $\mathcal{B}$-items overseas. Next, we predict demand for SKUs of each $\mathcal{A}$-item. Given limited SKU-level sales data,[4] we first predict total demand for each $\mathcal{A}$-item, then decompose it into SKU-level demand using an SKU curve that tracks each SKU's proportion of total demand.

Based on predictive analytics results, we use prescriptive analytics to develop models for optimizing inventory decisions for $\mathcal{A}$-items in overseas warehouses. BO's problem is essentially a single-period, multi-item inventory problem with transportation capacity constraints under two modes (light and heavy). We consider two optimization approaches: a deterministic model that ignores demand uncertainty by treating predicted demand as true demand, and a stochastic model that treats true demand as a random variable. The deterministic model is efficient to solve (as a linear program), but solution quality depends heavily on prediction precision. The stochastic model is more robust as it explicitly incorporates uncertainty, though it is less efficient to solve and requires knowledge of the demand distribution.

The remainder of the paper is organized as follows. Section 4.2 presents the practical problem and the solution framework. Section 4.3 presents the predictive analytical approaches for BO's data. In Sect. 4.4, we show the naïve model and the stochastic model. In Sect. 4.5, we apply the predictive and prescriptive results to solve BO's inventory issues, and study their effectiveness. Lastly, Sect. 4.6 concludes the paper.

[4] Many SKUs sell fewer than five units per season, making precise prediction difficult. Item-level sales data, aggregated across SKUs, are more abundant.

4.3 Predictive Analytics: Item Classification and Demand Prediction

In this section, we presents the predictive analytics applied to BO's data. Within BO's extensive product line, many items and SKUs are insufficiently profitable to be stored in overseas warehouses due to poor sales and high warehousing and logistics costs abroad. Therefore, the first step of our predictive analytics is to identify *which* items can be profitably stored overseas, thereby helping to optimize the item assortment before a selling season begins. The second step focuses on developing demand predictions for the SKUs of the selected items.

4.3.1 Data set

The predictive analytics is conducted using a data set provided by BO, containing transaction records over 12 selling seasons. Each record includes fields such as SKU ID, warehouse location, sale time, price, cost, and others. Table 4.1 presents descriptive statistics for demand and prices over past seasons, along with examples of item (i.e., apparel) attributes. Notably, the data contain many backorder records, allowing us to ignore demand censoring and assume that sales data capture all demand information.

Based on these data, we classify all items into one of two classes: $\mathcal{A}$ (profitable) and $\mathcal{B}$ (unprofitable). Table 4.2 shows that a large proportion of items (more than 70% in most recent seasons) belong to class $\mathcal{B}$ and should not be stored in overseas warehouses. This suggests that accurate pre-season classification can reduce BO's costs by shipping only $\mathcal{A}$-items overseas. Moreover, Table 4.2 indicates that BO continuously designs and launches new items (approximately 40% each season) for overseas markets. Without historical sales data, BO lacks a formal method to assess the profitability of these new items. We address this issue by using machine learning techniques to learn from the attributes of past items.

To ensure the quality of classification and demand prediction results, we consider various competing prediction techniques. We compare their effectiveness by randomly partitioning the complete data set into training and validation sets (using a 70%–30% split). After fitting the models on the training data, we evaluate each model based on its out-of-sample performance on the validation set.

4.3.2 Prediction of Item Classification

We now describe the method for predicting item classifications. Historical data reveal that items with specific attributes often sell well in particular markets or seasons. This observation motivates us to establish relationships between attributes and classifi-

Table 4.1 Descriptive statistics of demands, prices and attributes

Data	Mean	SD	Max	Min
SKU-level demand	10.19	38.63	2749.00	1.00
Item-level demand	80.59	439.66	20047.00	6.00
Selling price	27.26	150.72	2306.15	0.00
Attributes	Values			
Fabric	Chiffon, lace, tulle, spandex			
Collar	Crew, v-neck, scoop, heart, high neck			
Shoulder type	Off the shoulder, portrait, spaghetti-strap			
Dress type	A-line, mermaid, trumpet, sheath, column			
Back design	Hollow, zipper, backless, cross straps, lace-up			
Trimming	Beaded, embroidery, applique, bow			

Table 4.2 Item sales summary statistics over 12 selling seasons

Season	No. of Items	New Items	Class $\mathcal{A}$ (%)	Class $\mathcal{B}$ (%)
1	1815	–	26.61	73.39
2	1810	46.30	26.96	73.04
3	2071	47.46	25.88	74.12
4	2032	42.77	25.20	74.80
5	2020	45.05	30.20	69.80
6	2028	46.35	25.74	74.26
7	1595	39.69	22.76	77.24
8	2177	54.89	26.96	73.04
9	2201	44.48	24.81	75.19
10	2681	48.56	27.68	72.32
11	2668	42.39	26.01	73.99
12	1427	31.60	20.81	79.19

cations. Specifically, we aim to determine a function that takes attributes as inputs and outputs classifications. This approach allows the learned function to be applied to new items (which are often combinations of previously used attributes; see Table 4.1) even without historical sales data.

Following James et al. (2013), we treat this as a *supervised classification* problem. We fit a function to the data, using attributes as feature variables and the class designation $\mathcal{A}/\mathcal{B}$ as the response variable.[5] The learned function is then used to predict classifications for future seasons. We employ two machine learning techniques:

[5] The class $\mathcal{A}/\mathcal{B}$ is replaced by a dummy variable when fitting the model.

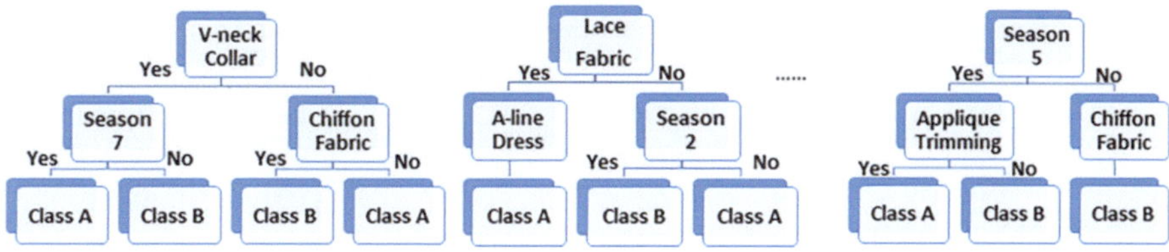

Fig. 4.3 An example of random forest for BO

logistic regression and random forest. The parametric model for logistic regression is as follows:

$$P(y = 1|\boldsymbol{x}, \boldsymbol{\theta}) = \frac{1}{1 + e^{-\sum_j \theta_j x_j}}, \tag{4.1}$$

where $y \in \{0, 1\}$ is the class label ("1" refers to class $\mathcal{A}$, and "0" refers to class $\mathcal{B}$), x_j is the value of attribute j, and θ_j is the weight of attribute j. In our fitting of a logistic regression model, we start with a set $\boldsymbol{x}$ of 70 attribute variables.[6] Then, we remove variables with zero variance, leaving 34 variables in $\boldsymbol{x}$.

Unlike the logistic regression, a random forest is a nonparametric method based on an ensemble of trees. In a random forest, each tree is established from a bootstrap random sample taken from the training set, each node represents a feature, a branch is split according to the rule of impurity reduction, and a leaf node represents the classification of an item (see Fig. 4.3).

We measure the out-of-sample performances of the two methods by the classification accuracy of class i, defined as $\frac{|C_{ii}|}{|C_i|} \times 100\%$, where $|C_{ii}|$ is the number of items that are truly class i and are predicted to be in class i, and $|C_i|$ is the number of actually observed i items (here, i is $\mathcal{A}$ or $\mathcal{B}$). Similarly, the overall classification accuracy is calculated as $\frac{|C_{\mathcal{AA}}|+|C_{\mathcal{BB}}|}{|C_{\mathcal{A}}|+|C_{\mathcal{B}}|}$. We summarize the classification accuracy of each season in Table 4.3. Clearly, the random forest provides classifications that are more accurate than those of the logistic regression. There are two possible reasons for this result. First, random forest is more flexible than logistic regression in terms of adapting to nonlinearities and jaggedness that might reside in the data. Second, the random forest adapts well in learning the interaction effects between feature variables. Thus, enterprises supplying extensive product offerings can benefit from using attribute information and machine learning to pre-position products, enabling them to store only profitable $\mathcal{A}$-items in overseas warehouses.

---

[6] These feature variables include fabric, collar type, shoulder type, skirt type, skirt length, sleeve shape, sleeve length, back design, ornament, color, size, and time, etc.

Table 4.3 Summary of out-of-sample performances of logistic regression and random forest

	Logistic regression			Random forest		
Season	Class $\mathcal{A}$ (%)	Class $\mathcal{B}$ (%)	Overall (%)	Class $\mathcal{A}$ (%)	Class $\mathcal{B}$ (%)	Overall (%)
1	88.15	65.71	76.73	89.66	81.21	85.16
2	85.19	62.86	73.82	90.70	79.79	84.16
3	76.88	71.35	73.96	84.71	86.96	85.99
4	73.61	77.01	75.53	86.11	87.57	86.92
5	83.59	77.16	80.67	92.71	76.92	85.48
6	77.78	68.59	73.86	90.51	81.00	85.20
7	64.65	85.71	76.15	91.92	84.77	87.60
8	80.12	75.60	77.88	88.51	85.05	86.60
9	60.75	83.72	71.79	89.71	83.33	86.23
10	78.50	69.34	73.94	78.54	82.94	80.89
11	74.74	71.05	72.92	78.24	83.93	81.14
12	57.14	85.81	74.77	93.42	83.55	86.84

4.3.3 Prediction of Item Demand

Given the set of $\mathcal{A}$-items, we next predict the demand for the SKUs of each item, which are important inputs in models for optimizing inventory decisions. A direct approach of predicting demand is to fit a model to the SKU-level data, with attributes as feature variables. However, such an approach is pragmatically problematic in terms of efficiency and effectiveness, given the number of SKUs (approximately 21600 SKUs) and the scarcity of SKU-level data (94.75% of SKUs have less than five sales units in a selling season). Therefore, we employ an indirect approach here. That is, we first predict the demand for an item (we have sufficient item-level data), and then disaggregate the predicted demand into that for each SKU, based on an SKU curve that tracks the proportion of an SKU's demand of the total demand. Note that the SKUs in an item are differentiated by color and size. The preferences for colors and the distributions of sizes can be better estimated using historical sales data or expert experience. Thus, we obtain the SKU curves by performing simple estimation techniques, such as frequency counting. The indirect approach is more efficient to implement, and has good interpretability (by showing the substitution effect between SKUs).

Figure 4.4 compares the demand predictions generated by the indirect and direct approaches. Clearly, the indirect approach generates better predictions than those of the direct method. There are two possible reasons for this: (i) the item demand prediction is more reliable than the SKU demand prediction; (ii) the SKU curve can be estimated using historical sales data or expert experience, because different SKUs of an item are differentiated only in terms of color and size, where the color preferences

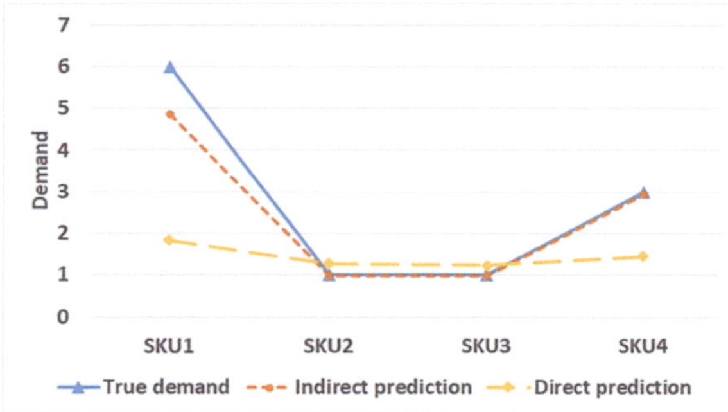

Fig. 4.4 An example of comparing demand predictions generated by the indirect and direct approaches

and size distributions in a market of consumers can be relatively certain. As such, the indirect approach can properly decompose the aggregate demand prediction into reliable SKU demand predictions.

Three methods are considered to predict the demand for an item: moving-average forecasting, linear regression, and random forest. Moving-average forecasting is widely used in practice, including at BO, owing to its simplicity. The method predicts the demand $\hat{D}_{it}$ for item i in season t as the average demand of the previous T seasons; that is, $\hat{D}_{it} = \sum_{\gamma=1}^{T} D_{i,t-\gamma}/T$. For BO's data, we found that T equal to three provides the best out-of-sample performance. A disadvantage of the moving-average method is that it cannot predict the demand for a new item without historical data.

A linear regression sets up a linear function between the demand and the attributes (i.e., $\hat{D} = \alpha + \sum_j \beta_j \cdot x_j$), where β_j is the coefficient of attribute j, and α is the intercept term. As before, we start with a set $\boldsymbol{x}$ of 70 variables. To avoid overfitting, we conducted a stepwise regression on the training set, cross-validated against the validation set, to select a subset of predictors. This process resulted in a linear regression model based on 12 selected variables.

The third method is a random forest using the 70 binary feature variables and the same training and validation sets as those of the linear regression. In contrast to the two previous methods, the random forest captures the substitution effect between items. Recall that the random forecast partitions the data according to items' feature variables into several segments, which also reflect consumers' preferences for items. To compare the different methods, we measure the forecast accuracy of each using a popular error metric in the literature, namely, the relative root mean squared error over the mean demand (relative RMSE: $\sqrt{\frac{1}{N_t}\sum_{i=1}^{N_t}(\hat{D}_{it} - D_{it})^2}/(\frac{1}{N_t}\sum_{i=1}^{N_t} D_{it})$). Figure 4.5 shows the prediction results.

Based on the relative RMSE, except for season 4, there are significant reductions in the forecasting errors of the random forest method in comparison with those of the other two methods. Moreover, the moving-average method outperforms the linear regression forecasting method in most seasons. These results suggest that although attributes and demand are closely linked, it is a complex nonlinear relationship, best captured by the flexible nonparametric random forest method.

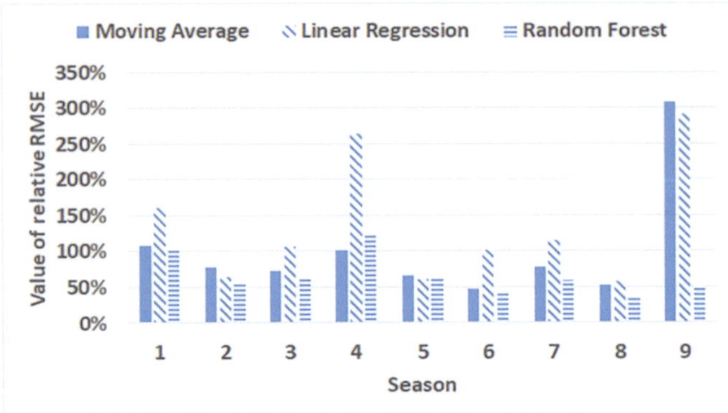

Fig. 4.5 Summary of demand prediction accuracy

4.3.4 Prediction of Moment Information

Our results indicate that while the random forest method generally performs well against the moving-average method, no prediction technique can fully eliminate demand risks for $\mathcal{A}$-items by providing perfectly precise forecasts. Ideally, we would like to estimate the full demand distribution to better model uncertainty; however, this is challenging with only 12 seasons of data. By examining daily demand patterns across seasons, we find that daily demand can be reasonably treated as independently and identically distributed. This allows us to estimate partial distributional information—specifically, the mean and variance of daily demand—which enables robust modeling under uncertainty (Bertsimas & Thiele, 2006; Maglaras & Eren, 2015). From a managerial perspective, incorporating moment information (mean and variance) into inventory planning offers a more resilient approach than relying solely on point forecasts. This is particularly valuable in cross-border e-commerce, where demand volatility is high and forecast errors are costly.

Specifically, we calculate the mean and variance of daily demand for each item in each season. We then fit the previously described models (moving-average, linear regression, and random forest) to historical moment data, using item attributes as feature variables to predict future moments. When using random forest, the training set includes attributes and moment information for the target item as well as all other items in the same assortment from past seasons. Importantly, the random forest captures substitution effects between items by considering the attributes of both the focal item and other items in the assortment. Its nonlinear structure allows it to model complex substitution patterns that linear methods may miss.

A practical consideration is that historical sales data include both $\mathcal{A}$- and $\mathcal{B}$-items, whereas after classification, only $\mathcal{A}$-items will be stocked overseas. This means substitution effects learned from historical data are influenced by the presence of $\mathcal{B}$-items, which could distort estimates of substitution among $\mathcal{A}$-items. However,

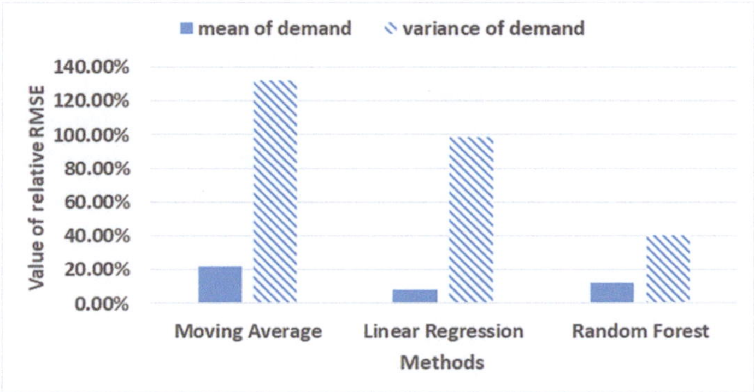

Fig. 4.6 Forecast results of demand mean and variance

since $\mathcal{B}$-items typically have low sales volumes, their impact as "noise" is limited, allowing reasonably accurate predictions of substitution between $\mathcal{A}$-items.

Figure 4.6 presents the prediction results for demand mean and variance. For mean demand, all three methods perform similarly, with linear regression achieving the smallest prediction error (8.46%). For demand variance, however, the random forest method shows a clear advantage, reducing prediction error to around 40%. This superior performance likely stems from its ability to capture substitution effects and consumer preference heterogeneity. Compared to direct demand forecasting, predicting moment information provides a more robust foundation for managing demand risk, as it explicitly quantifies variability. Given that daily demands are i.i.d., seasonal moment information can be easily derived from daily moments.

4.3.5 Summary of Predictive Analytics

We provide a brief summary of our predictive results, which provide the foundation for subsequent prescriptive analytics. First, for item classification, random forest delivers high accuracy, enabling BO to avoid shipping unprofitable $\mathcal{B}$-items to overseas warehouses. This directly reduces warehousing and logistics costs while focusing resources on high-potential items. Second, although random forest outperforms moving-average and linear regression in SKU demand prediction, forecast errors remain substantial. Relying solely on point forecasts in a deterministic inventory model may lead to unreliable stocking decisions. This highlights the limitation of purely forecast-driven approaches in volatile settings. Third, while full demand distributions are difficult to estimate precisely, moment information (mean and variance) can be predicted with reasonable accuracy. This allows the adoption of robust optimization models that use moment information rather than assuming known distributions—a more pragmatic approach given data limitations. Fourth, the moment information predicted by random forest implicitly captures substitution effects between items. This not only improves forecast realism but also simplifies the generation of maximum-entropy (ME) distributions in the prescriptive phase, supporting more robust and implementable inventory policies. Overall, our predictive analytics demonstrate that combining attribute-based learning with moment-level forecasting offers a balanced approach: it improves decision quality while acknowledging and mitigating inherent uncertainties in cross-border e-commerce demand.

4.4 Prescriptive Analytics

In this section, we develop models that address BO's inventory decisions for $\mathcal{A}$-items, based on the results of the prescriptive analytics. Let N be the number of $\mathcal{A}$-items being stored in an overseas warehouse, and N_i be the number of SKUs in the i-th item. Before the selling season, BO needs to decide the quantity q_{ij} of the j-th SKU in the i-th item being shipped to the warehouse, where $i \in [N]$ and $j \in [N_i]$.[7] During the season, customers demand $D_{ij} = s_{ij} D_i$ for this SKU, where D_i is the demand for the i-th item, and s_{ij} is the proportion of the demand for the j-th SKU of that for the i-th item. To fill the demand, BO pays the logistics cost l_{ij} to deliver the SKUs to customers, per unit. If the inventory q_{ij} exceeds the demand D_{ij}, the retailer pays a holding cost h_{ij} per unit[8]; if the demand D_{ij} exceeds the inventory q_{ij}, only a proportion θ_{ij} of unmet demand can be backlogged by the domestic warehouse. Furthermore, the retailer pays the backorder cost b_{ij} (including the costs of placing expedited orders and delivering the SKUs to customers from the domestic warehouse) per unit. Moreover, we do not consider the cost of lost sales in this model, because BO ignores this cost in its inventory management.

At the end of the season, BO receives the sale revenue $p_{ij} \cdot [\min\{q_{ij}, D_{ij}\} + \theta_{ij} \cdot (D_{ij} - q_{ij})^+]$, where p_{ij} is the price per unit, and pays the logistics cost $l_{ij} \cdot \min\{q_{ij}, D_{ij}\}$, holding cost $h_{ij} \cdot (q_{ij} - D_{ij})^+$, backorder cost $b_{ij} \cdot \theta_{ij} \cdot (D_{ij} - q_{ij})^+$, and ordering cost $c_{ij} q_{ij}$, where c_{ij} is the order cost per unit.

In addition to the inventory cost, BO must consider the cost of transporting these SKUs. In particular, there are two transportation modes (light and heavy) available to BO. Under the light mode, BO is allowed to ship items with a total weight within the range $[L_1, U_1]$ at a fare rate of r_1 per unit weight. Under the heavy mode, BO is allowed to ship items with a total weight within the range $[L_2, U_2]$ at a rate r_2, where $L_2 \geq U_1$ and $r_2 < r_1$. Given a mode $z \in \{1, 2\}$, BO's transportation cost is $r_z \sum_{i \in [N]} \sum_{j \in [N_i]} w_{ij} q_{ij}$, where $L_z \leq \sum_{i \in [N]} \sum_{j \in [N_i]} w_{ij} q_{ij} \leq U_z$, and w_{ij} is the unit weight of an SKU. Clearly, it is more cost effective for BO to choose the heavy mode and, thus, achieve economies of scale when more SKUs are shipped. Thus, given an assortment of $\mathcal{A}$-items, BO's profit function for selling these items in overseas markets is:

---

[7] The notation $[X]$, where X is a nonnegative integer, means the set $\{1, \ldots, X\}$.

[8] This logistics cost is commonly observed for cross-border e-commerce firms selling on the Amazon platform, who use the logistics service provided by Amazon (known as fulfillment-by-Amazon (FBA) program) and pay a logistics fee to Amazon.

$$\Pi(\boldsymbol{D}, \boldsymbol{q}, x) = \sum_{i \in [N]} \sum_{j \in [N_i]} \Big\{ (p_{ij} - l_{ij}) \min\{q_{ij}, D_{ij}\} + (p_{ij} - b_{ij})\theta_{ij}(D_{ij} - q_{ij})^+ \\ - h_{ij}(q_{ij} - D_{ij})^+ \\ - c_{ij}q_{ij} - [xr_1 + (1-x)r_2]w_{ij}q_{ij} \Big\}, \tag{4.2}$$

where $x \in \{0, 1\}$, $\boldsymbol{D} := \{D_{ij}\}_{i \in [N], j \in [N_i]}$ is the matrix of SKU demands, and $\boldsymbol{q} := \{q_{ij}^N\}_{i \in [N], j \in [N_i]}$ is the matrix of inventory decisions for these SKUs. Following BO's practice, we assume $p_{ij} > b_{ij} > l_{ij}$. To ensure tractability, the decision variable q_{ij} is treated as a continuous variable rather than as an integer in our analysis. The obtained continuous solution can be rounded up to a near-optimal integer solution for implementation.

4.4.1 Deterministic Model

We start with a naïve model in which the predictions for the demands of SKUs are treated as the true demands for making the inventory decisions. Actually, this model is adopted by BO's operation manager when planning inventory decisions in the past seasons with predictions generated by the moving-average method (see Sect. 4.5 for a detailed discussion). Following this idea, there are no uncertainties incorporated in the model (for clarity, the notation D_{ij} is replaced with d_{ij} here), and the inventory problem can be modeled as a deterministic one:

$$\begin{aligned} & \max\{\Pi(\boldsymbol{d}, \boldsymbol{q}, x)\}, \\ & s.t., \\ & xL_1 + (1-x)L_2 \le \sum_{i \in [N]} \sum_{j \in [N_i]} w_{ij}q_{ij} \le xU_1 + (1-x)U_2, \\ & q_{ij} \ge 0, i \in [N], j \in [N_i], \\ & x \in \{0, 1\}. \end{aligned} \tag{4.3}$$

Proposition 4.1 *By defining $\boldsymbol{q}_x^N$ and V_x^N ($x \in \{1, 2\}$) as the optimal solution and maximum value of the following problem:*

$$
\begin{aligned}
& \max\{\Pi(\boldsymbol{d}, \boldsymbol{q}, x)\}, \\
& = \max \sum_{i \in [N]} \sum_{j \in [N_i]} \Big\{(p_{ij} - l_{ij})Z_{ij} + (p_{ij} - b_{ij})\theta_{ij}(d_{ij} - Z_{ij}) \\
& \qquad\qquad - h_{ij}(q_{ij} - Z_{ij}) - c_{ij}q_{ij} - r_z w_{ij} q_{ij}\Big\}, \\
& s.t., \\
& L_x \le \sum_{i \in [N]} \sum_{j \in [N_i]} w_{ij} q_{ij} \le U_x, \\
& Z_{ij} \le q_{ij}, Z_{ij} \le d_{ij}, \\
& q_{ij} \ge 0, i \in [N], j \in [N_i],
\end{aligned} \tag{4.4}
$$

where Z_{ij} are auxiliary variable, we obtain:
(i) if $V_1^N > V_2^N$, $\boldsymbol{q}^N = \boldsymbol{q}_1^N$;
(ii) otherwise, $\boldsymbol{q}^N = \boldsymbol{q}_2^N$.

Proof Proofs are provided in Appendix A.3.1.

Proposition 4.1 shows the optimal solution for the naïve model, which results from a comparison between the maximum profits (V_1^N, V_2^N) under the two modes. Clearly, Problem (4.4) is a linear program which can be efficiently solved.

4.4.2 Stochastic Model with ME Distribution

Although the naïve model is efficient to solve, the solution of this model highly relies on the quality of the demand predictions. From the predictive study, we know that the predictions are not suffciently precise even when using the machine learning techniques. To solve this problem, it is necessary to know the distribution of D_{ij}. From our predictive analytics, we found that it is hard to obtain precise distribution information, but it is easy to obtain precise moment information. Motivated by this fact, we consider the regenerating of demand distributions only using the moment information.

As mentioned previously, we will regenerate the demand distribution following the principle of maximum entropy, which has been shown to be a powerful tool to estimate an unknown probability distribution from limited information (Andersson et al., 2013; Fleischhacker & Fok, 2015a, b; Maglaras & Eren, 2015). Given a discrete random variable X over support $\Theta_X := \{x_1, \ldots, x_K\}$, we regenerate a discrete distribution $\mathbb{P}_X$ from a set of distributions subject to certain constraints (such as support and moment constraints) with the goal of maximizing the entropy over this set of distributions:

$$
- \sum_{x_k \in \Theta_X} P_{x_k} \ln P_{x_k}, \tag{4.5}
$$

where P_{x_k} is the probability that x_k happens. In our problem, given support and reliable predictions of the first two moments of the demand distribution, we can regenerate the demand distributions following this principle. Generally speaking, given an assortment of K items, a straightforward way of regenerating the distribution is to maximize the following entropy:

$$\max_{\{P_{d_1,\ldots,d_N}\}} \left\{ - \sum_{d_1 \in \Theta_{D_1}, \ldots, d_N \in \Theta_{D_N}} P_{d_1,\ldots,d_N} \ln P_{d_1,\ldots,d_N} \right\}, \tag{4.6}$$

where Θ_{D_k} is the support of the demand of the k-th item, and $P_{d_1,\ldots,d_N}$ is the probability that the item demands in the assortment is $\{d_1, \ldots, d_N\}$. However, Problem (4.6) is not scalable as the number of the items increases. For example, for an assortment with $N = 5$ items and demand support $\Theta_{x_k} = \{1, \ldots, 20\}$, there are 5^{20} variables in Problem (4.6).

To ensure the scalability of our model, we generate the marginal distribution of the demand D_i for item i based on the moment information (m_1^i, m_2^i) by considering the following entropy maximization problem (Andersson et al., 2013):

$$\begin{aligned} &\max_{\{P_{d_k}\}} \left\{ - \sum_{d_k \in \Theta_{D_i}} P_{d_k} \ln P_{d_k} \right\}, \\ &s.t., \\ &\sum_{d_k \in \Theta_{D_i}} P_{d_k} = 1, \\ &\sum_{d_k \in \Theta_{D_i}} d_k P_{d_k} = m_1^i, \\ &\sum_{d_k \in \Theta_{D_i}} d_k^2 P_{d_k} = m_2^i, \\ &P_{d_k} \geq 0, \end{aligned} \tag{4.7}$$

where P_{d_k} is the probability that $D_i = d_k$ happens. Recall that the moment information (m_1^i, m_2^i) predicted by the random forest already captures the demand correlation. Thus, we argue that the joint distribution which is a union of the marginal distributions generated by (4.7) serves as an approximation of the joint distribution generated by (4.6). More importantly, the burden of computing the regenerated distributions scales linearly as the number of items increases. Because Problem (4.7) is a concave function maximization problem with equality constraints, which can be solved by employing the Lagrangian multiplier approach, the solution of Problem (4.7) is

$$P_{d_k}^* = \exp\left(\lambda_0 + \lambda_1 d_k + \lambda_2 d_k^2\right), \tag{4.8}$$

where λ_0 is the Lagrangian multiplier for equality $\sum_{d_k \in \Theta_{D_i}} P_{d_k} = 1$, λ_1 is that for equality $\sum_{d_k \in \Theta_{D_i}} d_k P_{d_k} = m_1^i$, and λ_2 is that for equality $\sum_{d_k \in \Theta_{D_i}} d_k^2 P_{d_k} = m_2^i$.

With the ME demand distribution, we can develop a risk-averse inventory model for optimizing inventory decisions for each SKU. Here, we follow the literature (e.g., Rockafellar & Uryasev (2000)) and use CVaR as the risk measure because of its advantages relative to other risk measures (e.g., VaR measure, semi-deviation measure). The risk-averse retailer's utility for the random profit $\Pi(\boldsymbol{D}, \boldsymbol{q})$ under the CVaR criteria is

$$\text{CVaR}[\Pi(\boldsymbol{D}, \boldsymbol{q}, x)] = \max_{v} \left\{ v - \frac{\mathbf{E}[v - \Pi(\boldsymbol{D}, \boldsymbol{q}, x)]^+}{\eta} \right\}, \tag{4.9}$$

where η is the parameter characterizing the degree of risk aversion, i.e., the retailer becomes more risk averse as η decreases. Moreover, a special case is $\eta = 1$ where $\text{CVaR}[\Pi(\boldsymbol{D}, \boldsymbol{q})] = \mathbf{E}[\Pi(\boldsymbol{D}, \boldsymbol{q})]$, which means the retailer is risk neutral. Correspondingly, the retailer's inventory problem becomes

$$\begin{aligned} & \max\{\text{CVaR}[\Pi(\boldsymbol{D}, \boldsymbol{q}, x)]\}, \\ & s.t., \\ & xL_1 + (1-x)L_2 \leq \sum_{i \in [N]} \sum_{j \in [N_i]} w_{ij} q_{ij} \leq xU_1 + (1-x)U_2, \\ & q_{ij} \geq 0, i \in [N], j \in [N_i], \\ & x \in \{0, 1\}. \end{aligned} \tag{4.10}$$

Note that the concavity of CVaR leads to the concavity of our inventory problem and the uniqueness of the optimal solution. Let q^{ME} be the optimal solution for Problem (4.10) with the regenerated distribution, which is given by the following result:

Proposition 4.2 *By defining $\boldsymbol{q}_x^{ME}$ and V_x^{ME} $(x \in \{1, 2\})$ as the optimal solution and maximum value of the following problem:*

$$\begin{aligned} & \max\{CVaR[\Pi(\boldsymbol{D}, \boldsymbol{q}, x)]\}, \\ & s.t., \\ & L_x \leq \sum_{i \in [N]} \sum_{j \in [N_i]} w_{ij} q_{ij} \leq U_x, \\ & q_{ij} \geq 0, i \in [N], j \in [N_i], \end{aligned} \tag{4.11}$$

we obtain:
(i) if $V_1^{ME} > V_2^{ME}$, $\boldsymbol{q}^{ME} = \boldsymbol{q}_1^{ME}$;
(ii) otherwise, $\boldsymbol{q}^{ME} = \boldsymbol{q}_2^{ME}$.

Proof Proofs are provided in Appendix A.3.2.

From Proposition 4.2 we can see that the solution for Problem (4.10) results from a comparison of the maximum expected profits of the two subproblems under the two modes. Moreover, Subproblem (4.11) is a variant of the multi-item newsvendor problem under the ME distribution, which can be solved using techniques of convex optimization (such as under KKT conditions).

4.5 Application

In Sect. 4.3, we assessed the predictive classification and demand prediction methods using BO's data. In this section, for an overseas warehouse, we study the effectiveness of a full-phase implementation of the two-stage predictive model (classification and demand/moment predictions), leading to our prescriptive modeling approaches. Our study is based on a simulated study using a data set of 12 selling seasons. After cleaning up the data, we observe 1935 items and 21584 SKUs in this warehouse over the 12 seasons. We also learned that the historical inventory decisions for old SKUs were made based on demand predictions for SKUs following the moving-average method. The inventory decisions for new SKUs are determined following a conservative method, that is, using a minimum order quantity of three or five units. We summarize the two-phase method in the following algorithm.

Algorithm 4.1 Algorithm for our approach

Input: item attributes, historical sales, prices, and cost parameters.
Output: item classification and inventory decisions.
Begin
1. Predict the classification ($\mathcal{A}$ or $\mathcal{B}$) for every item in each overseas warehouse in the coming selling season, and only ship $\mathcal{A}$ items to overseas warehouses;
2. For $\mathcal{A}$ items, predict their demand levels and the moment information in the coming selling season;
3. Calculate the inventory decision for every $\mathcal{A}$ item in each overseas warehouse following the deterministic/stochastic models using the predicted demand levels/moment information.
End

In the following analysis, the cost parameters (e.g., holding and delivering cost rates) are initialized using cost data published by Amazon[9]. This is because BO rents Amazon's warehouses to keep its inventories, and pays warehousing fares for using Amazon's logistics service under the latter's fulfillment-by-Amazon program. Specifically, given that apparel is usually of standard size and delivered in small packages, the cost parameters are as follows: $l_{ij} = 2.41\$$, $h_{ij} = 0.69\$$ in the first nine seasons, and $h_{ij} = 2.40\$$ in the last three seasons.

[9] source:https://services.amazon.com/fulfillment-by-amazon/pricing.html

4.5.1 Effectiveness of Predictive Classification

We first evaluate the impact of predictive classification on inventory performance. Using a rolling horizon approach, we predict item classifications for an upcoming season based on data from previous seasons. For example, for the third season, we use data from the first two seasons. In the simulated scenario, a $\mathcal{B}$-item is not shipped to overseas warehouses and thus does not generate profit. We then compare this scenario with the historical outcome: if the item was originally shipped, we compute its actual historical profit. The effectiveness of predictive classification is measured as the profit difference between the simulated and historical scenarios, as shown in Fig. 4.7.

Although the classification is not perfectly accurate, the high proportion of $\mathcal{B}$-items—most of which are unprofitable when stored overseas—means that overall profit still increases when $\mathcal{B}$-items are excluded. This highlights the strategic importance of accurate product-market positioning before launching products in foreign markets. Prior to using predictive classification, the profit per unit cost (i.e., cost-profitability) varied significantly across seasons. Lower original cost-profitability indicates weaker cost control and greater potential for profit improvement through classification. Since classification accuracy (Table 4.3) is relatively stable across seasons, the effectiveness of predictive classification (Fig. 4.7) is inversely related to the original cost-profitability and varies seasonally. Notably, in season 1, where cost-profitability was close to one, the revenue increase from classification reached 50%.

Fig. 4.7 The effectiveness of predictive classification over 9 selling seasons

Table 4.4 Performance loss of the feasible integer solutions from continuous approximation

Ex	No. of SKUs	Performance loss relative to the optimal value (%)			Performance loss relative to the upper bound(%)		
		η=1	η=0.1	η=0.01	η=1	η=0.1	η=0.01
1	2	0.01	0.00	0.00	0.01	0.00	0.00
2	4	0.00	2.10	0.13	0.01	1.16	0.10
3	6	0.08	0.58	5.36	0.05	0.25	1.53
4	8	1.71	3.58	0.01	1.77	3.50	0.36
5	10	1.66	0.02	1.75	1.71	0.03	2.22
6	20	–	–	–	0.02	1.94	3.28
7	30	–	–	–	1.91	2.02	12.26
8	40	–	–	–	5.17	0.11	5.81

4.5.2 *Effectiveness of Continuous Approximation*

We next evaluate the effectiveness of using continuous approximation for the integer decision variables q_{ij} in the inventory model. Continuous approximations are computationally efficient, and their solutions can be rounded to obtain feasible integer solutions for the original problem. We examine whether these rounded solutions are near-optimal for the original integer model.

We begin with small-scale problems (2 to 10 SKUs), where the original integer model can be solved to optimality using mixed-integer programming. The optimal value of the continuous approximation provides an upper bound. As shown in Table 4.4 (Experiments 1–5), the performance loss of the rounded feasible solutions relative to both the true optimum and the upper bound is very small. We then test larger problems (20 to 40 SKUs), where the integer model cannot be solved within reasonable time, but the continuous approximation remains tractable. Here, we measure performance loss only relative to the upper bound. Results (Experiments 6–8) show that the loss remains acceptable, with an average across all experiments of just 1.60%. This confirms that continuous approximation is a reliable and scalable approach for practical implementation.

4.5.3 *Effectiveness of Inventory Decisions*

We now compare the effectiveness of inventory decisions generated by different models, using the optimal profit under perfect demand foresight as a benchmark. This comparison highlights the practical value of integrating advanced prediction methods with robust optimization in volatile settings. First, we consider the deterministic model with predictions from the moving-average (MA) method, which represents BO's current practice. We then evaluate a deterministic model using random for-

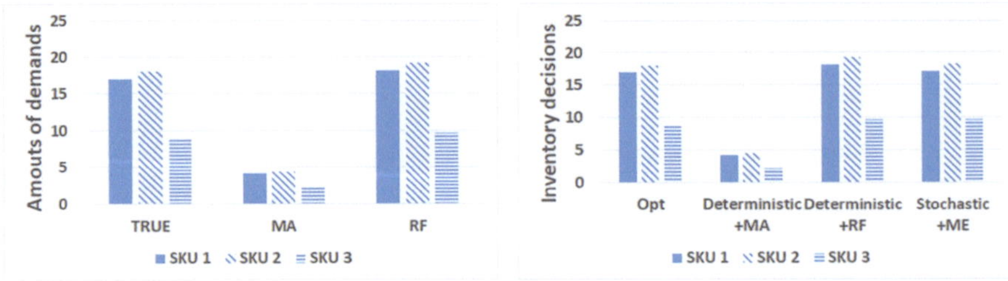

(a) (b)

Fig. 4.8 **a** Demand predictions across SKUs: the true (historical) demands, the moving-average (MA) predictions, and the random forest (RF) predictions. **b** Inventory decisions: the optimal in hindsight; under the deterministic model with MA predictions; under the deterministic model with RF predictions; under ME distribution

est (RF) predictions, which are generally more accurate. Finally, we examine the stochastic model using maximum-entropy (ME) distributions, which incorporates demand uncertainty explicitly.

Figure 4.8a compares the true demand with predictions for three representative SKUs of one item. The moving-average forecasts exhibit noticeable deviation from actual demand, particularly for SKU 2 and SKU 3. In contrast, the random forest predictions align more closely with the true demand pattern, demonstrating its ability to capture nonlinear relationships and substitution effects. Figure 4.8b shows the corresponding inventory decisions under risk neutrality ($\eta = 1$). Decisions based on RF predictions are closer to the hindsight optimum than those based on MA predictions, illustrating how improved forecasting can directly enhance inventory positioning. More importantly, the stochastic model with ME distributions—despite not relying on precise point forecasts—produces decisions nearly identical to the optimum. This demonstrates that a properly specified stochastic model can effectively hedge against demand variability, even when point forecasts are imperfect.

Figure 4.9 aggregates profit outcomes across the three SKUs. The deterministic model with RF predictions improves profit by approximately 18% relative to the MA baseline, confirming the value of enhanced forecasting. However, the stochastic model with ME distributions achieves a profit level within 2% of the perfect-information optimum, outperforming both deterministic approaches. This result underscores a key insight: in high-variability environments, modeling uncertainty explicitly can be more impactful than refining point forecasts alone. For managers, this suggests that efforts to characterize demand variability (e.g., estimating variances) may be as important as improving demand means.

To generalize these findings, we conduct 14 experiments with SKU counts ranging from 2 to 15, summarized in Table 4.5. The results reveal several important patterns. First, the stochastic model consistently yields the smallest performance loss across all risk aversion levels ($\eta = 1, 0.1, 0.01$), with an average loss of only 3.07% and a minimum of 0.00%. This robustness makes it a reliable choice for diverse operational settings. Second, the deterministic model with RF predictions generally outperforms

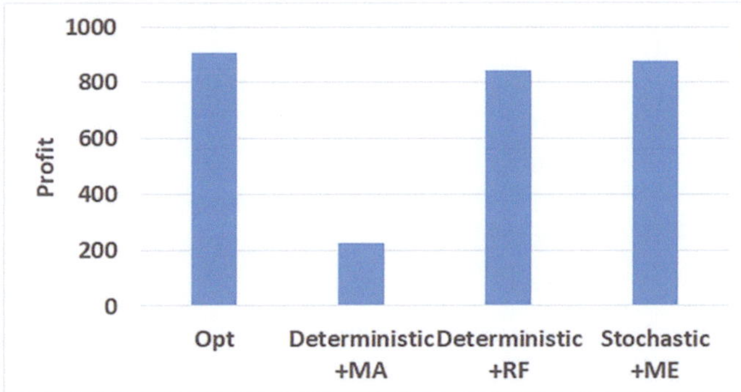

Fig. 4.9 Profit comparisons with the optimal profit in hindsight, the suboptimal profit resulting from the deterministic model with moving-average method, the suboptimal profit resulting from the deterministic model with random forest, and the suboptimal profit resulting from the stochastic model with ME distributions

the MA-based model, but its performance varies significantly with forecast accuracy. For instance, in Experiment 5 and 11, where RF predictions are highly accurate, the deterministic model achieves losses below 0.5%. However, in experiments with larger forecast errors (e.g., Experiments 2 and 13), its loss exceeds 20%. This variability highlights the risk of relying solely on point forecasts in volatile markets. Third, we observe that as risk aversion increases (lower η), the performance gap between the stochastic model and deterministic models often widens, particularly in experiments with higher demand variability. This indicates that the stochastic model better accommodates risk preferences, making it suitable for firms with varying risk tolerances. Finally, the results suggest that when SKU count increases, the stochastic model maintains stable performance, whereas deterministic models occasionally deteriorate (e.g., Experiment 13). This scalability is valuable for retailers managing large assortments.

Table 4.5 thus provides strong evidence that a stochastic formulation based on moment information can effectively mitigate forecast inaccuracy, delivering reliable performance across different problem scales and risk attitudes. For practitioners, this implies that adopting robust optimization can be a more sustainable strategy than continually seeking marginal improvements in forecasting, especially in environments where demand is inherently uncertain.

4.6 Conclusion

In this study, we have examined a challenging decision faced by cross-border e-commerce retailers in terms of managing the inventory for their thousands of items overseas, many of which have no historical sales data. We implement predictive analytics, followed by prescriptive analytics. In the first part of our predictive ana-

Table 4.5 The effectiveness of inventory decisions generated by different models with various numbers of SKUs

Ex	No. of SKUs	Det+ MA(%)	Det+ RF(%)	Sto+ME(%)		
				η=1	η=0.1	η=0.01
1	2	21.56	8.40	0.81	1.08	1.04
2	3	28.72	30.42	13.86	10.93	10.93
3	4	13.45	15.22	0.41	1.64	2.85
4	5	4.51	1.40	0.39	1.46	3.63
5	6	5.30	0.35	0.90	4.44	11.48
6	7	1.05	0.44	0.38	0.04	0.61
7	8	3.42	0.79	0.41	0.14	0.37
8	9	0.80	1.12	0.68	0.00	2.34
9	10	0.68	1.12	0.79	0.33	0.52
10	11	7.33	8.57	0.36	7.15	11.15
11	12	0.04	1.30	0.16	1.26	1.50
12	13	3.36	8.77	0.25	5.08	7.74
13	14	15.19	20.45	0.47	6.71	13.08
14	15	0.67	1.07	1.02	0.37	0.08

lytics, we classify each item into one of two classes, according to its profitability, and predict its classification based on its attributes. We found that the random forest method provides better classification than the logistic regression method does. After the classification, we predicted the SKU demand for items classified as profitable ($\mathcal{A}$-items). Three demand prediction methods were considered: the moving-average method, linear regression, and random forest. For both the classification stage and the demand prediction stage, the random forest method was found to outperform its competitors. However, there is still too much uncertainty in the demand predictions. As such, we focused on predicting the moment information in terms of the distribution mean and variance. The random forest method proved to be the best choice in this case, substantially outperforming its competitors in the prediction of demand variance.

Using these predictions, we proceeded to the prescriptive analytics phase to solve the inventory decisions for $\mathcal{A}$-items to be held in overseas warehouses. We developed a deterministic (naïve) model, as well as a stochastic model. The naïve model simply views the predicted demand as the deterministic demand, and is solved as a standard linear program. In contrast, the stochastic model considers demand as a random variable and applies the principle of ME to generate a demand distribution before solving the newsvendor problem.

In our simulation study, we find that pre-classifying items can result in 20% cost savings for cross-border e-commerce retailers. For these $\mathcal{A}$-items, we applied the results of the prediction to our models to solve the inventory decisions and to calculate the corresponding profit in each case. From an experiment on 14 data sets, we find that the effectiveness of the naïve model depends heavily on the prediction accuracy. However, in most cases, the stochastic model achieves a profit level very close to the optimal profit.

Our research solves a multi-item overseas inventory risk management problem of wide concern and interest to both practitioners and researchers. We make four contributions to the literature. First, we study operations analytics for a real-life scenario in which the demand data are small discrete values that fluctuate significantly. As such, subtle changes have a tremendous impact on corporate decision-making. Second, we demonstrate that classification predictive analytics alone can provide considerable cost savings for an enterprise. Third, we develop a stochastic model under a robust distribution that can overcome the predictive loss, and that can provide near-optimal inventory decisions.

References

Andersson, J., Jornsten, K., Nonas, S. L., Sandal, L., & Uboe, J. (2013). A maximum entropy approach to the newsvendor problem with partial information. *European Journal of Operational Research, 228*(1), 190–200.

Ban, G. Y., & Rudin, C. (2018). The big data newsvendor: Practical insights from machine learning. *Operations Research.*

Ben-Tal, A., Golany, B., Nemirovski, A., & Vial, J. P. (2005). Retailer-supplier flexible commitments contracts: A robust optimization approach. *Manufacturing & Service Operations Management, 7*(3), 248–271.

Bertsimas, D., Brown, D. B., & Caramanis, C. (2011). Theory and applications of robust optimization. *SIAM Review, 53*(3), 464–501.

Bertsimas, D., Kallus, N., & Hussain, A. (2016). Inventory management in the era of big data. *Production and Operations Management, 25*(12), 2006–2009.

Bertsimas, D., & Thiele, A. (2006). A robust optimization approach to inventory theory. *Operations Research, 54*(1), 150–168.

Choudhary, D., & Shankar, R. (2015). The value of VMI beyond information sharing under time-varying stochastic demand. *International Journal of Production Research, 53*(5), 1472–1486.

Disney, S. M., & Towill, D. R. (2003). On the bullwhip and inventory variance produced by an ordering policy. *Omega, 31*(3), 157–167.

Ferreira, K. J., Lee, B. H. A., & Simchi-Levi, D. (2015). Analytics for an online retailer: Demand forecasting and price optimization. *Manufacturing & Service Operations Management, 18*(1), 69–88.

Fleischhacker, A. J., & Fok, P. W. (2015). On the relationship between entropy, demand uncertainty, and expected loss. *European Journal of Operational Research, 245*(2), 623–628.

Fleischhacker, A. J., & Fok, P. W. (2015). An entropy-based methodology for valuation of demand uncertainty reduction. *Decision Sciences, 46*(6), 1165–1198.

Gessner, G. H., & Snodgrass, C. R. (2015). Designing e-commerce cross-border distribution networks for small and medium-size enterprises incorporating Canadian and US trade incentive programs. *Research in Transportation Business & Management, 16*, 84–94.

Giuffrida, M., Mangiaracina, R., Perego, A., & Tumino, A. (2017). Cross-border B2C e-commerce to Greater China and the role of logistics: a literature review. *International Journal of Physical Distribution & Logistics Management, 47*(9), 772–795.

Gomez-Herrera, E., Martens, B., & Turlea, G. (2014). The drivers and impediments for cross-border e-commerce in the EU. *Information Economics and Policy, 28*, 83–96.

Hartely, V. R. (1976). *Operations research-A managerial emphasis* (pp. 7–315). GoodYear.

Hou, S., Wang, X., Xiao, J., Zhang, Y., & Cheng, F. (2019). *Cluster Analysis and Overseas Warehouse Assignment of Chinese Smartphones under "The Belt and Road" Initiative* (pp. 203–227). The New Silk Road Leads through the Arab Peninsula: Mast ering Global Business and Inovation. Emerald Publishing Limited.

James, G., Witten, D., Hastie, T., & Tibshirani, R. (2013). *An introduction to statistical learning* (Vol. 112, p. 18). Springer.

Jönsson, H., & Silver, R. (1987). Stock allocation among a central warehouse and identical regional warehouses in a particular push inventory control system. *International Journal of Production Research,25*(2), 191–205.

Levi, R., Perakis, G., & Uichanco, J. (2015). The data-driven newsvendor problem: New bounds and insights. *Operations Research, 63*(6), 1294–1306.

Liu, X., Chen, D., & Cai, J. (2015). The operation of the cross-border e-commerce logistics in China. *International Journal of Intelligent Information Systems, 4*(2), 15–18.

Maglaras, C., & Eren, S. (2015). A maximum entropy joint demand estimation and capacity control policy. *Production and Operations Management, 24*(3), 438–450.

Natarajan, K., Sim, M., & Uichanco, J. (2017). Asymmetry and ambiguity in newsvendor models. *Management Science, 64*(7), 3146–3167.

Pakkala, T. P. M., & Achary, K. K. (1992). A deterministic inventory model for deteriorating items with two warehouses and finite replenishment rate. *European Journal of Operational Research, 57*(1), 71–76.

Rabah, M. Y., & Mahmassani, H. S. (2002). Impact of electronic commerce on logistics operations: A focus on vendor managed inventory (VMI) strategies (No. SWUTC/02/167227-1). *University of Texas at Austin. Center for Transportation Research.*

Rockafellar, R. S., & Uryasev, S. (2000). Optimization of conditional value-at-risk. *Journal of Risk, 2*, 21–42.

Saghafian, S., & Tomlin, B. (2016). The newsvendor under demand ambiguity: Combining data with moment and tail information. *Operations Research, 64*(1), 167–185.

Sarma, K. V. S. (1987). A deterministic order level inventory model for deteriorating items with two storage facilities. *European Journal of Operational Research, 29*(1), 70–73.

Shuyan, C., & Lisi, X. (2013). *Research on the overseas warehouse construction of cross-border e-commerce*. Association for Information Systems AIS Electronic Library (AISeL) WHICEB 2013 Proceedings.

Valarezo, A., Perez-Amaral, T., Garin-Munoz, T., Garcia, I. H., & Lopez, R. (2018). Drivers and barriers to cross-border e-commerce: Evidence from Spanish individual behavior. *Telecommunications Policy, 42*(6), 464–473.

van Heel, B., Lukic, V., & Leeuwis, E. (2014). *Cross-border e-commerce makes the world flatter*. The Boston Consulting Group.

Wu, G. (2016, May). Build Cross-border E-commerce "Overseas warehouse" Platform Effectively. In *In 2016 2nd international conference on social science and technology education (ICSSTE 2016)*. Atlantis Press.

Xue, W., Li, D., & Pei, Y. (2016). The development and current of cross-border e-commerce. *International Journal of Enterprise Information Systems, 14*(2), 56–76.

Zhan, X., Zhang, Q., & Xie, W. (2018). Dynamic performance and stability research of VMI-APIOBPCS in apparel industry based on control theory. In *Wuhan international conference on e-Business 2016 proceedings* (Vol. 53).

Zhou, Y. W. (2003). A multi-warehouse inventory model for items with time-varying demand and shortages. *Computers & Operations Research, 30*(14), 2115–2134.

Appendix

A.1 Appendix for Chap. 2

A.1.1 Proof of Lemma 2.1

The RAO-WCVaR problem is equivalent to a robust assortment optimization problem over uncertainty sets (Proposition 3 in Li and Ke (2019)):

$$\max_{\mathbf{x}\in\{0,1\}^n} \min_{\bar{\mathbf{v}}\in\mathcal{V}} \frac{\mathbf{r}_{\mathbf{x}}^T \bar{\mathbf{v}}}{1+\mathbf{x}^T\bar{\mathbf{v}}} \tag{A.1}$$

where $\mathcal{V} = \left\{\bar{\mathbf{v}} : \bar{\mathbf{v}} = \mu + \sqrt{\frac{1-\epsilon}{\epsilon}}\Sigma^{\frac{1}{2}}\mathbf{z},\ 1+\mathbf{x}^T\bar{\mathbf{v}} \geq 0,\ ||\mathbf{z}|| \leq 1, \mathbf{z} \in \mathbb{R}^n\right\}$. Let $S^*(\mathcal{V})$ and $Z^*(\mathcal{V})$ denote the optimal assortment and the optimal value of problem (A.1) under the uncertainty set $\mathcal{V}$, respectively. The uncertainty set $\mathcal{V}$ is convex and compact. To ensure its positivity, that is, each $\bar{v}_i > 0$, there should be a requirement for ϵ:

$$\min_{i,\mathbf{z}} \left\{\bar{v}_i : \bar{v}_i = \mu_i + \sqrt{\frac{1-\epsilon}{\epsilon}} \sum_{j=1}^{n} \sigma_{ij} z_j,\ ||\mathbf{z}|| \leq 1, i = 1, ..., n\right\} > 0.$$

It requires $\min_i \mu_i - \sqrt{\frac{1-\epsilon}{\epsilon}\sum_{j=1}^n \sigma_{ij}^2} > 0$, which lead to $\epsilon > \max_i \frac{\sum_{j=1}^n \sigma_{ij}^2}{\mu_i^2+\sum_{j=1}^n \sigma_{ij}^2}$, where σ_{ij} is the element in the ith row and jth column of $\Sigma^{\frac{1}{2}}$ and $\sum_{j=1}^n \sigma_{ij}^2 = \Sigma_{ii}$.

For any $\mathcal{V} \subset \mathbb{R}_{++}^n$, i.e., $\epsilon > \underline{\epsilon} = \max_i \frac{\Sigma_{ii}}{\mu_i^2+\Sigma_{ii}}$, we first prove that $\{i : r_i > Z^*(\mathcal{V})\} \subseteq S^*(\mathcal{V})$. Suppose on the contrary that there exists a product i such that $r_i > Z^*(\mathcal{V})$ and $i \notin S^*(\mathcal{V})$. Consider an arbitrary model parameter vector $\mathbf{v} \in \mathcal{V}$, by definition of $S^*(\mathcal{V})$, we have $\frac{\sum_{i\in S^*(\mathcal{V})} r_i v_i}{1+\sum_{i\in S^*(\mathcal{V})} v_i} \geq Z^*(\mathcal{V})$. Suppose that $r_i > \frac{\sum_{i\in S^*(\mathcal{V})} r_i v_i}{1+\sum_{i\in S^*(\mathcal{V})} v_i}$, in which case, it follows from Lemma 3.1 in Rusmevichientong and Topaloglu (2012) that $\frac{\sum_{i\in S^*(\mathcal{V})\cup\{i\}} r_i v_i}{1+\sum_{i\in S^*(\mathcal{V})\cup\{i\}} v_i} > \frac{\sum_{i\in S^*(\mathcal{V})} r_i v_i}{1+\sum_{i\in S^*(\mathcal{V})} v_i} \geq Z^*(\mathcal{V})$. On the other

Y. Yu et al., *Platform Supply Chains 1*, Platform Supply Chains in the AI Era,
https://doi.org/10.1007/978-981-95-9965-3

Table A.1 Critical values of different significance levels for KPSS test

Significance level	0.100	0.050	0.025	0.010
Critical value	0.347	0.463	0.574	0.739

hand, if $r_i \leq \frac{\sum_{i \in S^*(\mathcal{V})} r_i v_i}{1+\sum_{i \in S^*(\mathcal{V})} v_i}$, we have $\frac{\sum_{i \in S^*(\mathcal{V}) \cup \{i\}} r_i v_i}{1+\sum_{i \in S^*(\mathcal{V}) \cup \{i\}} v_i} \geq r_i > Z^*(\mathcal{V})$ following Lemma 3.1 in Rusmevichientong and Topaloglu (2012). Thus, in both cases, we have $\frac{\sum_{i \in S^*(\mathcal{V}) \cup \{i\}} r_i v_i}{1+\sum_{i \in S^*(\mathcal{V}) \cup \{i\}} v_i} > Z^*(\mathcal{V})$. Because $\mathbf{v} \in \mathcal{V}$ is arbitrary and $\mathcal{V}$ is compact, it follows that $\min_{\mathbf{v} \in \mathcal{V}} \frac{\sum_{i \in S^*(\mathcal{V}) \cup \{i\}} r_i v_i}{1+\sum_{i \in S^*(\mathcal{V}) \cup \{i\}} v_i} > Z^*(\mathcal{V})$. This contradicts the optimality of $S^*(\mathcal{V})$, so we have $i \in S^*(\mathcal{V})$.

Then, we prove that $S^*(\mathcal{V}) \subseteq \{i : r_i > Z^*(\mathcal{V})\}$. Suppose on the contrary that there exists a product t such that $r_t \leq Z^*(\mathcal{V})$ and $t \in S^*(\mathcal{V})$. Consider an arbitrary model parameter vector $\mathbf{v} \in \mathcal{V}$, by definition of $S^*(\mathcal{V})$, we have $r_t \leq Z^*(\mathcal{V}) \leq \frac{\sum_{i \in S^*(\mathcal{V})} r_i v_i}{1+\sum_{i \in S^*(\mathcal{V})} v_i}$. Following Lemma 3.1 in Rusmevichientong and Topaloglu (2012), we have $\frac{\sum_{i \in S^*(\mathcal{V})} r_i v_i}{1+\sum_{i \in S^*(\mathcal{V})} v_i} < \frac{\sum_{i \in S^*(\mathcal{V}) \setminus \{t\}} r_i v_i}{1+\sum_{i \in S^*(\mathcal{V}) \setminus \{t\}} v_i}$. Because $\mathbf{v} \in \mathcal{V}$ is arbitrary, it follows that $\min_{\mathbf{v} \in \mathcal{V}} \frac{\sum_{i \in S^*(\mathcal{V}) \setminus \{t\}} r_i v_i}{1+\sum_{i \in S^*(\mathcal{V}) \setminus \{t\}} v_i} \geq \min_{\mathbf{v} \in \mathcal{V}} \frac{\sum_{i \in S^*(\mathcal{V})} r_i v_i}{1+\sum_{i \in S^*(\mathcal{V})} v_i} = Z^*(\mathcal{V})$, which implies that $S^*(\mathcal{V}) \setminus \{t\}$ is also an optimal robust assortment. However, this contradicts the hypothesis that $S^*(\mathcal{V})$ is the optimal robust assortment with the smallest cardinality. Thus, it must be the case that $t \notin S^*(\mathcal{V})$.

Hence, if $\epsilon > \underline{\epsilon} = \max_i \frac{\Sigma_{ii}}{\mu_i^2+\Sigma_{ii}}$, $S^*(\mathcal{V}) = \{i : r_i > Z^*(\mathcal{V})\}$. This indicates that the optimal assortment of the RAO-WCVaR problem is a revenue-ordered assortment of the form $\{1, 2, ..., i^*(\mathcal{V})\}$, where $i^*(\mathcal{V})$ is the last product whose revenue still exceeds $Z^*(\mathcal{V})$. **QED.**

A.2 Appendix for Chap. 3

A.2.1 KPSS Test and Unit-Root Test

Table A.2 presents the results of additional stationarity tests. For KPSS test, the statistic-value of the original data is 1.182, which is larger than 0.739, the critical value with a significance level of 0.010, shown in Table A.1. Hence, we conclude that the original demand series is nonstationary. Similarly, we can derive the conclusion that the demand series transformed with DET, DIT and PCT all become stationary (the null hypothesis that there is a unit root can be rejected at a significance level of 0.010). The p-values of the Unit-Root test in the last column of Table A.2 show the same results.

Table A.2 Results of KPSS test and Unit-Root test

Transformation method	Statistic-value of KPSS test	p-value of Unit-Root test
Original data	1.182	0.308
DET	0.333	<0.01
DIT	0.213	<0.01
PCT	0.092	<0.01

Table A.3 Descriptive statistics of weekly demand series in different years

Year	Mean (kg)	Max (kg)	Min (kg)	Standard deviation	CV
2017	10421	38437	1070	8178	0.785
2018	12648	48526	206	9744	0.770
2019	13216	52072	165	10550	0.798

A.2.2 Examination of Seasonal Effect

In order to figure out whether the original demand series and transformed demand series have a seasonal effect or weekly pattern, we collected sales data in the years 2018 and 2019 for FPs corresponding to the same SFP we studied before (the best-selling SFP in 2017 is also the best-selling SFP in 2018 and 2019). Using that data, we calculate the SFP's weekly demands. Table A.3 provides the descriptive statistics for the SFP's weekly demand series in 2017, 2018 and 2019. The Mean column reveals that the company's sales scale is expanding year by year, and the CV column shows that the demand fluctuations in 2018 and 2019 remain the same as in 2017.

To test seasonality in the demand series, we follow Franses (1991), Franses (1992) and Moineddin et al. (2003) in making use of seasonal dummy variables. In each year, we have demands data for 46 consecutive weeks. Treating these weeks as 45 dummy variables, we construct a regression model as follows:

$$D_t = \alpha + \sum_{i=1}^{n} \beta_i Week_i,$$

where $Week_i$ is a dummy variable and equals 1 when $t = i$ and 0 otherwise. β_i is the correlation coefficient between D_t and $Week_i$ and α is the intercept term. In addition to the original demand series, we also perform this regression model on the transformed demand series $\varepsilon_t^i (i \in \{DET, DIT, PCT\})$ as dependent variable. The results of correlation coefficients and corresponding significance levels are summarized in Table A.4. Asterisks in Table A.4 denote significance at $*p < 0.05, **p < 0.01, and *** p < 0.001$.

All the coefficients of the first 28 periodic factors $Week_i (i = 1, ..., 28)$ for the original demands and transformed demands fail the significance test, so we omit

Table A.4 Correlation coefficients between demands and periodic factor

	D_t	ε_t^{DET}	ε_t^{DIT}	ε_t^{PCT}
⋮	⋮	⋮	⋮	⋮
$Week_{29}$	10.844	16.043*	14.518*	13.011
$Week_{30}$	0.999	5.980	4.248	3.029
$Week_{31}$	0.011	4.768	2.847	1.907
$Week_{32}$	7.840	12.366	10.279	9.605
$Week_{33}$	10.259	14.546*	12.317	11.894
$Week_{34}$	−0.231	3.810	1.467	1.276
$Week_{35}$	−2.587	1.200	−1.228	−1.205
$Week_{36}$	12.283	15.807*	13.329*	13.541
$Week_{37}$	1.016	4.269	1.776	2.151
$Week_{38}$	12.240	15.214*	12.746	13.256
$Week_{39}$	1.510	4.195	1.793	2.407
$Week_{40}$	−2.618	−0.231	−2.521	−1.838
$Week_{41}$	−1.179	0.899	−1.232	−0.515
$Week_{42}$	−0.117	1.643	−0.278	0.433
$Week_{43}$	3.554	4.985	3.329	3.992
$Week_{44}$	14.295	15.386*	14.051*	14.622*
$Week_{45}$	−0.734	0.005	−0.949	−0.5177
$Week_{46}$	12.810	13.186	12.676	12.9178

their results in Table A.4. As the table shows, none of the periodic factors show a significant effect on original demands and only a few of the periodic factors (such as $Week_{28}$, $Week_{35}$ and $Week_{43}$) are significantly correlated with the transformed demands. Owing to this fact, we conclude that there is no substantial seasonality in this SFP's demand series. Therefore, the consideration of seasonality does not help to improve the production.

A.2.3 Proof of Lemma 3.1, Proposition 3.1 and Proposition 3.2

Proof. We prove the results related to DET, DIT and PCT models in Lemma 3.1, Proposition 3.1 and Proposition 3.2 sequentially.

A.2.3.1 DET Model

When the nonstationarity in demand series is handled by DET, the demand series can be characterized as $D_t = \gamma_t + \tau^{DET} + \varepsilon_t^{DET}$. By applying $\Pi_t(Y_t, D_t|d_{t-1}) = (p+b-w)Y_t - (p+b+h)(Y_t - D_t)^+ - bD_t$ to (7), the optimization problem in period T is:

$$V_T(d_{T-1}) = \max_{z, Y_T} \quad z - \frac{E[z - (p+b-w)Y_T + (p+b+h)(Y_T - D_T)^+ + bD_T]^+}{\eta},$$

By defining $\overline{z} = z - (p+b-w)Y_T$, the problem can be reformulated as:

$$\begin{aligned} &\max_{\overline{z}, Y_T} \quad \overline{z} + (p+b-w)Y_T - \frac{E[\overline{z} + (p+b+h)(Y_T - D_T)^+ + bD_T]^+}{\eta} \\ &= \max_{\overline{z}, Y_T} \quad \overline{z} + (p+b-w)Y_T \\ &\quad - \frac{\int_0^{Y_T} [\overline{z} + (p+b+h)(Y_T - D_T) + bD_T]^+ dG(D_t) + \int_{Y_T}^{\infty} [\overline{z} + bD_T]^+ dG(D_t)}{\eta}, \end{aligned}$$

where $G(\cdot)$ is the CDF of D_t. Define X_+ and X_- as the unique solution for the following two equations:

$$\overline{z} + (p+b+h)(Y_T - X_+) + bX_+ = 0, \overline{z} + bX_- = 0,$$

then the optimization problem can be further formulated as:

$$\begin{aligned} &\max_{\overline{z}, Y_T} \quad \overline{z} + (p+b-w)Y_T \\ &\quad - \frac{\int_0^{X_+} [\overline{z} + (p+b+h)(Y_T - D_T) + bD_T] dG(D_t) + \int_{X_-}^{\infty} [\overline{z} + bD_T] dG(D_t)}{\eta}, \end{aligned}$$

Since this objective function is joint concave and thus we can use the first-order condition (FOC) to derive the optimal solutions. The base-stock level Y_t^* is the unique solution for the following two equations:

$$G\left(\frac{\overline{z}^* + (p+b-w)Y_T^*}{p+h}\right) = \frac{p+b-w}{p+b+h}\eta, G\left(-\frac{\overline{z}^*}{b}\right) = 1 - \frac{h+w}{p+b+h}\eta,$$

Because $D_t = \gamma_t + \tau^{DET} + \varepsilon_t^{DET}$, following Table 4, the optimal inventory decision is $Y_T^* = \gamma_T + \tau^{DET} + \frac{(p+h)v^+ + bv^-}{p+b+h}$, and the optimal value in period T is:

$$
\begin{aligned}
V_T(d_{T-1}) &= \left(p - w - \frac{b}{\eta}\right)(\gamma_T + \tau^{DET}) + \frac{p+b-w}{p+b+h}(p+h)v^+ - \frac{h+w}{p+b+h}bv^- \\
&\quad - \frac{(p+h)I(v^+) + bI(v^-) - bv^- + bE(\varepsilon_t^{DET})}{\eta} \\
&= A_T^{DET}
\end{aligned}
$$

Since V_T is independent of d_{T-1}, we have $Y_t^* = \gamma_t + \tau^{DET} + \frac{(p+h)v^+ + bv^-}{p+b+h}$ for any period t, and the optimal value in period t is:

$$
\begin{aligned}
V_t &= \left(p - w - \frac{b}{\eta}\right)\sum_{k=t}^{T}\beta^{k-t}\gamma_k + \frac{1-\beta^{T-t+1}}{1-\beta}\left(\left(p - w - \frac{b}{\eta}\right)\tau^{DET} + S(p+h)v^+\right. \\
&\quad \left. - \frac{h+w}{p+b+h}bv^- - \frac{(p+h)I(v^+) + bI(v^-) - bv^- + bE(\varepsilon_t^{DET})}{\eta}\right) \\
&= A_t^{DET}
\end{aligned}
$$

We therefore complete the proof of item (i) in Lemma 3.1 and item (i) in Proposition 3.1.

A.2.3.2 DIT Model

When the nonstationarity in the demand series is handled by DIT, the demand series can be characterized as $D_t = D_{t-1} + \tau^{DIT} + \varepsilon_t^{DIT}$. In period T, the derivation process of optimal inventory policy is the same as that under demand pattern in the DET and $Y_T^* = d_{T-1} + \tau^{DIT} + \frac{(p+h)v^+ + bv^-}{p+b+h}$, so the optimal value in period T is:

$$
\begin{aligned}
V_T(d_{T-1}) &= \left(p - w - \frac{b}{\eta}\right)\tau^{DIT} + \frac{p+b-w}{p+b+h}(p+h)v^+ - \frac{h+w}{p+b+h}bv^- \\
&\quad - \frac{(p+h)I(v^+) + bI(v^-) - bv^- + bE(\varepsilon_t^{DIT})}{\eta} + \left(p - w - \frac{b}{\eta}\right)d_{T-1} \\
&= A_T^{DIT} + B_T^{DIT}d_{T-1}
\end{aligned}
$$

where $B_T^{DIT} = p - w - \frac{b}{\eta}$. By defining $\bar{z} = z - (p+b-w)Y_{T-1} - \beta A_T^{DIT}$, then the optimization problem in period $T-1$ is:

$$
\begin{aligned}
&V_{T-1}(d_{T-2}) \\
&= \max_{Y_{T-1}\geq 0} \; R_{T-1|d_{T-2}}\left[\Pi_{T-1}(Y_{T-1}, D_{T-1}|d_{T-2}) + \beta V_T(D_{T-1}|d_{T-2})\right] \\
&= \max_{z, Y_{T-1}} \; z - \frac{1}{\eta}\left(E[z - (p+b-w)Y_{T-1} + (p+b+h)(Y_{T-1} - D_{T-1})^+\right.
\end{aligned}
$$

$$
\begin{aligned}
&+ bD_{T-1} - \beta A_T^{DIT} - \beta B_T^{DIT} D_{T-1}]^+ \Big) \\
&= \beta A_T^{DIT} + \max_{\overline{z}, Y_{T-1}} \overline{z} + (p+b-w)Y_{T-1} \\
&\quad - \frac{E[\overline{z} + (p+b+h)(Y_{T-1} - D_{T-1})^+ + (b - \beta B_T^{DIT})D_{T-1}]^+}{\eta} \\
&= \beta A_T^{DIT} + \max_{\overline{z}, Y_{T-1}} \overline{z} + (p+b-w)Y_{T-1} \\
&\quad - \frac{1}{\eta}\Big(\int_0^{Y_{T-1}} [\overline{z} + (p+b+h)(Y_{T-1} - D_{T-1}) + (b - \beta B_T^{DIT})D_{T-1}]^+ dG(D_t) \\
&\quad + \int_{Y_{T-1}}^{\infty} [\overline{z} + (b - \beta B_T^{DIT})D_{T-1}]^+ dG(D_t)\Big)
\end{aligned}
$$

where $G(\cdot)$ is the CDF of D_t. Define X_+ and X_- as the unique solution for the following two equations:

$$
\overline{z} + (p+b+h)(Y_{T-1} - X_+) + (b - \beta B_T^{DIT})X_+ = 0, \overline{z} + (b - \beta B_T^{DIT})X_- = 0,
$$

(i) If $B_T^{DIT} \leq -\frac{p+h}{\beta}$, then the function $\overline{z} + (p+b+h)(Y_{T-1} - X) + (b - \beta B_T^{DIT})X$ is an increasing function of X and $\overline{z} + (b - \beta B_T^{DIT})X$ is an increasing function of X. We further present the following discussion. (a) If $X_+ \leq Y_{T-1}$, which is equivalent to $\overline{z} + (b - \beta B_T^{DIT})Y_{T-1} \geq 0$, then $X_- \leq Y_{T-1}$. Note that βA_T^{DIT} is a constant, so the objective function of the optimization problem in period $T-1$ can be simplified to:

$$
\begin{aligned}
&\overline{z} + (p+b-w)Y_{T-1} - \\
&\frac{1}{\eta}\Big(\int_{X_+}^{Y_{T-1}} [\overline{z} + (p+b+h)(Y_{T-1} - D_{T-1}) + (b - \beta B_T^{DIT})D_{T-1}] dG(D_t) \\
&\quad + \int_{Y_{T-1}}^{\infty} [\overline{z} + (b - \beta B_T^{DIT})D_{T-1}] dG(D_t)\Big)
\end{aligned}
$$

Clearly, the above objective function is concave in $(\overline{z}, Y_{T-1})$. By applying the FOC, we obtain the optimizers $(\overline{z}^*, Y_{T-1}^*)$ for case (a):

$$
G\left(\frac{\overline{z}^* + (p+b+h)Y_{T-1}^*}{p+h+\beta B_T^{DIT}}\right) = 1 - \eta, G(Y_{T-1}^*) = 1 - \frac{h+w}{p+b+h}\eta
$$

(b) If $X_+ \geq Y_{T-1}$, which is equivalent to $\overline{z} + (b - \beta B_T^{DIT})Y_{T-1} \leq 0$, then $X_- \geq Y_{T-1}$, and the objective function of the optimization problem in period $T-1$ can be simplified to:

$$J(\overline{z}, Y_{T-1}) = \overline{z} + (p + b - w)Y_{T-1} - \frac{1}{\eta}\left(\int_{X_-}^{\infty} [\overline{z} + (b - \beta B_T^{DIT})D_{T-1}]dG(D_t)\right)$$

we can easily find that $J(\overline{z}, Y_{T-1})$ is increasing with Y_{T-1}, which implies that the optimizer of Y_{T-1} for case (b) is X_-. Thus, case (b) is dominated by case (a). Based on the above discussion, if $B_T^{DIT} \le -\frac{p+h}{\beta}$, the optimal base-stock level is $Y_{T-1}^* = d_{T-2} + \tau^{DIT} + v^-$ and the optimal value in period $T-1$ is:

$$\begin{aligned}
&V_{T-1}(d_{T-2}) \\
&= \beta A_T^{DIT} + \left(p - w + \beta B_T^{DIT} - \frac{b - \beta B_T^{DIT}}{\eta}\right)\tau^{DIT} \\
&\quad + (p + h + \beta B_T^{DIT})\overline{v} - (h + w)v^- - \frac{(p + b + h)(\overline{v} - v^-) + (b - \beta B_T^{DIT})\left(I(\overline{v}) - \overline{v} + E(\varepsilon_t^{DIT})\right)}{\eta} \\
&\quad + \left(p - w + \beta B_T^{DIT} - \frac{b - \beta B_T^{DIT}}{\eta}\right)d_{T-2} \\
&= A_{T-1}^{DIT} + B_{T-1}^{DIT} d_{T-2}
\end{aligned}$$

where $B_{T-1}^{DIT} = p - w + \beta B_T^{DIT} - \frac{b - \beta B_T^{DIT}}{\eta}$.

(ii) If $-\frac{p+h}{\beta} \le B_T^{DIT} \le \frac{b}{\beta}$, then the function $\overline{z} + (p + b + h)(Y_{T-1} - X) + (b - \beta B_T^{DIT})X$ is a decreasing function of X and $\overline{z} + (b - \beta B_T^{DIT})X$ is an increasing function of X. We further present the following discussion. (a) If $X_+ \le Y_{T-1}$, which is equivalent to $\overline{z} + (b - \beta B_T^{DIT})Y_{T-1} \ge 0$, then $X_- \ge Y_{T-1}$, and the objective function of the optimization problem in period $T-1$ can be simplified to:

$$\begin{aligned}
&\overline{z} + (p + b - w)Y_{T-1} \\
&\quad - \frac{1}{\eta}\left(\int_0^{X_+} [\overline{z} + (p + b + h)(Y_{T-1} - D_{T-1}) + (b - \beta B_T^{DIT})D_{T-1}]dG(D_t)\right. \\
&\quad \left. + \int_{X_-}^{\infty} [\overline{z} + (b - \beta B_T^{DIT})D_{T-1}]dG(D_t)\right)
\end{aligned}$$

Clearly, the above objective function is concave in $(\overline{z}, Y_{T-1})$. By applying the FOC, we obtain the optimizers $(\overline{z}^*, Y_{T-1}^*)$ for case (a):

$$G\left(\frac{\overline{z}^* + (p + b + h)Y_{T-1}^*}{p + h + \beta B_T^{DIT}}\right) = \frac{p + b - w}{p + b + h}\eta,\ G\left(-\frac{\overline{z}^*}{b - \beta B_T^{DIT}}\right) = 1 - \frac{h + w}{p + b + h}\eta$$

(b) If $X_+ \ge Y_{T-1}$, which is equivalent to $\overline{z} + (b - \beta B_T^{DIT})Y_{T-1} \le 0$, then $X_- \le Y_{T-1}$, and the objective function of the optimization problem in period $T-1$ can be simplified to:

$$\begin{aligned}&\overline{z}+(p+b-w)Y_{T-1}\\&\quad-\frac{1}{\eta}\bigg(\int_0^{Y_{T-1}}[\overline{z}+(p+b+h)(Y_{T-1}-D_{T-1})+(b-\beta B_T^{DIT})D_{T-1}]dG(D_t)\\&\quad+\int_{Y_{T-1}}^{\infty}[\overline{z}+(b-\beta B_T^{DIT})D_{T-1}]dG(D_t)\bigg)\end{aligned}$$

We can easily find that the optimizer for case (b) is $\eta = 1$. Thus, case (b) is dominated by case (a). Based on the above discussion, if $-\frac{p+h}{\beta} \leq B_T^{DIT} \leq \frac{b}{\beta}$, the optimal base-stock level is $Y_{T-1}^* = d_{T-2} + \tau^{DIT} + \frac{(p+h)v^+ + bv^-}{p+b+h}$ and the optimal value in period $T-1$ is:

$$\begin{aligned}&V_{T-1}(d_{T-2})\\&=\beta A_T^{DIT}+\left(p-w+\beta B_T^{DIT}-\frac{b-\beta B_T^{DIT}}{\eta}\right)\tau^{DIT}+\frac{p+b-w}{p+b+h}(p+h+\beta B_T^{DIT})v^+\\&\quad-\frac{h+w}{p+b+h}(b-\beta B_T^{DIT})v^-\\&\quad-\frac{(p+h+\beta B_T^{DIT})I(v^+)+(b-\beta B_T^{DIT})\left(I(v^-)-v^-+E(\varepsilon_t^{DIT})\right)}{\eta}\\&\quad+\left(p-w+\beta B_T^{DIT}-\frac{b-\beta B_T^{DIT}}{\eta}\right)d_{T-2}\\&=A_{T-1}^{DIT}+B_{T-1}^{DIT}d_{T-2}\end{aligned}$$

where $B_{T-1}^{DIT} = p - w + \beta B_T^{DIT} - \frac{b-\beta B_T^{DIT}}{\eta}$.

(iii) If $B_T^{DIT} > \frac{b}{\beta}$, then the function $\overline{z} + (p+b+h)(Y_{T-1} - X) + (b - \beta B_T^{DIT})X$ is a decreasing function of X and $\overline{z} + (b - \beta B_T^{DIT})X$ is a decreasing function of X. We further present the following discussion. (a) If $X_+ \geq Y_{T-1}$, which is equivalent to $\overline{z} + (b - \beta B_T^{DIT})Y_{T-1} \geq 0$, then $X_- \geq Y_{T-1}$, and the objective function of the optimization problem in period $T-1$ can be simplified to:

$$\begin{aligned}&\overline{z}+(p+b-w)Y_{T-1}\\&\quad-\frac{1}{\eta}\bigg(\int_0^{Y_{T-1}}[\overline{z}+(p+b+h)(Y_{T-1}-D_{T-1})+(b-\beta B_T^{DIT})D_{T-1}]dG(D_t)\\&\quad+\int_{Y_{T-1}}^{X_-}[\overline{z}+(b-\beta B_T^{DIT})D_{T-1}]dG(D_t)\bigg)\end{aligned}$$

Clearly, the above objective function is concave in $(\overline{z}, Y_{T-1})$. By applying the FOC, we obtain the optimizers $(\overline{z}^*, Y_{T-1}^*)$ for case (a):

$$G(Y_{T-1}^*) = \frac{p+b-w}{p+b+h}\eta, G\left(-\frac{\overline{z}^*}{b-\beta B_T^{DIT}}\right) = \eta$$

(b) If $X_+ \le Y_{T-1}$, which is equivalent to $\overline{z} + (b - \beta B_T^{DIT})Y_{T-1} \le 0$, then $X_- \le Y_{T-1}$, and the objective function of the optimization problem in period $T-1$ can be simplified to:

$$\begin{aligned} &J(\overline{z}, Y_{T-1}) \\ &= \overline{z} + (p+b-w)Y_{T-1} \\ &\quad - \frac{1}{\eta}\left(\int_0^{X^+} [\overline{z} + (p+b+h)(Y_{T-1} - D_{T-1}) + (b - \beta B_T^{DIT})D_{T-1}]dG(D_t)\right) \end{aligned}$$

Clearly, the above objective function is concave in $(\overline{z}, Y_{T-1})$. Given Y_{T-1}, the optimizer $\overline{z}(Y_{T-1}) = \arg\max_{\overline{z}} J(\overline{z}, Y_{T-1})$ satisfies $G(X^+(\overline{z}(Y_{T-1}), Y_{T-1})) = \eta$. From that, we can easily find that $J(\overline{z}, Y_{T-1})$ is decreasing with Y_{T-1}, which implies that the optimizer of Y_{T-1} for case (b) is X_+. Thus, case (b) is dominated by case (a). Based on the above discussion, if $B_T^{DIT} > \frac{b}{\beta}$, the optimal base-stock level is $Y_{T-1}^* = d_{T-2} + \tau^{DIT} + v^+$ and the optimal value in period $T-1$ is:

$$\begin{aligned} V_{T-1}(d_{T-2}) &= \beta A_T^{DIT} + \left(p - w + \beta B_T^{DIT}\right)\tau^{DIT} + (p+b-w)v^+ + (\beta B_T^{DIT} - b)v \\ &\quad - \frac{(p+b+h)I(v^+) + (\beta B_T^{DIT} - b)I(v)}{\eta} + \left(p - w + \beta B_T^{DIT}\right)d_{T-2} \\ &= A_{T-1}^{DIT} + B_{T-1}^{DIT} d_{T-2} \end{aligned}$$

where $B_{T-1}^{DIT} = p - w + \beta B_T^{DIT}$.

Recursively, by defining $A_{T+1}^{DIT} = B_{T+1}^{DIT} = 0$, we can infer that for demand pattern in the DIT, the optimal value function can be simplified to $V_t(d_{t-1}) = A_t^{DIT} + B_t^{DIT} \cdot d_{t-1}$, and for period T, the optimal stock level is $Y_T^* = d_{T-1} + \tau^{DIT} + \frac{(p+h)v^+ + bv^-}{p+b+h}$, while for period $t < T$,

(i) if $B_{t+1}^{DIT} \le -\frac{p+h}{\beta}$, then $Y_t^* = d_{t-1} + \tau^{DIT} + v^-$ and $B_t^{DIT} = p - w + \beta B_{t+1}^{DIT} - \frac{b - \beta B_{t+1}^{DIT}}{\eta}$;

(ii) if $-\frac{p+h}{\beta} \le B_{t+1}^{DIT} \le \frac{b}{\beta}$, then $Y_t^* = d_{t-1} + \tau^{DIT} + \frac{(p+h)v^+ + bv^-}{p+b+h}$ and $B_t^{DIT} = p - w + \beta B_{t+1}^{DIT} - \frac{b - \beta B_{t+1}^{DIT}}{\eta}$;

(iii) if $B_{t+1}^{DIT} \ge \frac{b}{\beta}$, then $Y_t^* = d_{t-1} + \tau^{DIT} + v^+$ and $B_t^{DIT} = p - w + \beta B_{t+1}^{DIT}$.

We therefore complete the proof of item (ii) in Lemma 3.1 and item (ii) in Proposition 3.1.

A.2.3.3 PCT Model

When the nonstationarity in demand series is handled by PCT, the demand series can be characterized as $D_t = D_{t-1}e^{\tau^{PCT}}e^{\varepsilon_t^{PCT}}$. In period T, the derivation process of the optimal inventory policy is the same as that for demand pattern in the DET and $Y_T^* = e^{\tau^{PCT}} \frac{(p+h)v^+ + bv^-}{p+b+h} d_{T-1}$, so the optimal value in period T is:

$$
\begin{aligned}
&V_T(d_{T-1})\\
&= e^{\tau^{PCT}}\left(Sv^{+} - (1-S)bv^{-} - \frac{(p+h)I(v^{+}) + bI(v^{-}) - bv^{-} + bE(e^{\varepsilon_t^{PCT}})}{\eta}\right)d_{T-1}\\
&= B_T^{PCT} d_{T-1}
\end{aligned}
$$

where

$$
\begin{aligned}
&B_T^{PCT}\\
&= e^{\tau^{PCT}}\left(S(p+h)v^{+} - (1-S)bv^{-} - \frac{(p+h)I(v^{+}) + bI(v^{-}) - bv^{-} + bE(e^{\varepsilon_t^{PCT}})}{\eta}\right)
\end{aligned}
$$

Set $y_t = \frac{Y_t}{e^{\tau^{PCT}} d_{t-1}}$, $\xi_t = \frac{D_t}{e^{\tau^{PCT}} d_{t-1}}$ and $\overline{z} = \frac{z}{e^{\tau^{PCT}} d_{t-1}} - (p+b-w)y_{T-1}$. Then, the optimization problem in period $T-1$ is:

$$
\begin{aligned}
&V_{T-1}(d_{T-2})\\
&= \max_{Y_{T-1}\geq 0} \quad R_{T-1|d_{T-2}}\left[\Pi_{T-1}(Y_{T-1}, D_{T-1}|d_{T-2}) + \beta V_T(D_{T-1}|d_{T-2})\right]\\
&= \max_{z, Y_{T-1}} \quad \Bigg\{z -\\
&\frac{E[z - (p+b-w)Y_{T-1} + (p+b+h)(Y_{T-1} - D_{T-1})^{+} + bD_{T-1} - \beta B_T^{PCT} D_{T-1}]^{+}}{\eta}\Bigg\}\\
&= e^{\tau^{PCT}} d_{T-2} \max_{\overline{z}, y_{T-1}} \quad \overline{z} + (p+b-w)y_{T-1}\\
&\quad - \frac{E[\overline{z} + (p+b+h)(y_{T-1} - \xi_{T-1})^{+} + (b - \beta B_T^{PCT})\xi_{T-1}]^{+}}{\eta}\\
&= e^{\tau^{PCT}} d_{T-2} \max_{\overline{z}, y_{T-1}} \quad \Bigg\{\overline{z} + (p+b-w)y_{T-1}\\
&\quad - \frac{1}{\eta}\Bigg(\int_0^{y_{T-1}} [\overline{z} + (p+b+h)(y_{T-1} - \xi_{T-1}) + (b - \beta B_T^{PCT})\xi_{T-1}]^{+} dF(\xi_t)\\
&\quad + \int_{y_{T-1}}^{\infty} [\overline{z} + (b - \beta B_T^{PCT})\xi_{T-1}]^{+} dF(\xi_t)\Bigg)\Bigg\}
\end{aligned}
$$

where $F(\cdot)$ is the CDF of ξ_t. Define X_+ and X_- as the unique solution for the following two equations:

$$
\overline{z} + (p+b+h)(y_{T-1} - X_+) + (b - \beta B_T^{DIT})X_+ = 0, \overline{z} + (b - \beta B_T^{DIT})X_- = 0,
$$

(i) if $B_T^{PCT} \leq -\frac{p+h}{\beta}$, then the function $\overline{z} + (p+b+h)(y_{T-1} - X) + (b - \beta B_T^{PCT})X$ is an increasing function of X and $\overline{z} + (b - \beta B_T^{PCT})X$ is an increasing function of X. We further present the following discussion. (a) If $X_+ \leq y_{T-1}$, which is equivalent to $\overline{z} + (b - \beta B_T^{PCT})y_{T-1} \geq 0$, then $X_- \leq y_{T-1}$. Note that $e^{\tau^{PCT}} d_{T-2}$

is a constant, so the objective function of the optimization problem in period $T-1$ can be simplified to:

$$\bar{z}+(p+b-w)y_{T-1}$$
$$-\frac{1}{\eta}\left(\int_{X_+}^{y_{T-1}}[\bar{z}+(p+b+h)(y_{T-1}-\xi_{T-1})+(b-\beta B_T^{PCT})\xi_{T-1}]dF(\xi_t)\right.$$
$$\left.+\int_{y_{T-1}}^{\infty}[\bar{z}+(b-\beta B_T^{PCT})\xi_{T-1}]dF(\xi_t)\right)$$

Clearly, the above objective function is concave in $(\bar{z}, y_{T-1})$. By applying the FOC, we obtain the optimizers $(\bar{z}^*, y_{T-1}^*)$ for case (a):

$$F\left(\frac{\bar{z}^*+(p+b+h)y_{T-1}^*}{p+h+\beta B_T^{PCT}}\right)=1-\eta,\ F(y_{T-1}^*)=1-\frac{h+w}{p+b+h}\eta$$

(b) If $X_+\geq y_{T-1}$, which is equivalent to $\bar{z}+(b-\beta B_T^{PCT})y_{T-1}\leq 0$, then $X_-\geq y_{T-1}$, and the objective function of the optimization problem in period $T-1$ can be simplified to:

$$J(\bar{z}, y_{T-1})=\bar{z}+(p+b-w)y_{T-1}-\frac{1}{\eta}\left(\int_{X_-}^{\infty}[\bar{z}+(b-\beta B_T^{PCT})\xi_{T-1}]dF(\xi_t)\right)$$

We can easily find that $J(\bar{z}, y_{T-1})$ is increasing with y_{T-1}, which implies that the optimizer of y_{T-1} for case (b) is X_-. Thus, case (b) is dominated by case (a). Based on the above discussion, if $B_T^{PCT}\leq-\frac{p+h}{\beta}$, the optimal base-stock level is $y_{T-1}^*=e^{\tau^{PCT}}v^-d_{T-2}$ and the optimal value in period $T-1$ is:

$$\begin{aligned}V_{T-1}(d_{T-2})&=e^{\tau^{PCT}}\left((p+h+\beta B_T^{PCT})\bar{v}-(h+w)v^-\right.\\&\left.-\frac{(p+b+h)(\bar{v}-v^-)+(b-\beta B_T^{PCT})\left(I(\bar{v})-\bar{v}+E(\xi_t)\right)}{\eta}\right)d_{T-2}\\&=B_{T-1}^{PCT}d_{T-2}\end{aligned}$$

where

$$\begin{aligned}B_{T-1}^{PCT}&=e^{\tau^{PCT}}\left((p+h+\beta B_T^{PCT})\bar{v}-(h+w)v^-\right.\\&\left.-\frac{(p+b+h)(\bar{v}-v^-)+(b-\beta B_T^{PCT})\left(I(\bar{v})-\bar{v}+E(\xi_t)\right)}{\eta}\right)\end{aligned}$$

(ii) If $-\frac{p+h}{\beta} \le B_T^{PCT} \le \frac{b}{\beta}$, then the function $\overline{z} + (p+b+h)(y_{T-1} - X) + (b - \beta B_T^{PCT})X$ is a decreasing function of X and $\overline{z} + (b - \beta B_T^{PCT})X$ is an increasing function of X. We further present the following discussion. (a) If $X_+ \le y_{T-1}$, which is equivalent to $\overline{z} + (b - \beta B_T^{PCT})\xi_{T-1} \ge 0$, then $X_- \ge y_{T-1}$, and the objective function of the optimization problem in period $T-1$ can be simplified to:

$$\begin{aligned}
&\overline{z} + (p+b-w)y_{T-1} \\
&\quad - \frac{1}{\eta}\bigg(\int_0^{X_+} [\overline{z} + (p+b+h)(y_{T-1} - \xi_{T-1}) + (b - \beta B_T^{PCT})\xi_{T-1}] dF(\xi_t) \\
&\quad + \int_{X_-}^{\infty} [\overline{z} + (b - \beta B_T^{PCT})\xi_{T-1}] dF(\xi_t)\bigg)
\end{aligned}$$

Clearly, the above objective function is concave in $(\overline{z}, y_{T-1})$. By applying the FOC, we obtain the optimizers $(\overline{z}^*, y_{T-1}^*)$ for case (a):

$$F\left(\frac{\overline{z}^* + (p+b+h)y_{T-1}^*}{p+h+\beta B_T^{PCT}}\right) = \frac{p+b-w}{p+b+h}\eta,\ F\left(-\frac{\overline{z}^*}{b - \beta B_T^{PCT}}\right) = 1 - \frac{h+w}{p+b+h}\eta$$

(b) If $X_+ \ge y_{T-1}$, which is equivalent to $\overline{z} + (b - \beta B_T^{PCT})\xi_{T-1} \le 0$, then $X_- \le y_{T-1}$, and the objective function of the optimization problem in period $T-1$ can be simplified to:

$$\begin{aligned}
&\overline{z} + (p+b-w)y_{T-1} \\
&\quad - \frac{1}{\eta}\bigg(\int_0^{y_{T-1}} [\overline{z} + (p+b+h)(y_{T-1} - \xi_{T-1}) + (b - \beta B_T^{PCT})\xi_{T-1}] dF(\xi_t) \\
&\quad + \int_{y_{T-1}}^{\infty} [\overline{z} + (b - \beta B_T^{PCT})\xi_{T-1}] dF(\xi_t)\bigg)
\end{aligned}$$

We can easily find that the optimizers for case (b) is $\eta = 1$. Thus, case (b) is dominated by case (a). Based on the above discussion, if $B_T^{PCT} \le \frac{b}{\beta}$, the optimal base-stock level is $Y_{T-1}^* = e^{\tau^{PCT}} \frac{(p+h)v^+ + bv^-}{p+b+h} d_{T-2}$ and the optimal value in period $T-1$ is:

$$\begin{aligned}
&V_{T-1}(d_{T-2}) \\
&= e^{\tau^{PCT}}\bigg(\frac{p+b-w}{p+b+h}(p+h+\beta B_T^{PCT})v^+ - \frac{h+w}{p+b+h}(b - \beta B_T^{PCT})v^- \\
&\quad - \frac{(p+h+\beta B_T^{PCT})I(v^+) + (b - \beta B_T^{PCT})\big(I(v^-) - v^- + E(\xi_t)\big)}{\eta}\bigg)d_{T-2} \\
&= B_{T-1}^{PCT} d_{T-2}
\end{aligned}$$

where

$$B_{T-1}^{PCT}$$
$$= e^{\tau^{PCT}}\left(\frac{p+b-w}{p+b+h}(p+h+\beta B_T^{PCT})v^+ - \frac{h+w}{p+b+h}(b-\beta B_T^{PCT})v^-\right.$$
$$\left. - \frac{(p+h+\beta B_T^{PCT})I(v^+) + (b-\beta B_T^{PCT})\left(I(v^-) - v^- + E(\xi_t)\right)}{\eta}\right)$$

(iii) If $B_T^{PCT} > \frac{b}{\beta}$, then the function $\overline{z} + (p+b+h)(y_{T-1} - X) + (b - \beta B_T^{PCT})X$ is a decreasing function of X and $\overline{z} + (b - \beta B_T^{PCT})X$ is a decreasing function of X. We further present the following discussion. (a) If $X_+ \geq y_{T-1}$, which is equivalent to $\overline{z} + (b - \beta B_T^{PCT})\xi_{T-1} \geq 0$, then $X_- \geq y_{T-1}$, and the objective function of the optimization problem in period $T-1$ can be simplified to:

$$\overline{z} + (p+b-w)y_{T-1}$$
$$- \frac{1}{\eta}\left(\int_0^{y_{T-1}} [\overline{z} + (p+b+h)(y_{T-1} - \xi_{T-1}) + (b - \beta B_T^{PCT})\xi_{T-1}]dF(\xi_t)\right.$$
$$\left. + \int_{y_{T-1}}^{X_-} [\overline{z} + (b - \beta B_T^{PCT})\xi_{T-1}]dF(\xi_t)\right)$$

Clearly, the above objective function is concave in $(\overline{z}, y_{T-1})$. By applying the FOC, we obtain the optimizers $(\overline{z}^*, y_{T-1}^*)$ for case (a):

$$F(y_{T-1}^*) = \frac{p+b-w}{p+b+h}\eta,\ F\left(-\frac{\overline{z}^*}{b - \beta B_T^{PCT}}\right) = \eta$$

(b) If $X_+ \leq y_{T-1}$, which is equivalent to $\overline{z} + (b - \beta B_T^{PCT})\xi_{T-1} \leq 0$, then $X_- \leq y_{T-1}$, and the objective function of the optimization problem in period $T-1$ can be simplified to:

$$J(\overline{z}, y_{T-1})$$
$$= \overline{z} + (p+b-w)y_{T-1}$$
$$- \frac{1}{\eta}\left(\int_0^{X^+} [\overline{z} + (p+b+h)(y_{T-1} - \xi_{T-1}) + (b - \beta B_T^{PCT})\xi_{T-1}]dF(\xi_t)\right)$$

Clearly, the above objective function is concave in $(\overline{z}, y_{T-1})$. Given y_{T-1}, the optimizer $\overline{z}(y_{T-1}) = \arg\max_{\overline{z}} J(\overline{z}, y_{T-1})$ satisfies $G(X^+(\overline{z}(y_{T-1}), y_{T-1})) = \eta$, so we can easily find that $J(\overline{z}, y_{T-1})$ is decreasing with y_{T-1}, which implies that the optimizer of y_{T-1} for case (b) is X_+. Thus, case (b) is dominated by case (a). Based on the above discussion, if $-\frac{p+h}{\beta} \leq B_T^{PCT} > \frac{b}{\beta}$, the optimal base-stock level is $Y_{T-1}^* = e^{\tau^{PCT}} v^+ d_{T-2}$ and the optimal value in period $T-1$ is:

$$
\begin{aligned}
&V_{T-1}(d_{T-2}) \\
&= e^{\tau^{PCT}}\left((p+b-w)v^+ + (\beta B_T^{PCT} - b)v - \frac{(p+b+h)I(v^+) + (\beta B_T^{PCT} - b)I(v)}{\eta}\right)d_{T-2} \\
&= B_{T-1}^{PCT} d_{T-2}
\end{aligned}
$$

where

$$
\begin{aligned}
&B_{T-1}^{PCT} \\
&= e^{\tau^{PCT}}\left((p+b-w)v^+ + (\beta B_T^{PCT} - b)v - \frac{(p+b+h)I(v^+) + (\beta B_T^{PCT} - b)I(v)}{\eta}\right)
\end{aligned}
$$

Recursively, by defining $B_{T+1}^{PCT} = 0$, we can infer that for demand pattern in the PCT, the optimal value function can be simplified to $V_t(d_{t-1}) = B_t^{PCT} \cdot d_{t-1}$, and for period T, the optimal stock level is $Y_T^* = e^{\tau^{PCT}} \frac{(p+h)v^+ + bv^-}{p+b+h} d_{T-1}$, while for period $t < T$,
(i) if $B_t^{PCT} \le -\frac{p+h}{\beta}$, then $Y_t^* = e^{\tau^{PCT}} v^- d_{t-1}$ and

$$
\begin{aligned}
B_{t+1}^{PCT} = e^{\tau^{PCT}}\Bigg((p+h+\beta B_{t+1}^{PCT})\overline{v} - (h+w)v^- \\
- \frac{(p+b+h)(\overline{v} - v^-) + (b - \beta B_{t+1}^{PCT})\left(I(\overline{v}) - \overline{v} + E(\xi_t)\right)}{\eta}\Bigg)
\end{aligned}
$$

(ii) if $-\frac{p+h}{\beta} \le B_{t+1}^{PCT} \le \frac{b}{\beta}$, then $Y_t^* = e^{\tau^{PCT}} \frac{(p+h)v^+ + bv^-}{p+b+h} d_{t-1}$ and

$$
\begin{aligned}
&B_t^{PCT} \\
&= e^{\tau^{PCT}}\Bigg(\frac{p+b-w}{p+b+h}(p+h+\beta B_{t+1}^{PCT})v^+ - \frac{h+w}{p+b+h}(b - \beta B_{t+1}^{PCT})v^- \\
&\quad - \frac{(p+h+\beta B_{t+1}^{PCT})I(v^+) + (b - \beta B_{t+1}^{PCT})\left(I(v^-) - v^- + E(\xi_t)\right)}{\eta}\Bigg)
\end{aligned}
$$

(iii) if $B_{t+1}^{PCT} \ge \frac{b}{\beta}$, then $Y_t^* = e^{\tau^{PCT}} v^+ d_{t-1}$ and

$$
\begin{aligned}
&B_t^{PCT} \\
&= e^{\tau^{PCT}}\left((p+b-w)v^+ + (\beta B_{t+1}^{PCT} - b)v - \frac{(p+b+h)I(v^+) + (\beta B_{t+1}^{PCT} - b)I(v)}{\eta}\right)
\end{aligned}
$$

We therefore complete the proof of item (iii) in Lemma 2.1 and Proposition 3.2.

A.2.4 Proof of Corollary 3.1 and Corollary 3.2

Proof. For Corollary 3.1 and Corollary 3.2, properties (i) and (ii) are easy to prove. Therefore, we focus on proving (iii). If $y_t^* = \frac{(p+h)v^+ + bv^-}{p+b+h}$, then studying the behavior of the optimal stock level with respect to η is equivalent to studying the following fractional term:

$$l(\eta) = \frac{(p+h)F^{-1}\left(\frac{p+b-w}{p+b+h}\eta\right) + bF^{-1}\left(1 - \frac{h+w}{p+b+h}\eta\right)}{p+b+h}$$

so the derivative of $l(\eta)$ with respect η is:

$$l'(\eta) = b(h+w)F^{-1'}(S\eta)\frac{\frac{(p+h)S}{b(1-S)} - \frac{F^{-1'}(1-\eta+S\eta)}{F^{-1'}(S\eta)}}{(p+b+h)^2}$$

where $S = \frac{p+b-w}{p+b+h}$. From the above equation, it suffices to study the sign of the following term:

$$\frac{(p+h)S}{b(1-S)} - \frac{F^{-1'}(1-\eta+S\eta)}{F^{-1'}(S\eta)}$$

where $0 < S < 1$.

(a) With the additive demand patterns (in the DET and DIT), since $\varepsilon_t^i (i \in \{DET, DIT\})$ is a normally distributed random variable, then $F(\cdot)$ is the CDF of a normal distribution with mean 0. It is easy to verify that $\frac{F^{-1'}(1-\eta+S\eta)}{F^{-1'}(S\eta)}$ is increasing in $\eta \in (0, 1)$ for $S < 0.5$, while decreasing in $\eta \in (0, 1)$ for $S > 0.5$.

Case 1: When $S \leq 0.5$, $\frac{F^{-1'}(1-\eta+S\eta)}{F^{-1'}(S\eta)} < 1$. Note that $\frac{(p+h)S}{b(1-S)} > 1$, then $\frac{(p+h)S}{b(1-S)} - \frac{F^{-1'}(1-\eta+S\eta)}{F^{-1'}(S\eta)} > 0$, and hence, $l(\eta)$ is increasing with η;

Case 2: When $S > 0.5$, $\frac{F^{-1'}(1-\eta+S\eta)}{F^{-1'}(S\eta)} < \lim_{\eta \to 0} \frac{F^{-1'}(1-\eta+S\eta)}{F^{-1'}(S\eta)} = \frac{S}{1-S}$. Note that $\frac{S}{1-S} < \frac{(p+h)S}{b(1-S)}$, then $\frac{(p+h)S}{b(1-S)} - \frac{F^{-1'}(1-\eta+S\eta)}{F^{-1'}(S\eta)} > 0$, and hence, $l(\eta)$ is increasing with η.

These facts complete the proof of property (iii) in Corollary 3.1.

(b) With multiplicative demand pattern (in the PCT), since $e^{\varepsilon_t^{PCT}}$ is a random variable with lognormal distribution, then $F(\cdot)$ is the CDF of a lognormal distribution. It is easy to verify that $\frac{F^{-1'}(1-\eta+S\eta)}{F^{-1'}(S\eta)}$ is decreasing in $\eta \in (0, 1)$ for any S. Therefore, $1 < \frac{F^{-1'}(1-\eta+S\eta)}{F^{-1'}(S\eta)} < \frac{F^{-1'}(1)}{F^{-1'}(0)}$.

Case 1: When $\frac{(p+h)S}{b(1-S)} \geq \frac{F^{-1'}(1)}{F^{-1'}(0)}$, $l(\eta)$ is increasing with η;

Case 2: When $1 < \frac{(p+h)S}{b(1-S)} < \frac{F^{-1'}(1)}{F^{-1'}(0)}$, $l(\eta) = 0$ has one root $\tilde{\eta}$, then $l(\eta) < 0$ for $\eta < \tilde{\eta}$, while $l(\eta) > 0$ for $\eta > \tilde{\eta}$.

The above completes the proof of property (iii) in Corollary 3.2.

A.2.5 Proof of the Results is Table 6

Proof. Since Proposition 3.1 and Proposition 3.2 are derived without any assumptions about the distribution for demand noise terms (i.e., $\varepsilon_t^i(i \in \{DET, DIT, PCT\})$), v^+, v^- and $\frac{(p+h)v^+ + bv^-}{p+b+h}$ are still the possible solutions for y_t^*.

A.2.5.1 Uniform Distribution of Noise Terms

For $i \in \{DET, DIT\}$, if ε_t^i is uniformly distributed with a mean of zero and a variance of σ_i^2, then the specific support is given by $[-\sqrt{3}\sigma_i, \sqrt{3}\sigma_i]$. Thus, $v^+ = (2S\eta - 1)\sqrt{3}\sigma_i$, $v^- = (1 - 2(1 - S)\eta)\sqrt{3}\sigma_i$ and $\frac{(p+h)v^+ + bv^-}{p+b+h} = \frac{2(p-w)\eta - (p-b+h)}{p+b+h}\sqrt{3}\sigma_i$. Obviously, v^+ and $\frac{(p+h)v^+ + bv^-}{p+b+h}$ are increasing with η and v^- is decreasing with η.

For $i = PCT$, if ε_t^i is uniformly distributed with a mean of zero and a variance of σ_i^2, then $v^+ = e^{(2S\eta-1)\sqrt{3}\sigma_i}$, $v^- = e^{(1-2(1-S)\eta)\sqrt{3}\sigma_i}$ and $\frac{(p+h)v^+ + bv^-}{p+b+h} = \frac{(p+h)e^{(2S\eta-1)\sqrt{3}\sigma_i} + be^{(1-2(1-S)\eta)\sqrt{3}\sigma_i}}{p+b+h}$. Obviously, v^+ is increasing with η and v^- is decreasing with η. Studying the behavior of $\frac{(p+h)v^+ + bv^-}{p+b+h}$ with respect to η is equivalent to studying the following term:

$$l(\eta) = (p + h)e^{(2S\eta-1)\sqrt{3}\sigma_i} + be^{(1-2(1-S)\eta)\sqrt{3}\sigma_i}$$

so the derivative of $l(\eta)$ with respect to η is:

$$l'(\eta) = (1 - S)be^{(1-2\eta+2S\eta)\sqrt{3}\sigma_i}\left[\frac{(p + h)S}{b(1 - S)}e^{(\eta-1)2\sqrt{3}\sigma_i} - 1\right]2\sqrt{3}\sigma_i$$

Recalling that $S = \frac{p+b-w}{p+b+h}$,

$$\frac{(p + h)S}{b(1 - S)}e^{(\eta-1)2\sqrt{3}\sigma_i} - 1 = \frac{(p + b - w)(p + h)}{(h + w)b}e^{(\eta-1)2\sqrt{3}\sigma_i} - 1$$

then the only solution of $l'(\eta) = 0$ is $\tilde{\eta} = \frac{\ln\left[\frac{(h+w)b}{(p+b-w)(p+h)}\right]}{2\sqrt{3}\sigma_i} + 1$ and $0 < \tilde{\eta} < 1$. Therefore, if the demand pattern is derived from PCT and a uniform noise term, $\frac{(p+h)v^+ + bv^-}{p+b+h}$ is first decreasing with η for $\eta \in [0, \tilde{\eta}]$ and then increasing with η for $\eta \in [\tilde{\eta}, 1]$.

A.2.5.2 Logistic Distribution of Noise Terms

For $i \in \{DET, DIT\}$, if ε_t^i is logistically distributed with a mean of zero and a variance of σ_i^2, the parameter is $(0, \frac{\sqrt{3}\sigma_i}{\pi})$. Thus, $v^+ = -\ln\left(\frac{1}{S\eta} - 1\right)\frac{\sqrt{3}\sigma_i}{\pi}$, $v^- = -\ln\left(\frac{1}{1-(1-S)\eta} - 1\right)\frac{\sqrt{3}\sigma_i}{\pi}$ and $\frac{(p+h)v^+ + bv^-}{p+b+h} = -\frac{(p+h)\ln\left(\frac{1}{S\eta}-1\right) + b\ln\left(\frac{1}{1-(1-S)\eta}-1\right)}{p+b+h}\frac{\sqrt{3}\sigma_i}{\pi}$. Obviously, v^+ is increasing with η and v^- is decreasing with η. Studying the behavior of $\frac{(p+h)v^+ + bv^-}{p+b+h}$ with respect to η is equivalent to studying the following term:

$$l(\eta) = -(p+h)\ln\left(\frac{1}{S\eta} - 1\right) - b\ln\left(\frac{1}{1-(1-S)\eta} - 1\right)$$

The derivative of $l(\eta)$ with respect to η is:

$$l'(\eta) = \frac{(p+b+h)^2\,[p+b+h-(p+b-w)\eta]}{[p+b+h-(h+w)\eta]\,[p+b+h-(p+b-w)\eta]} > 0$$

Therefore, $\frac{(p+h)v^+ + bv^-}{p+b+h}$ is always increasing with η.

For $i = PCT$, if ε_t^i is logistically distributed with a mean of zero and a variance of σ_i^2, then $v^+ = \left(\frac{1}{S\eta} - 1\right)^{-\frac{\sqrt{3}\sigma_i}{\pi}}$, $v^- = \left(\frac{1}{1-(1-S)\eta} - 1\right)^{-\frac{\sqrt{3}\sigma_i}{\pi}}$ and $\frac{(p+h)v^+ + bv^-}{p+b+h} = \frac{(p+h)\left(\frac{1}{S\eta}-1\right)^{-\frac{\sqrt{3}\sigma_i}{\pi}} + b\left(\frac{1}{1-(1-S)\eta}-1\right)^{-\frac{\sqrt{3}\sigma_i}{\pi}}}{p+b+h}$. Obviously, v^+ is increasing with η and v^- is decreasing with η. Studying the behavior of $\frac{(p+h)v^+ + bv^-}{p+b+h}$ with respect to η is equivalent to studying the following term:

$$l(\eta) = (p+h)\left(\frac{1}{S\eta} - 1\right)^{-\frac{\sqrt{3}\sigma_i}{\pi}} + b\left(\frac{1}{1-(1-S)\eta} - 1\right)^{-\frac{\sqrt{3}\sigma_i}{\pi}}$$

The derivative of $l(\eta)$ with respect to η is:

$$l'(\eta) = \frac{\sqrt{3}\sigma_i}{\pi}\left\{(p+h)\left(\frac{1}{S\eta} - 1\right)^{-\frac{\sqrt{3}\sigma_i}{\pi}-1}\frac{1}{S\eta^2} - b\left(\frac{1}{1-(1-S)\eta} - 1\right)^{-\frac{\sqrt{3}\sigma_i}{\pi}-1}\frac{1-S}{(1-(1-S)\eta)^2}\right\}$$

and the derivative of $l'(\eta)$ with respect to η is:

$$l''(\eta) = \frac{\sqrt{3}\sigma_i}{\pi}\left(\frac{\sqrt{3}\sigma_i}{\pi}+1\right)\left\{(p+h)\left(\frac{1}{S\eta}-1\right)^{-\frac{\sqrt{3}\sigma_i}{\pi}-2}\frac{1}{S^2\eta^4}\right.$$
$$\left.+b\left(\frac{1}{1-(1-S)\eta}-1\right)^{-\frac{\sqrt{3}\sigma_i}{\pi}-2}\frac{(1-S)^2}{(1-(1-S)\eta)^4}\right\}>0$$

so $l'(\eta)$ is increasing with η. Recalling that $S=\frac{p+b-w}{p+b+h}$, we can easily obtain the following equations:

$$l'(1) = \frac{\sqrt{3}\sigma_i}{\pi}\left(\frac{1-S}{S}\right)^{-\frac{\sqrt{3}\sigma_i}{\pi}-1}\frac{p-w}{S^2}>0$$
$$\lim_{\eta\to 0} l'(\eta) = -b(1-S)\left(\frac{1-(1-S)\eta}{(1-S)\eta}\right)^{\frac{\sqrt{3}\sigma_i}{\pi}+1} \to -\infty$$

Based on the above analysis, $l'(\eta)=0$ has one root between 0 and 1. Hence, $\frac{(p+h)v^+ + bv^-}{p+b+h}$ is first decreasing with η for $\eta\in[0,\tilde{\eta}]$ and then increasing with η for $\eta\in[\tilde{\eta},1]$, where $l'(\tilde{\eta})=0$.

A.2.6 ARMA Model on Transformed Demand Series

As Table 2 shows, after being processed by DET, DIT or PCT, the original demand series becomes a stationary series, which can also be characterized by an ARMA model. To forecast demand in combination with an ARMA model, we first present the transformed demand series and its ACF and PACF plots in Fig. A.2.6. Generally, the ACF and PACF values of the transformed demand series tend to be zero when the lag orders exceed 0 for DET, exceed 3 for DIT and exceed 1 for PCT. Thus, we construct ARMA(0,0), ARMA(3,3) and ARMA(1,1) models for the three transformed series, respectively.

Transformed demand series and its ACF and PACF plots

Out-of-sample demand forecast performance with different modeling of transformed demand series

Following the same rolling-horizon pattern of splitting of training set and testing set, we forecast the transformed demand series using normal variables and ARMA models, and then calculate the forecast of the original nonstationary demand series based on the forecast of transformed demand series. The forecasting results in terms of MAPE and relative RMSE are displayed in Fig. A.2.6. Obviously, the out-of-sample demand forecast performance with transformed demand series handled by a normal random variable and characterized by an ARMA model is basically the same for DET, and the former is better than the latter for DIT and PCT.

A.2.7 Incorporation of Risk Parameter in Predictive Analytics

In this section, we try to incorporate decision makers' risk attitude to predictive analytics. The first idea we tried is updating the commonly used measures of forecasting accuracy, MAPE and relative RRMSE, to the asymmetric loss function. Specifically, the new loss function in the predictive analytics is given by

$$(1-\eta)(\hat{D}_t - D_t)^+ + \eta(D_t - \hat{D}_t)^+,$$

where $(\hat{D}_t - D_t)^+$ is the over-estimating loss and $(D_t - \hat{D}_t)^+$ is the under-estimating loss. Generally, a more risk-averse decision maker would prefer to give a more conservative demand forecasting that is usually less than the actual demand. Therefore, we set the coefficient of under-estimating loss to be η and the coefficient of over-estimating loss to be $1-\eta$. Based on this asymmetric loss function, a decision maker with a smaller η is more sensitive to over-estimating loss and a decision maker with a larger η is more sensitive to under-estimating loss. The out-of-sample demand forecast performance with this asymmetric loss function is summarized in Fig. A.2.7. As η increases from 0 to 1, DIT, PCT and DET alternately become the method with the least out-of-sample forecast error. However, because demand to inventory is not a simple linear conversion, the best-performing method in predictive analytics and the method that produces optimal inventory decisions in prescriptive analytics are not always consistent for different risk tolerance levels.

Summary of out-of-sample demand forecast performance with asymmetric loss function

Based on the above findings, we tried another idea that aligns the measures of demand forecasting and inventory solving. Specifically, we calculate predicted risk-adjusted profits, which is the maximum out-of-sample CVaR that can be obtained under a given risk tolerance level η and with realized demand replaced with predicted demand resulted from each method. We test the risk-adjusted application on the real demand series of this company's best-selling SFP. The result is summarized in Fig. A.2.7a. Since the relative size of three lines in Fig. A.2.7a is almost the same with that in Fig. A.2.7b, we can infer that the method results in the best predicted out-of-sample CVaR would also perform the best in profit realization with actual demand. This is because that the impact of decision makers' risk attitude on the inventory decision has been incorporated into the predicted risk-adjusted profits in the same way as it is incorporated into the actual risk-adjusted profits. Then, as long as the predicted demand is not much different from the actual demand, the risk-adjusted predictive analytics provides us with a better suggestion of choice of nonstationary transformation method and finally better inventory solution and risk-adjusted profit realization.

Summary of predicted and realized out-of-sample performance

A.2.8 Extension of DIT to ARIMA(p,d,q) Process

Proof. Here, we extend the DIT to a more general ARIMA (p,d,q) process. In this case, the demand series can be characterized as:

$$\left(1-\sum_{i=1}^{p}\phi_i L^i\right)(1-L)^d D_t=\left(1+\sum_{j=1}^{q}\theta_j L^j\right)\varepsilon_t,$$

where L is the lag operator, d is the degree of differencing and $L^d D_t = D_{t-d}$. The process of the ARIMA family suggests that D_t is linearly related to the history demands and residual terms. Hence, D_t can be reexpressed as follows:

$$\begin{aligned} D_t &= \tau^{ARMA}+\sum_{i=1}^{m}\lambda_i D_{t-i}+\sum_{j=1}^{n}\theta_j\varepsilon_{t-j}^{ARMA}+\varepsilon_t^{ARMA} \\ &= \tau^{ARMA}+\sum_{i=1}^{m}\lambda_i D_{t-i}+\zeta_t, \end{aligned}$$

where $\zeta_t=\sum_{j=1}^{n}\theta_j\varepsilon_{t-j}^{ARMA}+\varepsilon_t^{ARMA}$ is the cumulative error in period t with the CDF $F_\zeta(\cdot)$.

By applying $\Pi_t(Y_t, D_t|d_{t-m},...,d_{t-1})=(p+b-w)Y_t-(p+b+h)(Y_t-D_t)^+-bD_t$ to (7), the optimization problem in period T is:

$$V_T(d_{T-m},...,d_{T-1})=\max_{z,Y_T}\quad z-\frac{E[z-(p+b-w)Y_T+(p+b+h)(Y_T-D_T)^+ +bD_T]^+}{\eta},$$

By defining $\bar{z}=z-(p+b-w)Y_T$, the problem can be reformulated as:

$$\begin{aligned} &\max_{\bar{z},Y_T}\quad \bar{z}+(p+b-w)Y_T-\frac{E[\bar{z}+(p+b+h)(Y_T-D_T)^+ +bD_T]^+}{\eta} \\ &=\max_{\bar{z},Y_T}\quad \bar{z}+(p+b-w)Y_T \\ &\quad -\frac{\int_0^{Y_T}[\bar{z}+(p+b+h)(Y_T-D_T)+bD_T]^+dG(D_t)+\int_{Y_T}^{\infty}[\bar{z}+bD_T]^+dG(D_t)}{\eta}, \end{aligned}$$

where $G(\cdot)$ is the CDF of D_t. Define X_+ and X_- as the unique solution for the following two equations:

$$\bar{z}+(p+b+h)(Y_T-X_+)+bX_+=0,\bar{z}+bX_-=0,$$

then the optimization problem can be further formulated as:

$$\max_{\bar{z},Y_T} \quad \bar{z} + (p+b-w)Y_T$$
$$- \frac{\int_0^{X_+}[\bar{z} + (p+b+h)(Y_T - D_T) + bD_T]dG(D_t) + \int_{X_-}^{\infty}[\bar{z} + bD_T]dG(D_t)}{\eta},$$

Since this objective function is joint concave and thus we can use the first-order condition (FOC) to derive the optimal solutions. The base-stock level Y_t^* is the unique solution for the following two equations:

$$G\left(\frac{\bar{z}^* + (p+b-w)Y_T^*}{p+h}\right) = \frac{p+b-w}{p+b+h}\eta, G\left(-\frac{\bar{z}^*}{b}\right) = 1 - \frac{h+w}{p+b+h}\eta,$$

Because $D_t = \tau^{ARMA} + \sum_{i=1}^{m} \lambda_i D_{t-i} + \zeta_t$, following Table 4, the optimal inventory decision is $Y_T^* = \tau^{ARMA} + \sum_{i=1}^{m} \lambda_i d_{T-i} + \frac{(p+h)v^+ + bv^-}{p+b+h}$, and the optimal value in period T is:

$$\begin{aligned}
&V_T(d_{T-m}, ..., d_{T-1}) \\
&= \left(p - w - \frac{b}{\eta}\right)\tau^{ARMA} + \frac{p+b-w}{p+b+h}(p+h)v^+ - \frac{h+w}{p+b+h}bv^- \\
&\quad - \frac{(p+h)I(v^+) + bI(v^-) - bv^- + bE(\zeta_t)}{\eta} + \left(p - w - \frac{b}{\eta}\right)\sum_{i=1}^{m}\lambda_i d_{T-i} \\
&= A_T^{ARMA} + \sum_{i=1}^{m} B_{T,i}^{ARMA} d_{T-i}
\end{aligned}$$

where $B_{T,i}^{ARMA} = \left(p - w - \frac{b}{\eta}\right)\lambda_i$. By defining $\bar{z} = z - (p+b-w)Y_{T-1} - \beta A_T^{ARMA} - \beta\sum_{i=2}^{m} B_{T,i}^{ARMA} d_{T-i}$, then the optimization problem in period $T-1$ is:

$$\begin{aligned}
&V_{T-1}(d_{T-1-m}, ..., d_{T-2}) \\
&= \max_{Y_{T-1}\geq 0} \quad R_{T-1|d_{T-1-m},...,d_{T-2}}\left[\Pi_{T-1}(Y_{T-1}, D_{T-1}) + \beta V_T(d_{T-m}, ..., d_{T-2}, D_{T-1})\right] \\
&= \max_{z,Y_{T-1}} \quad z - \frac{1}{\eta}\Bigg(E[z - (p+b-w)Y_{T-1} + (p+b+h)(Y_{T-1} - D_{T-1})^+ + bD_{T-1} \\
&\quad - \beta A_T^{ARMA} - \beta\sum_{i=2}^{m} B_{T,i}^{ARMA} d_{T-i} - \beta B_{T,1}^{ARMA} D_{T-1}]^+\Bigg) \\
&= \beta A_T^{ARMA} + \beta\sum_{i=2}^{m} B_{T,i}^{ARMA} d_{T-i} + \max_{\bar{z},Y_{T-1}} \quad \bar{z} + (p+b-w)Y_{T-1} \\
&\quad - \frac{E[\bar{z} + (p+b+h)(Y_{T-1} - D_{T-1})^+ + (b - \beta B_{T,1}^{ARMA})D_{T-1}]^+}{\eta} \\
&= \beta A_T^{ARMA} + \beta\sum_{i=2}^{m} B_{T,i}^{ARMA} d_{T-i} + \max_{\bar{z},Y_{T-1}} \quad \bar{z} + (p+b-w)Y_{T-1}
\end{aligned}$$

$$-\frac{1}{\eta}\left(\int_0^{Y_{T-1}}[\bar{z}+(p+b+h)(Y_{T-1}-D_{T-1})+(b-\beta B_{T,1}^{ARMA})D_{T-1}]^+dG(D_t)\right.$$
$$\left.+\int_{Y_{T-1}}^{\infty}[\bar{z}+(b-\beta B_{T,1}^{ARMA})D_{T-1}]^+dG(D_t)\right)$$

where $G(\cdot)$ is the CDF of D_t. Define X_+ and X_- as the unique solution for the following two equations:

$$\bar{z}+(p+b+h)(Y_{T-1}-X_+)+(b-\beta B_{T,1}^{ARMA})X_+=0, \bar{z}+(b-\beta B_{T,1}^{ARMA})X_-=0,$$

(i) If $B_{T,1}^{ARMA}\le -\frac{p+h}{\beta}$, then the function $\bar{z}+(p+b+h)(Y_{T-1}-X)+(b-\beta B_{T,1}^{ARMA})X$ is an increasing function of X and $\bar{z}+(b-\beta B_{T,1}^{ARMA})X$ is an increasing function of X. We further present the following discussion. (a) If $X_+\le Y_{T-1}$, which is equivalent to $\bar{z}+(b-\beta B_{T,1}^{ARMA})Y_{T-1}\ge 0$, then $X_-\le Y_{T-1}$. Note that $\beta A_T^{ARMA}+\beta\sum_{i=2}^m B_{T,i}^{ARMA}d_{T-i}$ is a constant, so the objective function of the optimization problem in period $T-1$ can be simplified to:

$$\bar{z}+(p+b-w)Y_{T-1}$$
$$-\frac{1}{\eta}\left(\int_{X_+}^{Y_{T-1}}[\bar{z}+(p+b+h)(Y_{T-1}-D_{T-1})+(b-\beta B_{T,1}^{ARMA})D_{T-1}]dG(D_t)\right.$$
$$\left.+\int_{Y_{T-1}}^{\infty}[\bar{z}+(b-\beta B_{T,1}^{ARMA})D_{T-1}]dG(D_t)\right)$$

Clearly, the above objective function is concave in $(\bar{z}, Y_{T-1})$. By applying the FOC, we obtain the optimizers $(\bar{z}^*, Y_{T-1}^*)$ for case (a):

$$G\left(\frac{\bar{z}^*+(p+b+h)Y_{T-1}^*}{p+h+\beta B_{T,1}^{ARMA}}\right)=1-\eta, G(Y_{T-1}^*)=1-\frac{h+w}{p+b+h}\eta$$

(b) If $X_+\ge Y_{T-1}$, which is equivalent to $\bar{z}+(b-\beta B_{T,1}^{ARMA})Y_{T-1}\le 0$, then $X_-\ge Y_{T-1}$, and the objective function of the optimization problem in period $T-1$ can be simplified to:

$$J(\bar{z}, Y_{T-1})=\bar{z}+(p+b-w)Y_{T-1}-\frac{1}{\eta}\left(\int_{X_-}^{\infty}[\bar{z}+(b-\beta B_{T,1}^{ARMA})D_{T-1}]dG(D_t)\right)$$

we can easily find that $J(\bar{z}, Y_{T-1})$ is increasing with Y_{T-1}, which implies that the optimizer of Y_{T-1} for case (b) is X_-. Thus, case (b) is dominated by case (a). Based on the above discussion, if $B_{T,1}^{ARMA}\le -\frac{p+h}{\beta}$, the optimal base-stock level is $Y_{T-1}^*=\tau^{ARMA}+\sum_{i=1}^m\lambda_i d_{T-1-i}+v^-$ and the optimal value in period $T-1$ is:

$$
\begin{aligned}
&V_{T-1}(d_{T-1-m}, \ldots, d_{T-2}) \\
&= \beta A_T^{ARMA} + \left(p - w + \beta B_{T,1}^{ARMA} - \frac{b - \beta B_{T,1}^{ARMA}}{\eta}\right)\tau^{ARMA} \\
&\quad + (p + h + \beta B_{T,1}^{ARMA})\overline{v} - (h + w)v^{-} \\
&\quad - \frac{(p + b + h)(\overline{v} - v^{-}) + (b - \beta B_{T,1}^{ARMA})\left(I(\overline{v}) - \overline{v} + E(\varepsilon_t^{DIT})\right)}{\eta} \\
&\quad + \beta \sum_{i=1}^{m-1} B_{T,i-1}^{ARMA} d_{T-1-i} + \left(p - w + \beta B_{T,1}^{ARMA} - \frac{b - \beta B_{T,1}^{ARMA}}{\eta}\right) \sum_{i=1}^{m} \lambda_i d_{T-1-i} \\
&= A_{T-1}^{ARMA} + \sum_{i=1}^{m} B_{T-1,i}^{ARMA} d_{T-1-i}
\end{aligned}
$$

where $B_{T-1,i}^{ARMA} = \beta B_{T,i-1}^{ARMA} + \left(p - w + \beta B_{T,1}^{ARMA} - \frac{b-\beta B_{T,1}^{ARMA}}{\eta}\right)\lambda_i$ for $i = 1, \ldots, m-1$ and $B_{T-1,m}^{ARMA} = \left(p - w + \beta B_{T,1}^{ARMA} - \frac{b-\beta B_{T,1}^{ARMA}}{\eta}\right)\lambda_m$.

(ii) If $-\frac{p+h}{\beta} \le B_{T,1}^{ARMA} \le \frac{b}{\beta}$, then the function $\overline{z} + (p + b + h)(Y_{T-1} - X) + (b - \beta B_{T,1}^{ARMA})X$ is a decreasing function of X and $\overline{z} + (b - \beta B_{T,1}^{ARMA})X$ is an increasing function of X. We further present the following discussion. (a) If $X_+ \le Y_{T-1}$, which is equivalent to $\overline{z} + (b - \beta B_{T,1}^{ARMA})Y_{T-1} \ge 0$, then $X_- \ge Y_{T-1}$, and the objective function of the optimization problem in period $T-1$ can be simplified to:

$$
\begin{aligned}
&\overline{z} + (p + b - w)Y_{T-1} \\
&\quad - \frac{1}{\eta}\left(\int_0^{X_+} [\overline{z} + (p + b + h)(Y_{T-1} - D_{T-1}) + (b - \beta B_{T,1}^{ARMA})D_{T-1}]dG(D_t)\right. \\
&\quad \left. + \int_{X_-}^{\infty} [\overline{z} + (b - \beta B_{T,1}^{ARMA})D_{T-1}]dG(D_t)\right)
\end{aligned}
$$

Clearly, the above objective function is concave in $(\overline{z}, Y_{T-1})$. By applying the FOC, we obtain the optimizers $(\overline{z}^*, Y_{T-1}^*)$ for case (a):

$$
G\left(\frac{\overline{z}^* + (p + b + h)Y_{T-1}^*}{p + h + \beta B_{T,1}^{ARMA}}\right) = \frac{p + b - w}{p + b + h}\eta,\ G\left(-\frac{\overline{z}^*}{b - \beta B_{T,1}^{ARMA}}\right) = 1 - \frac{h + w}{p + b + h}\eta
$$

(b) If $X_+ \ge Y_{T-1}$, which is equivalent to $\overline{z} + (b - \beta B_{T,1}^{ARMA})Y_{T-1} \le 0$, then $X_- \le Y_{T-1}$, and the objective function of the optimization problem in period $T-1$ can be simplified to:

$$
\begin{aligned}
&\overline{z} + (p+b-w)Y_{T-1} \\
&\quad - \frac{1}{\eta}\left(\int_0^{Y_{T-1}} [\overline{z} + (p+b+h)(Y_{T-1} - D_{T-1}) + (b - \beta B_{T,1}^{ARMA})D_{T-1}]dG(D_t)\right. \\
&\quad \left. + \int_{Y_{T-1}}^{\infty} [\overline{z} + (b - \beta B_{T,1}^{ARMA})D_{T-1}]dG(D_t)\right)
\end{aligned}
$$

We can easily find that the optimizer for case (b) is $\eta = 1$. Thus, case (b) is dominated by case (a). Based on the above discussion, if $-\frac{p+h}{\beta} \leq B_{T,1}^{ARMA} \leq \frac{b}{\beta}$, the optimal base-stock level is $Y_{T-1}^{*} = \tau^{ARMA} + \sum_{i=1}^{m} \lambda_i d_{T-1-i} + \frac{(p+h)v^{+} + bv^{-}}{p+b+h}$ and the optimal value in period $T-1$ is:

$$
\begin{aligned}
&V_{T-1}(d_{T-1-m}, \ldots, d_{T-2}) \\
&= \beta A_{T}^{ARMA} + \left(p - w + \beta B_{T,1}^{ARMA} - \frac{b - \beta B_{T,1}^{ARMA}}{\eta}\right)\tau^{DIT} \\
&\quad + \frac{p+b-w}{p+b+h}(p+h+\beta B_{T,1}^{ARMA})v^{+} - \frac{h+w}{p+b+h}(b - \beta B_{T,1}^{ARMA})v^{-} \\
&\quad - \frac{(p+h+\beta B_{T,1}^{ARMA})I(v^{+}) + (b - \beta B_{T,1}^{ARMA})\left(I(v^{-}) - v^{-} + E(\varepsilon_t^{DIT})\right)}{\eta} \\
&\quad + \beta \sum_{i=1}^{m-1} B_{T,i-1}^{ARMA} d_{T-1-i} + \left(p - w + \beta B_{T,1}^{ARMA} - \frac{b - \beta B_{T,1}^{ARMA}}{\eta}\right)\sum_{i=1}^{m} \lambda_i d_{T-1-i} \\
&= A_{T-1}^{ARMA} + \sum_{i=1}^{m} B_{T-1,i}^{ARMA} d_{T-1-i}
\end{aligned}
$$

where $B_{T-1,i}^{ARMA} = \beta B_{T,i-1}^{ARMA} + \left(p - w + \beta B_{T,1}^{ARMA} - \frac{b - \beta B_{T,1}^{ARMA}}{\eta}\right)\lambda_i$ for $i = 1, \ldots, m-1$ and $B_{T-1,m}^{ARMA} = \left(p - w + \beta B_{T,1}^{ARMA} - \frac{b - \beta B_{T,1}^{ARMA}}{\eta}\right)\lambda_m$.

(iii) If $B_{T,1}^{ARMA} > \frac{b}{\beta}$, then the function $\overline{z} + (p+b+h)(Y_{T-1} - X) + (b - \beta B_{T,1}^{ARMA})X$ is a decreasing function of X and $\overline{z} + (b - \beta B_{T,1}^{ARMA})X$ is a decreasing function of X. We further present the following discussion. (a) If $X_{+} \geq Y_{T-1}$, which is equivalent to $\overline{z} + (b - \beta B_{T,1}^{ARMA})Y_{T-1} \geq 0$, then $X_{-} \geq Y_{T-1}$, and the objective function of the optimization problem in period $T-1$ can be simplified to:

$$
\begin{aligned}
&\overline{z} + (p+b-w)Y_{T-1} \\
&\quad - \frac{1}{\eta}\left(\int_0^{Y_{T-1}} [\overline{z} + (p+b+h)(Y_{T-1} - D_{T-1}) + (b - \beta B_{T,1}^{ARMA})D_{T-1}]dG(D_t)\right. \\
&\quad \left. + \int_{Y_{T-1}}^{X_{-}} [\overline{z} + (b - \beta B_{T,1}^{ARMA})D_{T-1}]dG(D_t)\right)
\end{aligned}
$$

Clearly, the above objective function is concave in $(\overline{z}, Y_{T-1})$. By applying the FOC, we obtain the optimizers $(\overline{z}^*, Y^*_{T-1})$ for case (a):

$$G(Y^*_{T-1}) = \frac{p+b-w}{p+b+h}\eta,\ G\left(-\frac{\overline{z}^*}{b-\beta B^{ARMA}_{T,1}}\right) = \eta$$

(b) If $X_+ \le Y_{T-1}$, which is equivalent to $\overline{z} + (b - \beta B^{ARMA}_{T,1})Y_{T-1} \le 0$, then $X_- \le Y_{T-1}$, and the objective function of the optimization problem in period $T-1$ can be simplified to:

$$\begin{aligned}
&J(\overline{z}, Y_{T-1})\\
&= \overline{z} + (p+b-w)Y_{T-1}\\
&\quad - \frac{1}{\eta}\left(\int_0^{X^+} [\overline{z} + (p+b+h)(Y_{T-1} - D_{T-1}) + (b - \beta B^{ARMA}_{T,1})D_{T-1}]dG(D_t)\right)
\end{aligned}$$

Clearly, the above objective function is concave in $(\overline{z}, Y_{T-1})$. Given Y_{T-1}, the optimizer $\overline{z}(Y_{T-1}) = \arg\max_{\overline{z}} J(\overline{z}, Y_{T-1})$ satisfies $G(X^+(\overline{z}(Y_{T-1}), Y_{T-1})) = \eta$. From that, we can easily find that $J(\overline{z}, Y_{T-1})$ is decreasing with Y_{T-1}, which implies that the optimizer of Y_{T-1} for case (b) is X_+. Thus, case (b) is dominated by case (a). Based on the above discussion, if $B^{ARMA}_{T,1} > \frac{b}{\beta}$, the optimal base-stock level is $Y^*_{T-1} = \tau^{ARMA} + \sum_{i=1}^m \lambda_i d_{T-1-i} + v^+$ and the optimal value in period $T-1$ is:

$$\begin{aligned}
&V_{T-1}(d_{T-1-m}, \ldots, d_{T-2})\\
&= \beta A^{ARMA}_T + \left(p - w + \beta B^{ARMA}_{T,1}\right)\tau^{DIT} + (p+b-w)v^+ + (\beta B^{ARMA}_{T,1} - b)v\\
&\quad - \frac{(p+b+h)I(v^+) + (\beta B^{ARMA}_{T,1} - b)I(v)}{\eta} + \beta\sum_{i=1}^{m-1} B^{ARMA}_{T,i-1} d_{T-1-i}\\
&\quad + \left(p - w + \beta B^{ARMA}_{T,1}\right)\sum_{i=1}^{m} \lambda_i d_{T-1-i}\\
&= A^{ARMA}_{T-1} + \sum_{i=1}^{m} B^{ARMA}_{T-1,i} d_{T-1-i}
\end{aligned}$$

where $B^{ARMA}_{T-1,i} = \beta B^{ARMA}_{T,i-1} + \left(p - w + \beta B^{ARMA}_{T,1}\right)\lambda_i$ for $i = 1, \ldots, m-1$ and $B^{ARMA}_{T-1,m} = \left(p - w + \beta B^{ARMA}_{T,1}\right)\lambda_m$.

Recursively, by defining $A^{ARMA}_{T+1} = B^{ARMA}_{T+1,i} = 0$ $(i = 1, \ldots, m)$, we can infer that for ARMA(m,n) demand pattern, the optimal value function can be simplified to $V_t(d_{t-m}, \ldots, d_{t-1}) = A^{ARMA}_t + \sum_{i=1}^m B^{ARMA}_{t,i} d_{t-i}$, and for period T, the optimal stock level is $Y^*_T = \tau^{ARMA} + \sum_{i=1}^m \lambda_i d_{T-i} + \frac{(p+h)v^+ + bv^-}{p+b+h}$, while for period $t < T$,

(i) if $B^{ARMA}_{t+1,1} \le -\frac{p+h}{\beta}$, then $Y^*_t = \tau^{ARMA} + \sum_{i=1}^{m} \lambda_i d_{t-i} + v^-$,
$B^{ARMA}_{t,i} = \beta B^{ARMA}_{t+1,i-1} + \left(p - w + \beta B^{ARMA}_{t+1,1} - \frac{b-\beta B^{ARMA}_{t+1,1}}{\eta}\right)\lambda_i$ for i=1, ..., $m-1$
and
$B^{ARMA}_{t,m} = \left(p - w + \beta B^{ARMA}_{t+1,1} - \frac{b-\beta B^{ARMA}_{t+1,1}}{\eta}\right)\lambda_m$;

(ii) if $-\frac{p+h}{\beta} \le B^{ARMA}_{t+1,1} \le \frac{b}{\beta}$, then $Y^*_t = \tau^{ARMA} + \sum_{i=1}^{m} \lambda_i d_{t-i} + \frac{(p+h)v^+ + bv^-}{p+b+h}$,
$B^{ARMA}_{t,i} = \beta B^{ARMA}_{t+1,i-1} + \left(p - w + \beta B^{ARMA}_{t+1,1} - \frac{b-\beta B^{ARMA}_{t+1,1}}{\eta}\right)\lambda_i$ for i=1, ..., $m-1$
and
$B^{ARMA}_{t,m} = \left(p - w + \beta B^{ARMA}_{t+1,1} - \frac{b-\beta B^{ARMA}_{t+1,1}}{\eta}\right)\lambda_m$;

(iii) if $B^{ARMA}_{t+1,1} \ge \frac{b}{\beta}$, then $Y^*_t = \tau^{ARMA} + \sum_{i=1}^{m} \lambda_i d_{t-i} + v^+$,
$B^{ARMA}_{t,i} = \beta B^{ARMA}_{t+1,i-1} + (p - w + \beta B^{ARMA}_{t+1,1})\lambda_i$ for $i = 1, ..., m-1$ and
$B^{ARMA}_{t,m} = (p - w + \beta B^{ARMA}_{t+1,1})\lambda_m$.

Thus, the optimal solution Y^*_t for Problem (8) under ARMA(m,n) can be summarized as $Y^*_t = \tau^{ARMA} + \sum_{i=1}^{m} \lambda_i d_{t-i} + y^*_t$, where

$$y^*_t = \begin{cases} v^-, & B^{ARMA}_{t+1,1} \le -\frac{p+h}{\beta} \\ \frac{(p+h)v^+ + bv^-}{p+b+h}, & -\frac{p+h}{\beta} < B^{ARMA}_{t+1,1} < \frac{b}{\beta} \\ v^+. & B^{ARMA}_{t+1,1} \ge \frac{b}{\beta} \end{cases}$$

which is similar with item (ii) in Proposition 3.1. Consequently, the risk parameter's effect on the inventory decision Y^*_t summarized in Corollary 3.1 still holds. Therefore, we reach the conclusion that our findings under the additive demand pattern of the DIT mode can be generalized to ARIMA(p,d,q) demand process, which includes ARMA(p,q) process (i.e., ARIMA with one-fold differencing).

A.2.9 Extension to Production Diseconomy Scenario

To investigate a more realistic cost structure that better aligns low and high demand periods, we also extend the dynamic risk-averse newsvendor problem to production diseconomy scenario, where the marginal cost for a fixed production capacity is increasing. In the literature (e.g., Eichenbaum (1989) and Anand and Mendelson (1997)), it is quite common to model production diseconomy using a quadratic production cost function as follows:

$$wY_t + \varpi Y_t^2$$

where the production cost function consists of a linear term and a quadratic term reflecting diseconomy of scale, and a larger ϖ resents a greater production diseconomy. Then the newsvendor's profit function in period t becomes

$$\Pi_t(Y_t, D_t|d_{t-1}) = p \cdot \min(D_t|d_{t-1}, Y_t) - b \cdot (D_t|d_{t-1} - Y_t)^+ \\ - h \cdot (Y_t - D_t|d_{t-1})^+ - w \cdot Y_t - \varpi \cdot Y_t^2,$$

Since there is a quadratic term of Y_t, the dynamic programming problem (8) has no mathematical analytical solution. We conduct several numerical experiments to explore the impact of production diseconomy on the optimal inventor decision and out-of-sample CVaR. Specifically, for the testing period, we randomly generate 1000 demands according to estimated distribution parameters for each of the three demand models. Then the optimal decisions z^* and Y_t^* can be solved to maximize V_t. Consequently, realized out-of-sample CVaR can be calculated with Y_t^*. We summarize the inventory decisions and out-of-sample CVaRs in production diseconomy scenario in Fig. A.2.9. First, compared with Fig. 5, it's obvious that consideration of production diseconomy will make the decision makers' inventory decisions more conservative, so that the inventory level in Fig. A.2.9a is generally lower than that in Fig. 5(a). Second, the inventory decisions in production diseconomy scenario also dynamically change with decision makers' risk attitude. In particular, as the decision makers become more risk-averse, they would order less with DET model and could order more or less with DIT and PCT models. Third, the DET model that incorporating the trend term achieves the greatest out-of-sample CVaR in most of the cases, but PCT model can outperform DET model when decision makers are highly risk-averse. These results are essentially the same as our main findings without production diseconomy.

Inventory decisions and out-of-sample performance with production diseconomy

A.2.10 Detailed Examination on Holding and Shortage Costs

In this section, we provide a more detailed observation of inventory cost by splitting it into holding cost and shortage cost. Similarly, taking the first experiment in Table 5 as an example, the corresponding costs with different nonstationary demand patterns and their ensemble are shown in Fig. A.2.10. Overall, when the decision maker is more risk-averse, the inventory decisions become more conservative, resulting in larger shortage costs and smaller holding costs. That is, holding cost is generally increasing with η while shortage cost is generally decreasing with η. As a result, if the forecast demand of a certain method tends to be greater than the actual demand, risk-averse decision makers usually pay less inventory costs than risk-neutral decision makers, and vice versa. In another word, the impact of over-estimating (under-estimating) error in predictive analysis on profit realization can be mitigated (strengthened) by decision makers' risk aversion behaviors. However, this conclusion does not always hold for ensemble inventory decisions, which are weighted combinations of individual inventory decisions and the weights vary with η. Moreover, owing to the nonmonotonic relationship between inventory decisions and η under PCT demand patterns, the shortage costs under this demand pattern are also nonmonotonically related to η when $\eta < 0.4$. Therefore, only when the demand structure's influence on forecast performance and on the sensitivity of inventory decisions to decision-makers' risk attitudes are both considered, we are able to figure out a better underlying demand pattern for the nonstationary demand series and then achieve a superior profit performance.

Franses, P. H. (1991). Seasonality, non-stationarity and the forecasting of monthly time series. *International Journal of Forecasting, 7*(2), 199–208.
Franses, P. H. (1992). Testing for seasonality. *Economics Letters, 38*(3), 259–262.
Moineddin, R., Upshur, R. E., Crighton, E., & Mamdani, M. (2003). Autoregression as a means of assessing the strength of seasonality in a time series. *Population Health Metrics, 1*(1), 10.

Holding costs and shortage costs with different nonstationary demand patterns and their ensemble

A.3 Appendix for Chap. 4

A.3.1 Proof of Proposition 4.1

Proof. Clearly, the optimal value of problem (3) is a comparison of the following two subproblems with $z \in \{1, 2\}$:

$$\max \sum_{i\in[N]} \sum_{j\in[N_i]} \left\{p_{ij} \min\{q_{ij}, d_{ij}\} - h_{ij}(q_{ij} - d_{ij})^+ - b_{ij}(d_{ij} - q_{ij})^+ - c_{ij}q_{ij} - r_z q_{ij} w_{ij}\right\},$$

$$s.t.,$$

$$L_z \leq \sum_{i\in[N]} \sum_{j\in[N_i]} q_{ij} w_{ij} \leq U_z,$$

$$q_{ij} \geq 0, i \in [N], j \in [N_i],$$

Note that the objective function is equivalent to $p_{ij} \min\{q_{ij}, d_{ij}\} - h_{ij}(q_{ij} - \min\{q_{ij}, d_{ij}\}) - b_{ij}(d_{ij} - \min\{q_{ij}, d_{ij}\}) - c_{ij}q_{ij} - r_z q_{ij} w_{ij}$, which is increasing in the term $\min\{q_{ij}, d_{ij}\}$. Therefore, by introducing an auxiliary variable Z_{ij} that is subject to $Z_{ij} \leq \min\{q_{ij}, d_{ij}\}$, or equivalently, $Z_{ij} \leq q_{ij}$, $Z_{ij} \leq d_{ij}$, we obtain an equivalent formulation of the above problem:

$$\max \sum_{i\in[N]} \sum_{j\in[N_i]} \left\{p_{ij} Z_{ij} - h_{ij}(q_{ij} - Z_{ij}) - b_{ij}(d_{ij} - Z_{ij}) - c_{ij}q_{ij} - r_z q_{ij} w_{ij}\right\},$$

$$s.t.,$$

$$L_z \leq \sum_{i\in[N]} \sum_{j\in[N_i]} q_{ij} w_{ij} \leq U_z,$$

$$Z_{ij} \leq q_{ij}, Z_{ij} \leq d_{ij},$$

$$q_{ij} \geq 0, i \in [N], j \in [N_i],$$

which completes the proof. □

A.3.2 *Proof of Proposition 4.2*

Proof. The proof is similar to that of Proposition 4.1, thus, the details are omitted here. □

MIX
Papier aus verantwortungsvollen Quellen
Paper from responsible sources
FSC® C105338

If you have any concerns about our products,
you can contact us on
ProductSafety@springernature.com

In case Publisher is established outside the EU,
the EU authorized representative is:
Springer Nature Customer Service Center GmbH
Europaplatz 3, 69115 Heidelberg, Germany

Printed by Libri Plureos GmbH
in Hamburg, Germany